The Impossible Woman

Television, Feminism, and the Future

KRISTEN HOERL

Rutgers University Press

New Brunswick, Camden, and Newark, New Jersey,

Oxford and London

Rutgers University Press is a department of Rutgers, The State University of New Jersey, one of the leading public research universities in the nation. By publishing worldwide, it furthers the University's mission of dedication to excellence in teaching, scholarship, research, and clinical care.

Library of Congress Cataloging-in-Publication Data

Names: Hoerl, Kristen, author
Title: The impossible woman : television, feminism, and the future / Kristen Hoerl.
Description: New Brunswick : Rutgers University Press, 2025. | Includes bibliographical references and index.
Identifiers: LCCN 2025012136 | ISBN 9781978842526 paperback | ISBN 9781978842533 hardback
Subjects: LCSH: Women on television | Sex role on television | Television—Social aspects—United States | Feminist criticism | LCGFT: Television criticism and reviews
Classification: LCC PN1992.8.W65 H64 2025
LC record available at https://lccn.loc.gov/2025012136

A British Cataloging-in-Publication record for this book is available from the British Library.

♾ The paper used in this publication meets the requirements of the American National Standard for Information Sciences—Permanence of Paper for Printed Library Materials, ANSI Z39.48–1992.

rutgersuniversitypress.org

Contents

Introduction: Sexist Realism and the Crises of Contemporary Feminism 1

1 Impossibly Resilient: *Parks and Recreation*'s Leslie Knope 25

2 Improbably Cheerful: The *Unbreakable Kimmy Schmidt* 46

3 Exquisitely Lonely: *The Marvelous Mrs. Maisel* and *The Queen's Gambit*'s Beth Harmon 63

4 Insanely Gifted: *Game of Thrones*'s Daenerys Targaryen 95

5 Gangster Girlboss: The *Queen of the South* 117

Epilogue 140

Acknowledgments 147

Notes 149

Index 175

The Impossible Woman

Introduction

Sexist Realism and the Crises of Contemporary Feminism

This book is about a story that has been told many times over the past decade. The protagonist of this story is a smart, talented (usually white) woman with some moderately feminist inclinations who faces difficult circumstances in what is often unfamiliar territory. Sometimes she is abandoned by her family, sometimes her closest family members are dead, or sometimes she would be better off if she had no family at all. With few people she can rely on for support, she must contend with demeaning treatment, ranging from everyday humiliations of sexism and economic precarity to sexual violence and physical assault. Simply by virtue of being a woman, she is disregarded, denigrated, and damaged. Incredibly, she overcomes a myriad of obstacles in her path. In fact, she is remarkably resilient, able to withstand increasingly virulent forms of abuse. She overcomes the damage caused by powerful figures who threaten her career, her livelihood, and often even her very life because she is not merely resilient; she is extraordinary. Her talents, insight, wisdom, and skills rival those of everyone around her, including the powerful men who wish her harm. Precisely because those men underestimate her, she is able to outperform them, deceive them, and sometimes even destroy them. And yet her goals are often very modest: to survive and to receive the same respect given to the mediocre men who surround her. Who she is and what she wants appear to be impossible.

If you have watched television with any regularity over the past decade, you have likely encountered this narrative. This storyline has appeared in scripted television programming across a range of genres. In the Netflix original comedy *Unbreakable Kimmy Schmidt*, the titular character survives kidnapping and sexual assault and seeks happiness in a world that is unfamiliar to her. Amazon Prime's comedy-drama *The Marvelous Mrs. Maisel* features a well-off, twenty-something mother of two who strives to break the glass ceiling of New York's stand-up comedy scene in the late fifties after her husband abruptly leaves her for his secretary. More recently, Netflix's original teen-horror series *Chilling Adventures of Sabrina* revives the comic book character Sabrina Spellman, a half human, half witch who goes to tremendous lengths to save the world from Satan. This character shares some magic in common with the character Eleven of Netflix's *Stranger Things*, who prevents the collapse of civilization and saves multiple children in her hometown through her enigmatic ability to contain the monsters of a fantastic realm of "the upside down." All the main characters in BBC America's crime thriller *Killing Eve* are women who are outmatched only by one another despite their male counterparts' certainty of their own self-mastery. These examples are just a few of the many scripted television programs and miniseries that have circulated over the past ten years to feature extraordinary women and girls motivated to overcome the strictures of often-violent and always-degrading instances of misogyny that are embedded with the institutions that direct these characters' lives.

Although internet streaming services have proliferated this character, she does not solely appear on streaming programs. This character has appeared in broadcast, cable, and premium-subscription services, ranging from the comedic portrayal of NBC's Leslie Knope of *Parks and Recreation* to HBO's fantastic depiction of Daenerys Targaryen in *Game of Thrones*. Although these characters are predominantly white, they are not exclusively so: CBS's 2021 reboot of *The Equalizer* featuring Queen Latifah and USA's remake of the Telemundo series *La Reina del Sur* (*Queen of the South*) respectively foreground Black and Latina women who beat death-defying odds as they survive brutally racist and misogynist treatment.

This book explores the rhetorical implications of the *impossible woman* figure crafted across a variety of scripted television shows. The impossible woman underscores two ways in which popular culture has given meaning to feminism in the past decade. First, it suggests feminism is impossible because the women who represent feminist virtues are superhuman. They are gifted beyond measure, and they manage to exceed the limits of the human body as they strive to reach their goals. Second, feminism is impossible because even these impossibly gifted women find that their personal advancement is incompatible with their feminist commitments. Not only are they constantly thwarted by patriarchal structures; they are also caught up between incompatible goals of self-advancement and support of others who are exploited and demeaned due to their gender, race, poverty, and/or sexuality. This book critically interprets the variety of impossible women who have lit up the small screen to highlight how seemingly feminist narratives offer a restrained fantasy to viewers who might take pleasure in the image of strong woman characters. Instead of serving as a sign of progress, the impossible woman foregrounds the limits of feminist advancement because it illustrates how even the most capable women cannot succeed under trenchantly patriarchal environments. The figure of the impossible woman illustrates how positive portrayals of feminist women may not actually provide empowering feminist messages. Indeed, these narratives are both restrained and restraining, as they train viewers to be satisfied with the paltry representations they offer under the banner of feminist empowerment.

I am interested in how these programs elicit contradictory pleasures for viewers compelled by the upsurge of seemingly feminist content in scripted television. On the one hand, they invite viewers to empathize with female characters' all-too-relatable struggles for recognition and justice within patriarchal institutions. During the early weeks of the pandemic in 2020, I soothed my frustrations by taking pleasure in how many of these characters used their sharp wits to expose and undermine sexism. I enjoyed the vicarious experience of witnessing the shock and surprise of characters' friends and family members who did not suspect that the mild-mannered woman in their midst was the most talented, and often fiercest, person among them. The proliferation of these programs after 2015 points to a market for feminist characters and storylines. It makes sense that this narrative would take hold in 2020. In the wake of Donald Trump's first presidential election and the media spectacle surrounding the *Access Hollywood* video in which Trump brags about his license to sexually assault women at will, these programs offer resonant storylines about the dehumanizing treatment women routinely encounter in all spheres of activity in their lives—at work, at home, in public—and from a myriad of people: coworkers, family members, and strangers. Storylines of women who outperform men who presume that they have the license to do whatever they please to those in less privileged positions promise some catharsis to deeply felt anxieties about cultural misogyny. These often riveting and deeply affective narratives lampoon familiar public figures who are unable or unwilling to recognize their own ineptitude; likewise, the programs demonize misogynist men by suggesting that these men deserve what's coming to them: punishment, disrespect, and loss of power. Soon enough, women will finally be recognized for who they are. And they are extraordinary.

The vicarious thrill of watching more-than-competent women show up their mediocre male counterparts is not the only pleasure elicited by these programs. There is something more sinister at work in programs oriented around impossible women. Although the protagonists across these programs are invariably more talented, smarter, stronger, and resilient than the mediocre men who surround them, their lives and their communities rarely ever experience meaningful change despite their determination to make a difference. Characters challenged by these extraordinary women rarely undergo transformation themselves. The narrative structures of these shows routinely defer or deny a satisfying closure or the development of new narrative tension. The more I watched these programs during the pandemic, the more I anticipated a feeling of catharsis that never came. Admittedly, the lack of resolution for the show's protagonists is likely influenced by the conventions and imperatives of serial programming in an era of peak television that aims to maintain audience investment beyond one episode or viewing season. Yet the serial narrative structure of contemporary television alone does not explain the phenomenon. Even in series finales, when there is no potential for further narrative development, these programs rarely offer satisfying resolutions for those of us primed to identify with the remarkable women on the small screen. Indeed, many series featuring extraordinary and magical women such as *Game of Thrones* and *Chilling Adventures of Sabrina* conclude by dramatically killing off their impossible women characters. Television cannot seem to imagine a world in which modest feminist outcomes are possible, even in its wildest fantasies. Offering limited opportunity to witness women's overcoming, these programs provide viewing pleasures grounded in watching well-intended women struggle, often painfully, in their efforts to achieve recognition, authority, and power, or sometimes just for survival in a deeply misogynist culture. There seems to be some enjoyment in watching women suffer.

These two contradictory pleasures evoke some of the tension in what Sarah Banet-Weiser has foregrounded in her attention to the dynamics between popular feminism and popular misogyny in public culture. As Banet-Weiser argues, the contemporary media landscape has given visibility to feminist expressions of female empowerment and inclusion within male-dominated economic spheres as means of resistance to structural gendered inequalities; a broadly defined idea of feminism has become popular precisely because it foregrounds "individual capacity" as the means of overcoming sexism, thus leaving deeper structures of inequity intact.[1] Banet-Weiser argues that such feminist visibilities are countered by virulent expressions of misogyny that revel in the devaluing and dehumanizing of women. These two social currents are embattled within contemporary networked media, "living side by side as warring, constantly moving contexts in an economy of visibility."[2]

Programs featuring impossible women illuminate how deeply enmeshed popular misogyny has become with popular feminism. In this book, I argue that much of the television content organized around the premise of its strong women characters responds and contributes to this ideological battlefield. It would be a mistake, I contend, to identify the trends in strong women characters on TV solely in terms of the market for feminist content. As these programs give narrative form to the ongoing cultural tensions between feminism and misogyny—between women's demands for recognition and the intense backlash against them—they elicit competing desires to empower and objectify women. They reveal that there is a market for images of strong women, but that market hasn't replaced Hollywood's tendency to turn women into disposable commodities. Recent programs with empowered feminist characters highlight a frontier of feminist imagination in popular culture that is conditioned by the omnipresence of popular misogyny.

In this book, I argue that the impossible woman is a rhetorical figure that embodies the principles underlying what I have termed *sexist realism*. I take inspiration from Mark Fisher's work on capitalist realism, which describes the "widespread sense that not only is capitalism the only viable political and economic system, but also that it is now impossible even to imagine a coherent alternative to it."[3] Taking a rhetorical approach to sexist realism, I attend to the narrative devices within scripted television that confirm patriarchy's inevitability. The impossible woman mediates the tension between feminism and misogyny by foregrounding feminist striving as a virtue for itself—as the best outcome one could hope for when achieving a more just and equitable world seems nearly impossible. This process appears in narratives of popular feminism that present sexual harassment and blatant acts of misogyny as routine and expected while also celebrating women's efforts to overcome damage within institutions premised on inequality. In reading television's impossible women as constitutive of sexist realism in popular culture, I suggest some revision of Banet-Weiser's temporal understanding of the dueling forces of feminism and misogyny in the contemporary era. Banet-Weiser sees the intensification of misogyny as a backlash response to liberal feminist gains since the 1960s and 1970s in attesting that while "popular feminism is *active* in shaping culture, . . . the 'popular' of popular misogyny is *reactive*."[4]

The narrative structure of these programs suggests that the relationship between these ideological forces may be less linear in their development, as they portray popular feminism itself as structured by patriarchy. Not only do characters' feminist orientations emerge in response to their dehumanizing treatment, but the programs' inability to depict justice on behalf of groups subordinated by sexism suggests that feminism is only thinkable in the presence of an overbearing diminution of women, not as a politics with a self-propelling agenda. Sexist realism suggests that feminist outcomes are unimaginable within the spaces of popular culture and that feminism is always reactive to an overbearing patriarchal present.

By tracing the recent cycle of scripted entertainment programs that foreground sexism as a precondition for feminist politics, this book explains how the impossible woman mediates the temporal crisis facing feminist activism and politics. In attending to television's investments in sexist realism, this book also considers the temporal frameworks that constrain feminist politics and organizing. Temporality is an important consideration for feminism. What we think about time and what we do with our time are enmeshed with gendered power dynamics and have figured centrally in historic struggles for women's rights, inclusion, and equity. One's time use is certainly impacted by other social divisions. As Sarah Sharma explains, working-class individuals' and migrant workers' time use is conditioned by the timing and needs of the primarily white, affluent people they serve.[5]

Narratives about impossible women's struggles engage viewers in a broader understanding of time as they contribute to social knowledge about feminism's past, present, and future. Feminist activism is predicated on the idea that social struggle is needed to achieve a more just and equitable future. Yet investments in future-oriented progress are themselves also products of inequality. Because progress narratives have historically been articulated to colonialist expansion, capitalist development, and the Enlightenment, movements toward "progress" tend to privilege groups in greater proximity to structures of power than others and often either ignore or exploit communities of color and women in the Global South. Consequently, liberal feminists have faced strong criticism for generalizing white Western affluent women's interests to the interests of all women. Nonetheless, most feminist-oriented movements—liberal, anti-racist, queer, or decolonial—are driven to create conditions that would promote more equitable conditions in the days and years ahead. We act now, albeit in a variety of often divergent ways, in anticipation that our actions will shape our lives and others' lives in the future.

Looking across a variety of television series, I explain how the impossible woman provides lessons that suggest women will inevitably fail if they attempt to become leaders of historically male-driven organizations. Although their temporal structures are varied, they all offer equally bleak outlooks for the lives of women and girls who resemble the "go-getters" featured in women's magazines and self-help literature. TV comedies feature strong women characters caught within an absurdly endless cycle of feminist struggle. Period dramas tell us that postfeminist assumptions are timeless because activism on behalf of women's inclusion into male-dominated institutions was never actually needed at all even if women will never be happy. Programs featuring women with magical powers suggest that we cannot even imagine a fantasy world in which a woman becomes a world leader. And some of the most diverse, multiracial action thrillers conclude that an early death is the inevitable outcome for women who react violently against the vicious patriarchal structures that seek to contain and control them. Stories that directly challenge the temporal frameworks that deny women's agency as change agents are often canceled after one season.[6] These temporal orientations have troubling implications for the lives of people subjected to patriarchy.

The emphasis on women's struggle as the telos rather than the driver of feminism mitigates the movement's transformative potential. Sexist realism tells women that it's cool that they want to change the world, but's also entirely naive for them to believe they might succeed. By failing to imagine a feminist future, it narrows the range of resources for viewers to conceptualize what justice looks like for themselves and others. For impossible women, there is only inexorable striving, and viewers are encouraged to celebrate such striving as consolation for the lack of meaningful change in their own lives. The cynicism at the root of sexist realism has implications for the future of feminist politics and organizing. If we believe feminism has no future, then feminism will have no future.

Of course, this is not the end of feminism's story. By centralizing the experiences of women subjected to misogynist practices and gendered violence, these TV series remind us that women deserve much better. Even though misogyny is the precondition for impossible women's agency, series featuring women's desires for justice provide some opening for resistive narratives to emerge. This book attends not only to how television has contributed to sexist realism but to how voices of resistance have found their way into these stories despite the appearance that feminist possibilities have been foreclosed.

The Crises Facing Contemporary Feminisms

The impossible woman has emerged out of interconnected developments in popular discourses about feminism and transformations in the production and circulation of scripted television entertainment, including the gendered imperatives driving television content development and previous TV shows with feminist themes. Television's impossible women both respond and contribute to the current cultural and political status of women and feminism. After a period of backlash in which young women largely hesitated to express feminist commitments, support for feminism has garnered positive attention in a variety of places, including enthusiasm for Hillary Clinton's U.S. presidential runs in 2008 and 2016, publicity surrounding the United Nations Women's HeForShe Alliance and its celebrity spokesperson Emma Watson, and the fervor surrounding #MeToo activism, which drew widespread attention to the omnipresence of sexual harassment and rape culture—particularly in Hollywood. These events foregrounded a variety of goals that have characterized liberal feminism: increasing women's leadership and inclusion in politics, media, and corporations; closing the gender pay gap; providing greater opportunities for women and girls; and protecting women and girls from sexual harassment and violence.

Despite the increased visibility of feminist advocacy in preceding decades, feminism continues to face backlash. Misogyny remains a popular sociocultural and political force, and the variety of cultural artifacts attesting to its presence contribute to sexist realism as a broader cultural phenomenon that exists beyond the small screen. Banet-Weiser argues that misogyny circulates in an economy of visibility now "more than ever before."[7] She elaborates that the "systematic devaluing and dehumanizing of women" takes place across a variety of spaces.[8] Its most obvious manifestations include extraordinary instances of gendered violence, "in death and rape threats expressed on social media platforms toward women who either identify as feminists . . . or those who enter into previously male-dominated professions such as game development and commentary . . . to revenge porn websites to a rise in men's rights organizations to an increase in global sex trafficking of women and girls."[9]

Misogyny is also advanced by more mundane practices and in political and legal arenas in which misogynist arguments are legitimated as "common sense."[10] The 2022 U.S. Supreme Court's overturning of the *Roe v. Wade* decision to protect abortion rights was a victory for groups who have sought to roll back the achievements of second-wave feminism. Long-standing misogynist attitudes among the U.S. electorate contributed to Donald Trump's popularity, as his openly hostile remarks about women journalists and his Democratic rivals Hillary Clinton and Kamala Harris have only seemed to bolster his credibility among many of his supporters. That in 2016 Trump won a greater share of white women voters than Clinton, a self-proclaimed feminist, attests to feminism's marginal status despite its visibility.[11]

In an opinion essay titled "The Future Isn't Female Anymore," *New York Times* columnist Michelle Goldberg chronicles signs of growing antifeminist backlash in public culture, including a 2021 poll commissioned by the Southern Poverty Law Center that found that even among young Democrats, enthusiasm for feminism has waned precipitously. The survey found that of the groups most likely to support feminist causes, 46 percent of Democratic men under fifty and nearly 25 percent of Democratic women thought feminism had done "more harm than good." Goldberg laments that for some self-professed feminists, the movement has "lacked a vision of a better world."[12] Recently, a United Nations report found that nine out of ten people surveyed across 85 percent of the global population hold "fundamental biases against women." According to the report, half of the population believes that men are more capable of political leadership, and 25 percent believe that it is acceptable for men to beat their wives.[13]

Gender inequities in the workforce also point to ongoing feminist struggles. The wage gap has remained virtually unchanged since 2002, when women on average earned eighty cents for every dollar a man earned. Wage inequities are greatest for Black and Hispanic women, who earn seventy and sixty-five cents on the dollar, and tend to increase for women as they age. Expectations holding women responsible for the care of children and other dependent family members are a major contributing factor, as women are more likely than men to leave the paid workforce to care for family members and suffer career-long wage penalties when they return.[14] The wage gap points to a fundamental tension in feminist organizing, as the goal of achieving parity with men has traded off with efforts to transform capitalist economies that benefit from gendered and racialized labor disparities. Formal inclusion of middle- and upper-class white cisgender women within upper ranks of paid employment cannot resolve broader structural inequities facing less privileged women; it also fails to support policies that enable middle-class women to pursue upward mobility without also relying on the care labor of others.

This second tension has grounded ongoing debates about whether women in white-collar positions can expect to successfully manage a career and family life. Nancy Fraser describes this as an issue of "feminist ambivalence," in which liberal feminism's emphasis on access to wage labor and financial independence contributed to the undervaluation of care labor.[15] The alignment of feminist struggles against gender hierarchy with neoliberal economics has obscured feminism's historic investments in economic justice. Reflecting on how other strands of the second wave, including socialist feminists and feminists of color, resisted marketization and organized around universal access to care work and wage labor, Fraser concludes that feminist emancipation must start by recognizing the ambivalence between the turn toward marketization and appeals for social protection.

Whereas Fraser regards liberal feminism as partly responsible for ongoing pay inequities, others have pointed to discourses that have popularized feminism while evacuating it of political meaning. In the past decade, liberal feminism has sat uneasily alongside proclamations of feminist identity that have lacked a specific policy agenda. Beyoncé's performance at the MTV Video Music Awards in 2014 with the word "feminist" lit behind her literally highlighted the emergence of popular feminism. Banet-Weiser explains that an "economy of visibility" bounded by corporate logics and desires has enabled an individualized image of feminism to gain traction in popular culture.[16] References to women's confidence and empowerment expressed in women's fashion magazines and commercial advertisements have advanced a model of feminism focused on the visible, thus commodifiable, body. Rosalind Gill observes that popular appeals to women's inclusion, representation, and authorship are relatively vacuous, as a variety of figures proclaim feminist identities "without specifying what that means in terms of some kind of politics."[17] Banet-Weiser's concern with what she refers to as the "economies" of feminist visibility makes a similar critique. Noting the difference between the politics of visibility in which marginalized groups demand recognition to draw attention to inequity and injustice, "economies of visibility fundamentally shift politics of visibility so that visibility becomes the end rather than a means to an end."[18]

The mainstream face of feminism that understands sexism as the problem of individual men or organizations also aligns with the goals and assumptions underlying neoliberal capitalism by avoiding concerns about structural inequities and cultural dimensions of women's subordination.[19] Wendy Brown explains that "invisible gender subordination" is intensified by neoliberalism because the individual pursuit of one's self-interests within a bourgeois household depends on the unacknowledged infrastructure of women's reproductive and care work. Since the neoliberal subject is putatively masculine, according to Brown, there is an unresolvable tension between feminism and neoliberalism as the latter cannot address feminist demands.[20] Drawing upon Brown's work, Catherine Rottenberg argues that neoliberal feminism resolves this tension by foregrounding women's self-reliance and efficiency. Pointing to popular press articles and self-help literature such as Sheryl Sandberg's bestseller *Lean In: Women, Work, and the Will to Lead*, Rottenberg notes that this literature presents "happy work-family balance" and women's pursuit of high-ranking corporate leadership roles as feminist ideals.[21] Neoliberal feminism puts a feminine face on the neoliberal subject by recognizing gendered imbalances yet presenting them as a private concern for individual women to manage.

Dispensing with concerns regarding structural inequities and systems that privilege white, able-bodied cisgender women, neoliberal feminism tasks women to become more resilient in the face of growing challenges. In "Notes on the Perfect," Angela McRobbie suggests that feminist action has been translated into calls for women's "inner drive" for personal achievement.[22] Emerging out of the neoliberal marketplace, popular feminism recognizes that gendered inequality exists while simultaneously buttressing "the political economic conditions that allow that inequality to be profitable."[23] In this process, structures of patriarchy are maintained in the name of feminist striving for success and achievement.

Resilience is a crucial disposition for putting feminism to work for the current economy. As Robin James explains, "Resilience is uniquely tailored to maximize women's productivity for neoliberal capitalism."[24] James attends to popular culture narratives featuring women who "spectacularly overcome" the "damage" caused by white supremacist patriarchy and receive rewards of capital and status in return.[25] Ironically, individual resilience is socially profitable for those hegemonic institutions responsible for inflicting damage on historically subordinated groups, such that sexism and racism become more firmly entrenched in society as social value is accorded to those who can demonstrate their resilience. For James, resilience "deregulates the work and effects of racialization, gendering, sexualization, and so on" by shifting the onus for inclusion and justice onto the very bodies of those who are excluded.[26]

The cultural emphasis on perfection, positivity, and resilience has implications for subjectivity and politics. James notes that if resilience is increasingly regarded as a desirable feminine trait, then damage itself is to be expected. Thus, "good girls" are the ones who demonstrate an active commitment to overcoming their damage. In turn, persistent sexism is rendered unavoidable, an expected norm and prerequisite for women's overcoming to establish their value. James concludes, "In a twist of particularly cruel irony, this actually *reinforces* and *strengthens* patriarchy. With the narrative of therapeutic overcoming, patriarchy has figured out how to convert so-called 'feminist' practices . . . into its own power supply."[27] As part of a broader set of neoliberal dispositions, resilience anchors feminism to conditions of patriarchy, making resilience dependent on the conditions it seeks to upend.

Sexist realism is not merely or solely the product of cultural misogyny, as it is also a by-product of popular feminism and its imbrications with white, neoliberal feminism. Impossible women's storylines are part of this broader conjunctural moment in feminist politics. Characters' problems illustrate the challenges and limitations of liberal and neoliberal feminist agendas when they are confounded by incompatible goals of personal advancement and serving the collective good. Likewise, these characters find it impossible to achieve positive recognition and inclusion while also promoting justice for others. Notably, these tensions have also animated disagreements and conflicts among feminists.

Black, radical, queer, and disability rights feminists have taken liberal feminist efforts to task for failing to address concerns that extend beyond issues facing white, middle- and upper-class cisgender women and for contributing to white supremacy.[28] As announcements of feminist identification by celebrities, fashion, and commerce have come to supplant a deeper political vision, mainstream media continue to marginalize or ignore the demands of groups who are less easily commodifiable: poor women, women of color, and disabled women. The controversy surrounding the sale of T-shirts reading "This is what a feminist looks like" foregrounded some of the problems associated with popular feminism. Shortly after *Elle UK*'s December 2014 issue featured Emma Watson proudly wearing the shirt on the cover, the *Daily Mail* reported that the shirts were manufactured in a sweatshop in Mauritius.[29] Three years later in the United States, the Women's March in Washington, D.C., drew criticism for being predominantly white and for backgrounding issues of race, immigration, worker's rights, and environmental justice.[30]

Later that year, Black activists critiqued mainstream coverage of #MeToo activism that credited Alyssa Milano for the movement instead of Tarana Burke, whose organization supported Black women and girl survivors of sexual assault over a decade before Milano's tweet. As Burke lamented in a *Washington Post* editorial at the height of #MeToo publicity, the voices of people of color, queer people, disabled people, and poor people often go unheard even though the individuals in these groups are most likely to experience sexual assault at some point in their lives.[31] Burke and other anti-racist activists spotlight how white women's concerns have garnered public attention at the expense of racial justice causes, and often emerge in direct opposition to them. These criticisms illustrate how mainstream feminist movements have failed to promulgate a more diverse movement because they have lacked intersectional awareness about the variety of identity positions that work together to impact people's lives and treatment by others.[32]

Despite anti-racist feminists' valid critiques, some white feminists have pointed to demands for intersectional awareness as an explanation for feminism's failures. For instance, in the aforementioned *New York Times* article, Goldberg cites her interview with Susan Faludi to explain that factionalism within the movement has come at the cost of feminist gains. The opinion piece glosses over the reason for such divisions—the mainstream movement's overarching failure to speak to the interests or concerns of working-class women of color—to suggest that unity around a liberal agenda is inherently valuable. Hostile responses to intersectional critiques of mainstream politics and education also contribute to sexist realism. Feminists oriented around intersectional concerns have provoked conservative backlash among critics such as Ben Shapiro, who believes that the concept of intersectionality works to devalue white men, and Florida Governor Ron DeSantis, who used the term as a reason for banning the College Board's Advanced Placement course in African American Studies.[33]

Television's impossible women both respond and contribute to the mediated discourses about feminism's difficulties over the past fifteen years. Rampant sexism within characters' storyworlds obliquely references the broader cultural malaise about the possibilities for feminist activism amid growing misogynist fervor, which was amplified by Trump's first election. Main characters' inability to protect vulnerable communities in their quests for power and the harm they cause to others also evokes the tensions between feminist goals of inclusion and structural transformation. By attending to various iterations of the impossible woman in scripted television since 2009, this book explains how entertainment has responded to this crisis in ways that both reproduce and admonish misogynist and racist attitudes about women's liberation.

Although it is centrally featured, sexism's omnipresence is not the only lesson that might be drawn from television's fascination with impossible women. Paradoxically, sexist realism may offer limited resources for thinking anew about feminist politics and organizing. The complicated problems facing television's impossible women do not solely function to teach us that feminism is doomed; they also point to the variety of reasons for feminism's failures that are within our control in the fight against sexism, racism, homophobia, and capitalist imperialism. By featuring the problems that follow when women pursue individual striving at all costs, the series invites viewers to think differently about the feminist agendas that have been popularized elsewhere by mainstream media and commercial advertisers.

The Strong Female Lead and Televised Feminism

As television has responded and contributed to an ongoing conversation about feminism, it has helped define the parameters by which feminism is made legible and meaningful to viewers,[34] but it does so with an eye toward promoting those aspects of feminism most relevant to its targeted viewers and from the vantage point of content that worked for the industry in the past. Although its cultural significance is grounded in its response to broader challenges within contemporary feminism, the impossible woman is also a creation of the entertainment television industry that has reinvented itself for the streaming era via an emphasis on the "strong female lead." The significance of this category for television producers and consumers helps explain why the impossible woman has become a recurring figure in scripted television.

The "strong female lead" is at once a reference to audience preferences and a representational strategy. Netflix executives foregrounded the phrase in response to their unique approach of developing content based on Netflix's proprietary algorithmic formula that predicts audiences' interests based on the viewing habits of its users. As of 2024, the streaming service had divided viewers into over 4,100 "taste communities" made up of people who exhibited similar viewing preferences, which directed Netflix's decisions for future content development.[35] The "strong female lead" taste community has become a dominant factor in shaping content. As streaming video on demand (SVOD) services enable more specialized attempts at narrowcasting, it has become desirable and possible for them to invest in products with feminist themes. There is a growing market for portrayals of complex female characters in streaming platforms that hold particular appeal to white, upper-middle-class women viewers. These platforms have expanded the range of portrayals of women even as they maintain television's overarching investments in white, upper-income viewers. Some data suggests that SVOD appeals to women television consumers in particular; one consumer data firm finds that streaming on demand viewers "skew female and are driven by the desire to live a life full of excitement."[36] Jane Shattuc avers that Netflix has maintained "race and gender as central categories for prediction, revealing the central role of identity politics in its streaming choices."[37] Julia Havas and Tanya Horeck note that Netflix's efforts to "brand itself as concerned with feminist issues" are enhanced by the platform's ability to release entire seasons concurrently.[38] Complex subjects difficult to unpack in episodic television can be addressed with more depth and nuance and are "bingeable" for "media-savvy and feminized audiences" likely to be drawn to such content.[39]

Beyond using it as a category of prediction and content designation, Netflix also promoted the "strong female lead" as a sign of the streaming service's cultural importance. In 2017, it produced a half-hour YouTube video featuring women actors on Netflix-supported programs touting strong female characters. The video begins with captions overlaying a montage of clips from their library: "Our greatest heroes have one thing in common: the F word. Focused. Fabulous, Fearless, Funny . . . Female."[40] The service likely sought to capitalize on the proliferation of positive attention given to women-centered television programming by critics and mainstream news sources. In 2015, *Variety* magazine tentatively declared that the number of Emmy-nominated television series featuring complex women characters such as *Downton Abbey*, *Mad Men*, and *Homeland* marked a "golden era of female characters on television."[41] Around this period, a variety of sources including Vulture provided lists of "the best" Netflix content featuring a "strong female lead."[42]

Other streaming services sought to compete with Netflix by developing their own original content featuring women characters, such as *The Handmaid's Tale* (Hulu) and *The Marvelous Mrs. Maisel* (Amazon Prime Video). That these were the first original series developed by Netflix's main competition speaks to the centrality of storylines about agentic women for television in the past decade. Popular culture's celebration of the strong female lead has become so ubiquitous that it has inspired satire from comedian Michelle Wolf, who spoofed Netflix's investments in the phrase in a sketch entitled "Featuring a Strong Female Lead" for her own Netflix-produced comedy talk show in 2018 (see fig. I.1). A voice-over for a mock trailer announces a new film about "one woman tough enough for the boy's club." Wearing a white pantsuit, Wolf declares, "I never sweat; I win. . . . I never sleep; I win."[43] Elsewhere, actors including Brit Marling, Tatiana Maslany, and Emily Blunt have publicly objected to the phrase.[44] As Marling pointedly remarks, "What we really mean when we say we want strong female leads is: 'Give me a man but in the body of a woman I still want to see naked.'"[45]

The proliferation of the "strong female lead" category demonstrates the confluence between television content and popular feminism, as viewers' "taste" for women characters reflects some of the virtues associated with neoliberal feminism: confidence, resilience, and resourcefulness. It also demonstrates that the industry has cultivated this taste preference by directing audiences to programming that foregrounds women characters with these dispositions. However, it's important to note that such "taste" preferences are also rooted in media culture's many-decades-long efforts to align feminism with consumerism.[46] Although it has gained prominence in the past decade, the much-touted "strong woman character" is not a new development in scripted television as much as it is an effort to market streaming television content to women who can afford to subscribe to one or more streaming services. The impossible woman is the product of a commercial industry's long-standing effort to maintain and grow its base of

FIG. I.1 Michelle Wolf spoofs the "strong female lead" programming trend. *The Break with Michelle Wolf*, season 1, episode 1, "Strong Female Lead," written by Christine Nangle, released May 27, 2018, Netflix Original.

predominantly affluent, white, and female viewers by reflecting and commenting upon feminist concerns—even as these concerns have also been mediated by television over the past forty-five years. Scripted television has featured assertive and independent women characters at least as early as the second wave.

A variety of strong women television characters have responded to feminist activism and the socioeconomic shifts impacting women's lives in different historic moments. Each successive development has helped inspire new iterations of strong female characters who struggle to manage difficult situations that are invariably related to feminist issues and causes. While broadcast television tended to feature women in domestic roles and in heteronormative relationships, *The Mary Tyler Moore Show* broke ground by centering a single, career-oriented woman. The series influenced the development of a variety of half-hour comedies with similar characters and overt references to the women's liberation movement.[47]

Crime dramas, science fiction, and fantasy series also responded to viewers' enthusiasm for depictions of liberated women after the second wave. *Charlie's Angels*, *The Bionic Woman*, and *Wonder Woman* featured characters who reflected many of the qualities of today's impossible women. These characters' superhuman abilities anticipated television's ongoing enthusiasm for portrayals of women who easily overcome men's attempts to control or harm them. They also illustrate television's conflicted relationship with feminism by presenting contradictions that have endured in subsequent series; while television's strong women characters are smart, independent, and confident, they are consistently young, white, and thin, reflecting normative standards for sexual attractiveness.[48] Television's strong women have almost always been amenable to the male gaze. The impossible woman continues this trend.

This enduring character construction also reflects television's investments in appealing to a mass consumer audience of white, middle-class "working women" at a time when women's entry into the paid workforce was not only desirable but a financial necessity for many households. This audience demographic became particularly desirable to television networks after advertising agencies identified "the Go-Getter" as a lucrative new mass market of conspicuous consumers. Advertisers conceptualized this "Go-Getter" as "aggressive, self-motivated, goal-oriented, and less influenced by the opinions of men in their lives [than domestically oriented women]."[49] As both daytime viewership dropped and as a sizable share of prime-time audiences began turning their attention from broadcast to cable, major television networks focused their attention on reaching the women who might see themselves reflected in this constructed image. From the "Go-Getter" to the "can-do" girl, television has embraced the most commodifiable elements of liberal feminism's second wave as it provided a fruitful platform for advertisers and network executives.[50] For Angela McRobbie, popular culture's celebration of women's achievements in education and employment illustrates "feminism taken into account."[51] That is, mainstream politics and pop culture have embraced liberal feminist investments in equal opportunities for women and girls in historically male-dominated institutions but have largely discredited or ignored radical feminists' calls for substantive changes to the social order.

During the 1980s, television adjusted to the growing conservatism of the decade. While a variety of programs sought to appeal to women viewers, the prominence of feminine-coded sitcoms featuring single, career-minded women gave way to masculine-coded dramas that acknowledged the influence of feminism without centralizing feminist protagonists.[52] A "new traditionalism" in television emerged during this period with dramas like *thirtysomething* that presented women's renewed embrace of domestic life as a preferable alternative to professional careers.[53] Media portrayals of the unhappy career woman turned contented housewife reinforced the antifeminist conservative backlash against feminism, as did portrayals of professional women such as *Murphy Brown* whose professional success came at the expense of a satisfying personal life.[54] These narratives circulated in tandem with journalistic reports about women's inability to "have it all": both professional careers and fulfilling home lives. The message that career success comes at the expense of a fulfilling family life and healthy romantic relationships is repeated in many impossible women's storylines. Ongoing doubt regarding the possibilities for women to "have it all" reveals the stability of sexist realism over the past several decades. As Sarah Kornfield finds, this debate has remained at the stasis of fact; public discourse has continued to suggest that women cannot have it all, even as it has ignored that "most women's lives do not fit neatly into this debate."[55]

Antifeminist backlash stories circulated alongside the ascendance of postfeminist discourses in popular culture that proliferated in the 1990s and early 2000s. Bonnie J. Dow concludes that postfeminist content represents television's ambivalent approach to feminism. In seeking to reach an increasingly fragmented mass market, the industry could neither afford to completely denigrate nor fully embrace the movement that was driven to restructure patriarchal relations throughout politics and culture.[56] A variety of TV shows including *Ally McBeal* and *Sex and the City* contributed to a broader cultural assumption that feminism had achieved its aims and was no longer needed. Robust scholarship has documented postfeminist television's emphasis on what Laurie Ouelette refers to as "postvictimization femininity," which presumes women's agency while "affirming their right to choose femininity."[57] An underlying lesson across many earlier programs is that individual choices, not structures, are the primary cause of women's unhappiness.[58] By denying the need for continued feminist action, postfeminist rhetoric advanced the neoliberal assumption that individual differences offer the best explanation for present inequalities, thus deflecting institutionalized and structural causes for gendered and racial disparities.

Television's impossible women draw on multiple themes and conventions of their predecessors. They are committed to advancing their professional careers and personal advancement even though this pursuit almost always comes at the cost of satisfying personal lives. However, unlike postfeminist expressions of women's agency, recent TV series featuring impossible women depict patriarchal structures and sexist men, not individual choices or feminism, as the cause of characters' problems. They feature feminist agendas even though feminist outcomes appear implausible within their storyworlds.

Television shows featuring impossible women are among a variety of scripted programs that have incorporated more expressly feminist content into their storylines since the 2008 economic recession. Prime-time TV shows such as *The Good Wife*, *Madam Secretary*, *Scandal*, and *Veep* featured the challenges women leaders face in U.S. electoral politics with varying lessons about women's leadership capabilities. For Allison Prasch, *Madam Secretary* offers a refreshing alternative to postfeminist portrayals by attending to both the unique challenges that female secretaries of state face and the everyday difficulties women experience in managing their professional and personal lives.[59] The proliferation of feminist themes on television has occurred alongside or within series featuring difficult and complicated female characters such as *The Killing*, *Outlander*, and *Orange Is the New Black*.[60] Julia Havas argues that recent programs have distinguished themselves by satirizing postfeminist gender scripts (in the cases of *30 Rock* and *Parks and Recreation*) or by illustrating "failed feminism" (in the cases of *The Good Wife* and *Orange Is the New Black*).[61] Havas observes a "tense relationship between historic feminist politics and female protagonists" in prestige television near the end of the 2010s.[62]

Michaela Meyer concurs that *The Good Wife* depicts feminism as "fatalistic," as women with feminist inclinations fail to meet their goals.[63] The emergence of women who pursue corrupt enterprises to advance their personal self-interests reflects the industry's efforts to innovate upon successful cable series featuring male antiheroes. While feminism failed women in postfeminist television, it is now women who fail to support feminism.

Unfortunately, television's feminist content is not equally matched by an interest in antiracism, and it rarely suggests that racism is also a woman's issue. Netflix's category codes lack intersectional awareness, suggesting they cannot understand that viewers who are interested in "women making history" may equally be drawn to "black stories," "gritty Latino dramas," or "Asian comedy icons."[64] Relatedly, the majority of television's strong and capable women are white, and their stories background or ignore the impacts that racism plays in the series' storyworlds. Thus, when people discuss feminist television, they are almost invariably talking about white feminism. Despite the omnipresence of white characters in TV shows featuring the strong woman trope, diverse representations of strong women do exist, aided by the impact of uberproducer Shonda Rhimes, the showrunner responsible for multiple hit series featuring diverse characters and storylines centering socially relevant issues.[65] "Shondaland's" *Scandal* was the first TV series with a Black woman headliner since 1974's *Get Christie Love*.[66] Critics have critiqued the color-blind and postracial logics of Rhimes's programs that avoid deep engagement with ongoing forms of racial injustice.[67] Such logics contribute to a television landscape in which sexism is inevitable and racism is unexamined even though the last chapter of this book illustrates that the horrors of anti-Black and anti-immigrant violence in the contemporary United States are not excluded altogether in television stories about impossible women.

Beyond their inclusion of feminist issues, the impossible woman appears alongside a variety of portrayals of women's struggles that wrestle with the limits of neoliberal popular feminism. Many of television's strong women characters of the past decade are notable for being unlikable. Television's recent depictions of selfish and misanthropic women have generated considerable attention among feminist media critics.[68] Analyzing *Game of Thrones*, *The Americans*, *Scandal*, and *Homeland*, Sarah Hagelin and Gillian Silverman observe that women characters suffer when they fail to perform traditionally feminine norms of selflessness, nurturance, and restraint. In pursuing political power, they are ultimately punished for their efforts. Observing that "the trajectory of the woman-in-power is largely downward, the mood more melancholic than triumphant,"[69] Hagelin and Silverman aver that "Ambition TV" hardly encourages viewers to idealize women characters with aspirational goals.[70] Instead, their stories provide evidence of misogynist backlash. The proliferation of female antiheroes who strive but fail to rise in the ranks of the powerful illustrates how scripted television cannot envision a world in which women's self-reliance and drive deliver positive outcomes.

The impossible woman extends this conversation by demonstrating that women characters don't necessarily need to pursue blind ambition to suffer, nor do they need to be unlikable to incur the wrath of others. Women characters across a variety of genres who are portrayed as likable, unbreakable, marvelous, magical, and lovable are also victims of misogynist backlash. They also make mistakes that set them back, put others in jeopardy, and sometimes cause grave harm to others more vulnerable than them. By featuring their maltreatment and flaws, television's impossible women embody the contradictory messages about women's agency in contemporary politics and commercial media.

Impossible women are unwitting illustrations of what Anita Harris and Amy Shields Dobson have termed "suffering actors": women who are neither completely empowered nor pure victims. Suffering actors name the experience of being female in a culture that recognizes women and girls as empowered while also subjecting them to patriarchal oppression. For these authors, contemporary girlhood is marked by girls' efforts to succeed and gain social acceptance in ways that violate normative expectations. While Harris and Dobson recommend the "suffering actor" as a conceptual tool to avoid the "pure agent/victim dichotomies" that have reduced our understandings of the experiences of girlhood and young womanhood,[71] the term is an apt descriptor of television's contradictory images of women characters who are extraordinarily equipped to rise above their patriarchal surroundings yet find themselves held down nonetheless.

By working with the resources of previous decades of empowered female characters alongside broader cultural discourses that have given meaning to feminism, television has helped establish the common sense of sexist realism. But that should not imply patriarchy's inevitability. The tensions that drive narratives featuring impossible women suggest that the television industry is not solely invested in pursuing a backlash account; rather, it is informed by the various competing agendas that have made feminism visible in the past fifteen to twenty years. In providing narratives that express feminism's impossibilities via a set of social and economic tensions, rather than by vacuous appeals to girl power presented in advertising and women's magazines, television's impossible women may also offer us some inchoate resources for thinking anew, prompting us to seek new narratives out of the ashes of feminist accounts that have been left for dead.

A Rhetorical Approach to Scripted Television

My background in rhetoric informs my approach to television portrayals of women and feminism. Rhetorical criticism is conventionally concerned with how public texts function for audiences within particular historical and social contexts. I am indebted to Bonnie J. Dow, whose groundbreaking book

Prime-Time Feminism helped justify the study of television as worthy of rhetorical criticism. Dow argues that entertainment television has played important social roles in "interpreting social change and managing cultural beliefs."[72] Dow draws from Lynn Spigel and Denise Mann, who suggest that television's "discursive functions" may be best understood by "attending to television's textual systems and to the specific historical frameworks in which television is received." Through this practice, television critics "might better understand how mass media help to produce, transmit, and at times transform the logic of cultural fantasies and practices."[73]

Other scholars have also laid the groundwork for thinking rhetorically about television. Drawing from Kenneth Burke, who considered literature as "equipment for living,"[74] Barry Brummett explains that fictionalized mass-mediated narratives offer lessons for how a culture might resolve widely shared problems, insofar as stories "follow discursively a pattern that people might follow in reality."[75] Critics may glean from a particular story the underlying representative anecdote that taps into the "essence of a culture's values, concerns and interests in regard to real-life issues."[76] Awareness of a given representative anecdote may thus offer deeper insight into how people manage their hopes and fears. Guided by this insight and rhetoric's historic interest in discourses of citizenship and national belonging, a variety of feminist critics have explored how popular culture contributes to discourses that shape viewers' political identities and beliefs. For Karrin Vasby Anderson, "the realm of pop politics" is worthy of rhetorical analysis because it "both reveals and reshape[s] citizens' understanding of feminist politics and female political figures." By studying popular culture, critics might learn how "important feminist work gets done."[77] Alternatively, television is also a site that routinely confirms misogynist assumptions about women's limited capacities for political leadership.[78] In other words, television can also help us understand why feminist progress has been slow and limited.

My work is also influenced by cultural studies' efforts to take popular culture seriously as a site of sociopolitical struggle. I draw cues from Douglas Kellner and others who have understood mediated texts as sites of hegemonic negotiation that may both "reproduce current relations of power, while also providing resources for the construction of identities and for empowerment, resistance, and struggle."[79] Like other cultural forms, scripted television is meaningful because it draws from "the same discourses that determine the substance and form of the everyday world."[80] In Michael Ryan and Douglas Kellner's language explaining the rhetoric of film, television "transcodes the discourses of social life" into televisual narratives.[81] These forms invite viewers to internalize such narratives and adapt their own subjectivities to the values and dispositions displayed on screen even though such processes are never final or guaranteed.

In the chapters that follow, I analyze a selection of scripted television series across a variety of genres, networks, and/or streaming services to highlight the breadth and scope of sexism realism on the small screen. The impossible woman's presence across network, cable, and streaming television responds to the conjunctural moment in popular feminism. I attend to the impossible woman as a response to the crisis in feminism, not to prioritize liberal feminism or its neoliberal husk, but because liberal and neoliberal feminist storylines predominate to the exclusion of alternative feminist orientations. These narratives establish parameters around which viewers may deliberate over the value and purpose of feminism. Although storylines about extraordinarily gifted women characters are not identical, they all focus on the characters' struggles to overcome the strictures placed on them by patriarchal institutions and neoliberal economics and balance their goals for personal self-advancement with their commitments to protect others from violence and exploitation.

Alongside many other rhetorical critics of television texts, I locate the meaning of television in the interplay of textual dimensions of particular programs and the broader context in which viewers consume them. My rhetorical approach to criticism diverges from approaches to feminist television criticism that locate meaning in the perspectives of individual writers and showrunners or in television critics' commentary. Attention to showrunners' explanations or critics' reviews has meaning insofar as these commentaries function as paratexts that guide or shape readers' experiences with a show, but I regard these as secondary concerns, largely because most viewers do not consume paratexts as their primary mode of engagement with television. My interpretive choices are geared toward analyzing texts in ways that most viewers engage with them because this offers the strongest insights into the cultural implications of these texts.

By looking at a variety of examples across the genres of comedy, period drama, fantasy, and thriller television, I point to the patterns that evince an underlying set of concerns and anxieties regarding the contemporary status of women and girls. Exploring the patterns that run across texts also points to the ongoing cultural and ideological significance of television in the streaming era. Given that the audience share of any television series is considerably smaller today than for popular series during the broadcast era, television's cultural power is no longer located in specific programs that draw national audiences. Furthermore, marketing and Nielsen data cannot give us deep insight into the audience size and demographics of programs housed by subscription-based streaming services. Analyzing specific "taste communities" such as the "strong female lead" that categorize a range of products provides a more helpful mechanism for recognizing television's cultural influence. Amanda Lotz suggests that TV programs' cultural and ideological work occurs through the "identifiable patterns [that] emerge across multiple texts."[82] From a rhetorical perspective, these patterns matter because they construct a "structured symbolic environment that circumscribes our shared resources" for making sense of and discussing pressing social problems with others.[83] Kenneth Burke understood that rhetoric was "a general body of identifications that owe their convincingness much more to trivial repetition and dull daily reinforcement than to exceptional rhetorical skill."[84] The variety of storylines featuring impossible women construct a dominant cultural framework for assessing the value and contributions of strong women with feminist orientations and concerns and illustrate how television continues to shape the cultural life of feminism in the streaming era by reinforcing sexist realism as common sense.

While my primary goal is to elucidate the patterns that compose the impossible woman in scripted television, I also attend to the specificities of individual series that give meaning to this figure. Each chapter focuses on dialogue, character, and narrative development across one or two series over the course of their multiple seasons. I am interested in character development because main characters are important points of identification for viewers. Typically, series position viewers to understand events through main characters' perspectives. When these characters espouse feminist values or are confronted by patriarchal power structures, they invite viewers to empathize with a feminist perspective. As they are a synecdoche for feminist politics, what happens to these characters offers implicit object lessons for contemporary feminist activism.

Circulating predominantly via streaming services, programs featuring impossible women tend to follow an episodic serial or serial structure.[85] I focus on the narrative arcs of main characters over the course of a series because they extend and elaborate upon images of popular feminism. If women are told to aspire and be empowered, the long story form presents viewers with a set of conflicts and problems that emerge for women when they attempt to do so. These stories necessarily extend beyond feminism's economies of visibility by giving meaning to the "goods" traded across popular culture's images of feminist agency: "self-esteem, confidence, [and] competence."[86] TV portrayals of women who share these qualities illustrate the extent to which such dispositions serve them or lead to personal fulfillment. I also observe the episodic storylines that inform stories about impossible women because patterns that run across individual episodes may convey overarching lessons more forcefully than a surprising or unexpected conclusion. For series that end due to declining ratings or negative responses from fans, episodic story patterns within early seasons are more likely to contribute to cultural meanings than a less widely viewed series finale.

Admittedly, my choices extend rhetoric's tendency to emphasize the verbal over televisual aesthetics of editing, lighting, and camerawork. My emphasis on narrative over aesthetics offers one among a variety of approaches that have provided meaningful explications of television culture's engagement with feminism. Other work has attended more closely to individual episodes, scenes, and shots to explore how women are often reduced to objects for audiences' viewing pleasure,[87] or to note how contemporary television has begun to centralize women's pleasure and agency.[88] Aesthetics is certainly important, but the limitations of scholarship that focuses on aesthetics are that it cannot illustrate how a particular scene is folded into a broader story arc, how viewers are invited to identify with or against a character over the course of a series, or how that identification shapes viewers' understandings of the resonant issues and outcomes of conflicts presented by the series' storyworlds. By focusing on character and narrative development, I point to a predominant mechanism by which television instructs viewers to think and feel about feminism.

I put narrative and character development in conversation with similar themes and issues addressed elsewhere in popular culture and politics. By understanding the significance of these representations within the broader contexts in which these programs were created and viewed, we can then consider how these stories provide viewers with faulty equipment for living in our deeply misogynist world. The meanings enabled by stories about impossible women are dependent upon these contexts. The problems that impossible women encounter resonate with the feminist-oriented problems and concerns that have animated contemporary political and journalistic discourses. These storylines transcode the discourses of popular feminism in ways that register cultural investments in women's resilience and growing recognition that popular feminism and its imbrications with neoliberalism cannot make good on its promises of fulfillment and personal happiness.

Chapter Previews

The first chapter focuses on an early iteration of the impossible woman: Leslie Knope of NBC's situation comedy *Parks and Recreation*. The character is a weakly satiric example of neoliberal feminist striving, as Knope tirelessly strives for a career in public service in the face of constant sexual discrimination and harassment. Knope's storyline mediates public controversies regarding the gendered dynamics of civic life at a time when neoliberal economics has eroded government commitment to the public good. Her character foregrounds the troubling implications of discourses that suggest sexism is an inevitability in electoral politics. The next case study chapter explores how the Netflix comedy *Unbreakable Kimmy Schmidt* expands upon the trope of feminist impossibility with a darkly satiric take neoliberal feminist striving. *Unbreakable* Kimmy is improbably cheerful despite her squalid living conditions and post-traumatic stress disorder. By pointing to the variety of industries that profit from the commodification of misogynist violence, the series portrays survivorship as a general condition of living as a woman or girl under neoliberal capitalism.

Subsequent chapters look at how more dramatic series have depicted women's impossible struggles against patriarchy. Chapter 3 analyzes the main characters of two original streaming period dramas: Amazon Prime's Miriam "Midge" Maisel from *The Marvelous Mrs. Maisel* and Netflix's Beth Harmon from the limited series *The Queen's Gambit*. These characters highlight television's fascination with what I have termed "trailblazer beauty": Midge and Beth are breathtakingly beautiful women who break the glass ceilings of their respective career fields prior to the second wave of feminism by virtue of their extraordinary, natural talent. Narratives about these trailblazer beauties point to a crisis of white feminist struggle in which women's striving for individual achievement isolates them from friends and family members. While white women's upward mobility depends on their debasement, it also relies on structural racism to prop them up.

The fourth chapter elaborates on television's ambivalent portrayals of empowered white women by interrogating the feminist status of Daenerys Targaryen on HBO's critically acclaimed and widely popular series *Game of Thrones*. As the "Mother of Dragons," Daenerys was one of the most magically gifted and beloved characters of the series, and yet the series finale concludes with her murder. This chapter argues that the character's contradictory goals explain both her popularity and her tragic demise. Daenerys's white feminism prevents her from recognizing that she cannot gain support from the world's most powerful white men and pursue liberation for the world's most oppressed at the same time. Her tragic demise highlights U.S. television's investments in white supremacy. Women might be able to pursue power, but they should expect a tragic conclusion should they seek to dismantle colonial relations altogether.

The final case study analyzes the character construction of Teresa Mendoza on the USA Network series *Queen of the South*. By featuring a Latina character from a poor city in northern Mexico, the program illustrates possibilities for television's impossible women who do not have the advantages of whiteness or U.S. citizenship. The series follows Teresa's transformation from the hapless wife of a drug runner to a calculating drug cartel boss. In the process, it illustrates how neoliberal economics and racial capitalism have shaped conditions of impossibility for poor Mexican women near the U.S.-Mexico border. The construction of Teresa aligns neoliberal feminism with what Sayak Valencia refers to as "gore capitalism," or organized crime's turn to violence to meet the demands of global capitalism.[89] Teresa's transformation illustrates how chasing power and wealth is a morally bankrupt and dangerous endeavor. In *Queen of the South*, neoliberal striving is, quite literally, a dead end. The conclusion reflects on the implications of sexist realism by contemplating how the absence of cultural narratives about feminist achievements restricts imaginative resources.

1

Impossibly Resilient

Parks and Recreation's Leslie Knope

The NBC situation comedy *Parks and Recreation* (hereafter *P&R*) marked the emergence of the impossible woman as a new development in the negotiation between neoliberal individualism and feminist concerns. First airing in 2009 and lasting for seven seasons, the series received acclaim from critics and academics for its favorable presentation of feminist themes. It features the character Leslie Knope (Amy Poehler) in her efforts to navigate a career in public service. Knope strives to emulate women who have served in national public office, including Hillary Clinton and Madeleine Albright, and her character is emblematic of liberal feminism's commitments to women's political inclusion, gender equity in the workplace, and the power of individuals to alter discriminatory policies against women. Knope struggles to overcome local townspeople's disdain for women in leadership positions, resulting in mixed and limited success. Media scholar Erika Engstrom concludes that the program is unique because its central character "actually breaks the status quo" by transforming patriarchal structures in her small town.[1] Writing for *Bitch* magazine, Kelsey Wallace applauds Knope's character as "a female comedic lead who is openly feminist, career-focused, kind, smart, optimistic, and multidimensional."[2]

P&R is a satiric portrait of a small Indiana city's Parks Department that Knope runs in her position as deputy director. Knope is a prototypical feminist character who meets incredibly high standards of achievement. The program's humor draws from the quirky personalities of the department's staff and from Knope's enduring resilience in the face of a shrinking parks budget, the unreasonable demands of local citizens, and corporate control over city governance. She works tirelessly in the face of seemingly insurmountable obstacles posed by sexist individuals and powerful corporations. She strives for perfection, maintains a positive attitude, and persists despite constant challenges. Over the course of the program's seven seasons, Knope strives to climb the ladder of city government and provide more opportunities to women and girls. It is only by virtue of her extraordinary talents that she earns a measure of recognition in public office. However, her career does not flourish because sexist policies and sexual harassment continually get in her way. This sexism is particularly pronounced when she opposes other city managers' procorporate agendas. In this regard, her storyline displays broader political tensions between feminism and neoliberalism. An overarching lesson across the program's multiple seasons is that feminist goals are beyond reach, even if they are worth striving for, because neoliberalism cannot countenance a feminist agenda.

P&R is the only program among those featured in this book that is expressly concerned with women's status in U.S. electoral politics. Cameos of political figures including Michelle Obama, Barbara Boxer, and Olympia Snowe contribute to the show's emphasis on women's participation in public office. The pilot episode aired ten months after Hillary Clinton formallyconceded to Barack Obama at the conclusion of the presidential primary campaign of 2008; the episode opens as Leslie Knope tells the camera "It's a great time to be a woman in politics" and then pushes an intransigent drunk man out of a children's tube-slide in a city park.[3] The program's satiric commentary is reinforced by Poehler's earlier work on the sketch comedy series *Saturday Night Live* in her role as a hilariously apoplectic Hillary Clinton in 2008. As Poehler's Clinton rails against the sexism that contributed to her campaign loss, Knope laments the misogyny within her hometown. Part of the humor across both programs is that Clinton/Knope are constantly derided despite their overwhelming qualifications. Through the interplay between fictionalized and real-world political figures, *P&R* mediates public controversies regarding the gendered dynamics of civic life at a time when neoliberal economics has eroded government commitment to the public good.

Knope's character mediates the tension between feminism and neoliberalism by foregrounding feminist striving as a virtue in itself—as the best outcome one could hope for when achieving a more just and equitable world seems nearly impossible. (I refer to this character as Leslie throughout the rest of the chapter because most of the other characters on the program identify her by her first name.) Leslie's irrepressible cheerfulness and tirelessness affirm a worldview in which women's virtues are marked by their spectacular struggle against patriarchy. However, she does not necessarily embrace neoliberal logics that have articulated feminism to a framework of individualist achievement and upward mobility because she is equally driven by her concern for others, invested in public life, and committed to serving her community. Her conflicting allegiance between her self-advancement and others' well-being illustrates how neoliberalism cannot subsume conditions of precarity and inequity or blind us to the limits of individualist striving. Despite her resistance to neoliberal imperatives, this character remains caught up in this dilemma until the program's final season. As a weakly satiric take on the impossible woman, *P&R* reveals the cultural ambivalence surrounding neoliberal feminism that paradoxically reifies the conditions of impossibility that it purports to critique.

Perfect and Productive

Notably, Leslie is talented in every activity she pursues. Although many men refuse to seriously consider her as a political leader, she successfully competes against them in hunting, golfing, dart throwing, and bowling. She is also a savvy politician. During season 3, she insists on delivering a speech to the Chamber of Commerce to raise funds for her signature project even though she has a severe case of the flu (see fig. 1.1). She is delirious with fever but manages to give a persuasive speech to rousing applause.

Leslie is also tirelessly productive. For example, her contribution to her city of Pawnee's time capsule is a thick book on the history "of everything that has

FIG. 1.1 Leslie Knope continues to work for the Parks Department even while being hospitalized for a severe case of the flu. *Parks and Recreation*, season 3, episode 2, "Flu Season," written by Norm Hiscock, original airdate January 27, 2011, NBC.

ever happened since Pawnee was founded," which she typed from memory.[4] A recurring joke is that Leslie never sleeps, yet the quality of her work continually exceeds the expectations of those around her. After her speech to the Chamber of Commerce, Parks Department Director Ron Swanson (Nick Offerman) admits, "The advantage of being Leslie's boss is that she does all the work and nothing ever goes wrong."[5] The joke pokes fun at sexist double standards, as Ron's job rests entirely on Leslie's boundless productivity. However, little ever happens to fundamentally challenge the dynamic between them until season 7. Instead, the program spotlights Leslie's work ethic. By portraying her as more than capable of accomplishing virtually any task before her, the program infers that only sexism prevents her from holding more prestigious job titles. The first season makes this explicit when Leslie explains to Ron that because she is a woman, she needs to hold herself "to a higher standard" than the men working in city government.[6] This double standard becomes all the more obvious in season 2 when the Indiana Organization of Women gives Ron the Woman of the Year Award in recognition of projects that Leslie initiated and developed.

Leslie's character contributes to neoliberal understandings of feminist politics after the Great Recession of 2008, a period of economic downturn that news coverage largely characterized in gendered terms because male-dominated industries including manufacturing were hit particularly hard. As the subprime mortgage crisis exposed the limits of neoliberal deregulation, many households became dependent on women's lower-paid employment.[7] As Michelle Rodino-Colocino observes, reports of the "Great He-Cession" reproduced "normative assumptions that men serve as breadwinners."[8] Rather than offering a counterpoint to the assumptions underlying the "He-Cession," neoliberal feminism has maintained structures of patriarchy in the name of feminist striving for success and achievement.

Leslie's unending talent, enduring commitment to hard work, and determination to overcome obstacles keep the male-driven Parks Department and city government running. Her indefatigable drive is an exaggerated portrayal of Sheryl Sandberg's neoliberal feminist subject. Just as *Lean In* calls upon women to strenuously pursue higher ranks of powerful institutions and emphasizes professional ambition as the key to individual feminist achievement, Leslie's feminism is linked to her aspirations to serve in a political office that requires her constant attention. Even when she is not getting paid, she is eager to work. At the beginning of a season 2 episode entitled "Budget Cuts," she recounts that she spent months on furlough brainstorming how she would improve the parks. Upon her return to the office, she presents each member of her staff with numerous color-coded, two-inch binders outlining her plans and presses them to get back to work. Leslie's approach to work during this episode illustrates the broader phenomenon of free labor "as a meritocratic investment in one's employment prospects" within a precarious and insecure job market.[9] In her analysis of women's "aspirational" labor as social media producers, Brooke Erin Duffy observes that "uncompensated, independent work" is often propelled by "the much-venerated ideal of *getting paid to do what you love*."[10] Duffy concludes that gender, race, and class hierarchies endure within this ideological framework that encourages women to embrace self-enterprise and passion even if financial returns are limited or nonexistent.

Emblematic of this ideal, Leslie frequently affirms that her passion for her job is based on her love of Pawnee. Although she is employed by the city throughout most of the series, her tirelessness does more to keep the wheels of government turning than it does to transform the city. After all, it takes ten years for her to transform an abandoned lot into a small park! Finding value in overcoming challenges brought about by economic insecurity, Leslie valorizes a particular performance of white femininity that maintains structural inequalities in her hometown. Her insistence that "Cool people make the rules. They don't break the rules" exemplifies her investments in working within existing institutions to create incremental social change.[11] She is an impossible woman because there are no limits to what she can do even though all she wants are the same opportunities and recognition as the mediocre white men who surround her. Yet this goal seems beyond reach.

Leslie's impossible talent and tirelessness give her the capacity for resilience as she bounces back from a myriad of dehumanizing and sexist affronts that threaten to obstruct her goals. She contends with a variety of degrading city laws—including the mandate that "all menstruating women shall be confined to their bathtubs"[12]—sexual harassment from city employees and local media personalities, and dismissive attitudes from public officials. Despite these routine obstacles and humiliations, Leslie remains "determined to bust up the boy's club of local government."[13] Her boundless optimism is a recurring point of humor as it contrasts with other characters' more pessimistic perspectives. During episode 2 of the first season, Leslie's mother tells the camera, "I always want my daughter to be successful, which is why I tell her there's nothing wrong with being a wife and mother."[14] Not even her own mother has faith that Leslie's drive and talent will lead to her career success.

The program's exaggerated portrayal of Leslie foregrounds the folly of white middle-class women's investments in the promise of liberal feminism and its grounding in the presumption of social mobility based on meritocracy. Her perseverance conforms to the genre of the situation comedy in which "personality is figured as a limited set of repetitions that will inevitably appear in new situations."[15] Lauren Berlant describes the situation comedy in terms of a subject whose "slapstick maladjustment" to a slightly destabilizing situation turns out "absurdly and laughably without destroying very much."[16] *P&R* is comedic insofar as Leslie continues to exude faith in her impending success despite all evidence to the contrary. From one angle, her resilience appears to be a maladjustment to the destabilizing situations caused by sexist policies, sexual harassment, and misogynist attitudes of citizens and city employees; Leslie's actions presume that meritocracy can overcome the strictures of sexism, which becomes laughable when she is faced with the absurdity of the beliefs and practices founded upon assumptions of women's inferiority to men.

But it might be more apt to read the situation in reverse. The subject of the program is patriarchy, which is destabilized by Leslie's tireless efforts. What is laughable is not the absurdity of the sexism she confronts but her commitment to working within sexist institutions as though the harder she works, the more likely those institutions will be to create room for her. The inclusion of women in lower ranks of government office is the maladjustment of a patriarchal order that must reckon with feminist challenges without fundamentally altering the gender hierarchy. As Berlant notes, the situation comedy evokes a world that enables its subjects to endure despite their flaws. Throughout the series, Leslie's resilience helps bind feminism to the sexism she seeks to upend. Because sexism endures despite her best efforts, she must withstand degrading situations with the expectation of small incremental changes at some point in the future. However, her commitments also yoke her to the institutions that are invested in her dehumanization.

Berlant's reflections on cruel optimism illuminate the troubling implications of the impossible woman. Berlant is interested in how the situation comedy genre has been transmuted in what she identifies as an emerging genre of the "situation tragedy" in nineties-era independent film. She observes that in the situation tragedy, characters at the bottom rungs of society do not convey expectations for future success but pursue proximity to the good life with "passionate attachment to a world in which they have no controlling share."[17] The situation tragedy illustrates Berlant's larger point that investing one's optimism in a desired project is misguided when that project is also "an obstacle" to one's "flourishing."[18] Berlant describes the experience of optimism as "an inclination to return to a scene of fantasy," such as upward mobility or political equality, that raises the expectation that proximity to the object/scene will lead toward personal or global transformation.[19] This optimism is cruel when that which "ignites a sense of possibility actually makes it impossible to attain the expansive transformation for which a person or a people risks striving."[20] By lampooning Leslie's feminist striving within a small town that is resistant to change, *P&R* provides a satire of the cruel optimism underlying feminist political agendas. Leslie learns, time and time again, that the individuals she needs to win over to achieve her goals are the people most invested in maintaining gender hierarchies.

The cruelty underlying Leslie's optimistic attachment to city government is most vividly illustrated in seasons 5 and 6 after she barely wins her election campaign for city council despite the obvious incompetence of her challenger

Bobby Newport (Paul Rudd), a man who is so unqualified for his job that he publicly announces that he voted for Leslie because he thinks it is illegal for candidates to vote for themselves. Her meeting with the election commissioner illustrates that her desire to work as an elected official is the primary obstacle to her success when the commissioner informs her that in the event of an exact tie, "the seat is awarded to the male candidate and the female candidate is put in jail."[21] The ridiculous and offensive law suggests that sexism is not ancillary to but is encoded within the operations of government.

This lesson is reinforced in subsequent episodes. After her election, Leslie faces resistance from city workers who resent her initiatives to provide more employment opportunities for women. During one episode, Sanitation Department head Steve (Michael McGill) resists Leslie's request that they hire women to haul trash. To prove that women are capable, Leslie and her assistant April Ludgate (Aubrey Plaza) nearly complete a collection route ahead of schedule until Steve sabotages them with the impossible task of moving an industrial-sized refrigerator to the city dump on their own (see fig. 1.2). The scene's humor emerges from Leslie and April's determination; because they have already accomplished numerous onerous projects, they do not recognize that no person could move the enormous appliance on their own. Once Leslie realizes that Steve set her up to fail, she solicits a crew of other women who work together to relocate the refrigerator. Given her success, the Sanitation Department is compelled to hire women trash haulers. Although the episode frames the conclusion as a win for Leslie, the Sanitation Department's disdain for her becomes part of the season's broader narrative arc that results in Leslie's ouster from city council.

Other men in city government also take issue with Leslie. She frequently butts heads with boorish city council member Jeremy Jamm (Jon Glaser), who relishes opportunities to "jam" Leslie's agenda. During season 5, Jamm recommends that the city hire his "alcoholic" friend, who he admits is "a bit grabby."[22] Leslie insists that the council consider April for the position, given her more extensive experience in city management. Jamm opens the confirmation proceedings by inciting his fellow men on the city council: "OK! Let's tear this chick a new one, shall we?"[23] Jamm's blatant misogyny, conveyed through his exaggerated expressions and open disdain for Leslie and April, presents a mockery of male entitlement in politics that is both abject and relatable. (Perhaps the least relatable aspect of Jamm's comments is that he referred to April as a "chick" instead of using obscenities commonly directed toward women in positions of authority.[24] The label of "chick" was likely chosen to conform to the series' prime-time slot on NBC, since more likely terms would be considered too offensive for family viewers.) Since the other city council members refuse to consider April for the job, she and Leslie adjust their strategy. They propose that animal control be moved under the direction of the Parks

FIG. 1.2 Leslie and April fruitlessly attempt to move an industrial refrigerator to prove that women are just as capable as men of hauling trash. *Parks and Recreation*, season 3, episode 2, "Women in Garbage," written by Harris Wittels, original airdate January 24, 2013, NBC.

Department, technically putting April in charge but without the title of director or a commensurate salary. Given that Jamm is an ardent supporter of small government, he reluctantly agrees. The episode's conclusion illustrates the tension between sexism and feminist resistance under neoliberal capitalism, a point I elaborate on in the next section of this chapter. Leslie responds to the city council's intransigent sexism by fostering the resilience of a new generation of women workers who must also endure routine sexism in return for their own demanding labor.

Leslie continues to demonstrate resilience in the face of sexist efforts to undermine her. The other white men on city council are chronic sexual harassers. When Leslie asks Councilman Milton (James Greene) to support her bill, he asks to kiss her in exchange for his vote. In a later episode, Milton does not recognize her as a member of the city council and instructs her to leave a meeting that she convened and to return with more snacks. Councilman Bill Dexhart (Kevin Symonds) also harasses women across multiple seasons of the program. A recurring joke revolves around Dexhart's numerous sex scandals; no matter how often he is caught having extramarital affairs with young women (including his babysitter), he continues to proposition women. Despite their scandalous behavior, these men continue to curry favor with voters. Their ongoing popularity is highlighted in season 6 when news breaks that Dexhart sent sexually suggestive text messages to over one hundred women. In a scene that anticipates Donald Trump's early political career, local journalist Shauna Malwae-Tweep (Alison Becker) informs Leslie that Dexhart's approval ratings only grew after the scandal broke and that Pawnee voters never seemed to care about Dexhart's long history of sexual harassment. Even Malwae-Tweep admits to her attraction to Dexhart. "He's kind of cute!" she confides to Leslie. "I just feel like I could fix him, you know?"[25]

Via its depiction of Steve, Jamm, and other members of the city council, the program mocks the dangerous influence of mediocre white men in U.S. politics and history. As Ijeoma Oluo reflects, "Women still spend a large portion of their lives battling men for their basic dignity and safety," yet "our entire society is built to ensure that white men hoard power."[26] Oluo emphasizes that it is not necessarily women who resemble Leslie but queer, transgender, and/or disabled women and people of color who are most harmed by oppressive systems that bolster white male supremacy. *P&R* avoids a more complicated and multifaceted story about interlocking systems of privilege by focusing solely on the plight of white women to illustrate the unequal, gendered dynamics underlying cultural expectations for achievement. White men are expected to succeed while cisgender white women are expected to struggle. The subject positions of nonwhite characters do not meaningfully shape the central conflict that drives the series' narratives.

The show contrasts Leslie's sheer competence and exceptional commitment to public service with her white male colleagues' lackluster performance and disregard for the citizens of Pawnee. Despite her strengths, the citizens of Pawnee turn against her. In an election recall, Leslie loses by an overwhelming margin. The program's humor is grounded in the irony that men's sexism continues with impunity while women toil to achieve a modicum of respect for their impeccable performance.

Leslie's humiliations in city council reinforce the program's overarching message that even someone as remarkable and kind as Leslie cannot overcome the limits imposed by patriarchy. The show is satirical insofar as no one could possibly be so industrious, yet the features of sexism she encounters are all too familiar. Her disposition of resilience is cultivated by her optimism in reforming a system that is intransigent to change. Ever the resilient feminist, Leslie resumes her efforts once she is removed from office through her position as deputy director of the Parks Department. When she laments that she "just can't seem to walk away" from the work, Ron remarks that she has always loved fixing the town. "You know it's an uphill battle, but you love the struggle."[27] This exchange finds virtue in Leslie's passionate striving, even as the consequences of such striving compromise her health and happiness. It presents an earnest illustration of Mark Neocleous's observation that "resilience is nothing if not an apprehension of the future, but a future imagined as disaster and then, more importantly, recovery from the disaster."[28] Leslie rebuilds her sense of purpose and emerges more resilient than ever—but the objective is always to *manage* ongoing crises, not to resolve or prevent them. Leslie Knope's constant ability to bounce back illustrates how resilience itself produces new forms of damage to bodies subjected to patriarchy.

Neoliberal Sexism

While Leslie's damage is most obviously caused by patriarchal culture, it is inextricable from the influence of neoliberalism. The program frequently illustrates how market-driven policies have subjected publicly accessible spaces to crass commercialization. As deputy director of the Parks Department, Leslie is as dedicated to her career in public service as she is to her own upward mobility. The obstacles to her flourishing are not solely the result of sexism, for the dehumanizing treatment she receives is often facilitated by corporate interests seeking to influence local politics. It is poignant that Leslie's conflicts revolve around the administration of public parks because access to common space has historically been a feminist concern. As Silvia Federici argues, women's survival has often depended on access to resources found in the commons. Federici explains that witch hunts were not entirely driven by superstitious beliefs but were a precondition for capitalist development as peasant women were dispossessed from their land.[29] *P&R* situates Leslie's feminist struggles on similar grounds, as she seeks to protect public spaces from the onslaught of corporate influence. In the process, the program illustrates how her dedication to public service is often at odds with her aspirations to serve in elected office. (Not too coincidentally, when Leslie challenges citizens for proffering sexist messages as the new town slogan, they respond by portraying her as a witch on a government website.)

During season 2, Leslie cannot prevent the sale of Sweetums's energy bars in the city's parks because the corporation's wholesome family image dissuades citizens from thinking critically about how unhealthy the bars really are. While Leslie presents a strong case against the sale of "Nutriyums" during a public forum,[30] she is outmatched by Sweetums CEO Nick Newport Jr. (Gary Weeks), who provides free candy to everyone in attendance. She is also thwarted by her boss, a character inspired by government appointees under the George W. Bush administration who did not believe in the mission of the branches they were overseeing.[31] An avowed libertarian, Ron is delighted when the attendees unanimously vote in favor of privatizing the city parks' concession stands. Leslie's struggles with corporate actors continue in subsequent seasons. For her first act as councilwoman, Leslie proposes a tax on sugary sodas to combat the city's childhood obesity epidemic. The representative for the Pawnee Restaurant Association, Kathryn Pinewood (Mary Faber), opposes the plan and threatens to deliver a press release announcing that one hundred restaurant employees would be laid off should Leslie's tax bill pass. Many citizens turn against Leslie in response, prompting the recall effort.

Corporate interests also drive Leslie's rivalry with Jamm, whose decisions are largely motivated by his efforts to broaden his orthodontist practice. He reckons that cavities from the sugar in Paunch Burger's enormously sized soft drinks and Sweetums products will lead more consumers to require dental work. Consequently, he finds a common cause with Paunch Burger and Sweetums representatives. There is some paradox in Jamm's support for corporations that would compromise the health of his patients. As someone who equates his responsibility as an elected official with his own personal ambitions, Jamm presents a caricature of *homo oeconomicus*, the full extension of a neoliberal subject who "cannot think public purposes or common problems in a distinctly political way." Wendy Brown elaborates that *homo oeconomicus*'s emphasis on market principles as a governing logic compromises the very idea of public life, as it "generates a condition of politics absent democratic institutions that would support a democratic public and all that such a public represents," such as informed deliberation and limitations on private influence.[32] While Leslie strives to foster democratic deliberation through interactive town hall meetings, Jamm and others often succeed by violating the norms of civic engagement. The contrast between Leslie's and Jamm's approaches to city management stages the conflict between the public good and the neoliberal public. Robert Asen advances a notion of the public good as "a *practice* that draws on *relationships* within and among publics and counterpublics" who are connected beyond "naturally occurring associations."[33] Asen insists that attention to relationships should foster attention to "(in)equality and difference by facilitating contestation."[34] Neoliberal publics impede such modes of engagement by valuing competition over coordinated action. As competition is premised upon personal success at the expense of another, neoliberalism depends on inequality. Consequently, neoliberal publics disavow difference in favor of a universal (white masculine) subject.

Although Leslie's encounters with sexism often occur separately from her conflicts with corporate figures, a variety of character dynamics suggest that these struggles are interconnected. Jamm is a pawn in a larger project of corporate influence over Pawnee city government. Working alongside Jamm, Pinewood and the Newport family lead the "Committee to Recall Leslie Knope" with talking points about her "unfair government regulations."[35] Pinewood and Sweetums CEO Jessica Wicks (Susan Yeagley) are blond women like Leslie, but they do not face the same humiliations. On the contrary, men tend to fawn over them. At the same time, Pinewood and Wicks ingratiate themselves to these men by gratifying their appetites for attractive women and junk food. While Leslie began her career as a tireless public employee, Jessica began hers as the winner of a Miss Pawnee beauty pageant, which led to her marriage to octogenarian Nick Newport Sr. By situating Pinewood and Wicks as foils for Leslie, the program suggests that the town's sexism operates in the service of neoliberal capitalism. Leslie is a problem for those seeking to profit from Pawnee's public health crises because she cannot be bought, so they leverage the town's proclivity for sexism to remove her from office.

Several scenes suggest that sexism is a by-product of neoliberalism, as some characters' demeaning treatment of Leslie is driven by their financial interests. After she is voted out of office, Jamm admits that he regards Leslie as one of his best friends, and he later solicits her help in ending a toxic relationship with his girlfriend. The shift in Jamm's behavior exemplifies Kate Manne's position that misogyny is rooted less in a general disregard for women's humanity than in women's failure to adequately serve men's desires for support, admiration, and attention. Manne suggests that privileged white women (those whose humanity is recognized in general) provoke hatred when they fail to put others' needs and interests ahead of their own.[36] Thus, when Leslie no longer threatens Jamm's finances but offers emotional support, Jamm loses his incentive to demean her.

The character construction of the town's local shock jock known as The Douche (Nick Kroll) vividly illustrates the economic incentives that facilitate Pawnee residents' misogyny. The Douche is a racist, sexist radio personality. In season 5, he agrees to quit teasing Leslie's best friend Ann Perkins (Rashida Jones) on air on the condition that Leslie stand in a tub of red Jell-O during his show. A few days later, The Douche reveals that his real name is Howard Tuttleman and that his offensive performance is an act. He explains to Leslie and Ann that he created The Douche in jest while studying semiotics at Northwestern, and the character snowballed into his career. With a disarming smile, he admits, "It's a silly thing to do, but it pays the bills."[37] The Douche turns out to be a persona, but the persona is integrated into Tuttleman's everyday life nonetheless as Tuttleman/The Douche toggles back and forth between engaging in earnest conversation and overt sexual objectification of Leslie and Ann.

Leslie's interactions with Jamm and The Douche illustrate that exploiting people's proclivity toward sexism is part of doing business. As cultural critic Henry A. Giroux notes, the "relentless public debasement of young girls and women" is a product of the "predatory mode" of politics "in which the logic of the marketplace is recalibrated to exploit society's most vulnerable."[38] *P&R*'s effort to expose the endearing qualities of figures who uttered some of the most deeply offensive comments during earlier seasons of the program depersonalizes their sexism, suggesting it is part of a larger political and economic system that privileges individual financial pursuits over the well-being of others.

The program's integration of corporate and sexist challenges to Leslie's agenda conveys that sexist realism is not merely a parallel to capitalist realism, but the two are intrinsically connected. Leslie's predicament is impossible because she is bound up in two fundamentally incompatible positions, caught between the ideal of neoliberal feminism and the material precarities that neoliberalism produces. Considered apart from her investments in promoting other women and public welfare, Leslie's career advancement might be achievable, but breaking through glass ceilings *and* providing social protections against the depredations of neoliberalism is impossible within her hometown.

This conflict highlights a new kind of feminist dilemma akin to highly mediated controversies during the eighties and nineties regarding whether women could "have it all": a fulfilling career and a satisfying home life.[39] *P&R* foregrounds a new iteration of feminist struggle: to have an upwardly mobile career trajectory and enable others to flourish at the same time. Leslie's struggle to have it all is a different kind of totality, but both are driven by women's conflicts between self-advancement and care for others in the absence of effective social supports that would make such "balance" more feasible. The impossible woman thus marks the limits of neoliberal feminism for gender justice as it situates this character between second-wave feminism's emphasis on women's access to waged labor and its concern for public protections from the marketplace. While Leslie's desire to climb the ladder of local government evokes aspects of liberal second-wave feminism's emphasis on women's inclusion within sectors of employment previously dominated by men, the program's farcical portrayal of her unremitting resolve and commitment to public service conveys that no amount of striving will lead to women's full emancipation. In this sense, the program obliquely points to other models of feminism premised around more fundamental challenges to the economic structures that undergird patriarchy. But as I explain in the next section, the program's vision for feminism is hazy at best.

Admittedly, I have not reviewed the full narrative of Leslie Knope's career. At the conclusion of the program's sixth season, federal officials recognize Leslie's good work and hire her to run a branch of the National Park Service. In her new role, she establishes a large area of formerly private property near Pawnee into a national park. The series' final episode suggests that either she or her spouse, Ben Wyatt (Adam Scott), eventually becomes president of the United States. One implication of Leslie's appointment at the federal level is that she had to transcend local politics to achieve her career goals. By locating sexist realism in white, rural America, the conclusion disavows broader structures of sexism shaping national political and social life to offer a glimpse of possibility for the impossible woman after all.

I do not think the series' final season necessarily negates the program's underlying sexism realism. The episodic structure across most of the individual episodes amplifies sexist realist themes well into season 7. The series' ending points to the ambivalences entailed by the impossible woman in popular culture, revealing that audiences want her to succeed yet may not be entertained by the narrative after she has done so. In celebrating the extraordinary effort that is required for women to gain recognition while also supporting others,

P&R invites viewers to both appreciate and mock the impossible woman's tireless striving.

Weak Satire

Thus far, I have attended to *P&R*'s narrative tensions to explore how the sitcom pokes fun at white, middle-class women's striving under neoliberalism. *P&R*'s emphasis on the difficulties Leslie faces creates some potential for the program to function as a representative anecdote about the limits of neoliberal feminism for managing contemporary political and economic crises. By witnessing Leslie's foibles, the program might invite viewers to reconsider their own maladjustments to increasingly demanding sociopolitical and economic circumstances. Viewers could recognize in Leslie's striving the limits to their own efforts to demonstrate perfection, positivity, and resilience under damaging, distressing, and prohibitive circumstances. However, I am not convinced that the program offers resources for sharp interrogation of neoliberal feminist virtues.

Instead, I argue that *P&R* is a form of weak satire that normalizes sexist realism even as it reveals and critiques it. My conceptualization of "weak" satire draws from Michelle Colpean and Meg Tully's critique of "weak reflexivity" in white feminist comedy that jokes about the privileged subjectivity of whiteness but fails to offer deeper critical examination. They conclude that such weak reflexivity ultimately reproduces dominant racial ideologies rather than dismantles them.[40] Taking a cue from this work but on a different register, weak satire identifies the process through which a text's satiric elements such as exaggeration foreground structural problems while simultaneously reproducing the logics that propel those very concerns. Several feminist scholars have explored how feminist content in late-night television entertainment and comedy sketch programs has used irony and satire to make pointed critiques of gender injustice, postfeminism, and patriarchal norms.[41] A satiric portrayal may be said to be "weak" when an object of criticism within a text is inadvertently or paradoxically reinforced by virtue of its relationship to other themes and messages within the text's diegesis. While *P&R* makes a clear mockery of sexism in politics and its imbrications with neoliberalism's influence on democracy, it stops short of offering a strong critique of neoliberal feminist striving. The show's biting commentary about sexism works alongside its gentler take on Leslie's resilience to reinforce the lessons of sexist realism.

The attempt to pin down the meaning of a satiric performance can be, well, prickly. As several rhetoric and media scholars note, satire is inherently polysemic and polyvalent.[42] Viewers may not recognize implicit criticism within a text's exaggerated portrayal or incongruous message, instead identifying with the expressed commitments and ideas represented. Lisa Glebatis-Perks argues that our understanding of satire's polysemic potential would be enhanced by recognizing the discursive interactions that activate polysemy within satiric texts. Rather than locate polysemy with the viewer, Glebatis-Perks finds it within the "scaffolding" of humorous texts that are composed of contrasting elements.[43] *P&R*'s discursive scaffolding involves contrasting storylines that juxtapose ironic elements with earnest portrayals of generosity, intimacy, and friendship. Rather than open up multiple potential interpretations, these elements narrow the range of available meanings of Leslie's character. In addition to her efforts in the workplace, Leslie works tirelessly for her friends. She organizes elaborate parties and makes handmade gifts to honor them. To celebrate "Galentine's Day," she gives each of her six girlfriends a mosaic portrait "made from the crushed bottles of [their] favorite diet soda" and "a personalized 5,000 word essay of why" they are "all so awesome."[44]

Leslie also has the devotion of several fellow city employees. Ron reluctantly volunteers for a local telethon because he owes her "like a thousand favors."[45] Even the city's police chief volunteers his force to serve at one of her events because "she's the kind of person who uses favors to help others."[46] The emphasis on Leslie's concern for others reflects a feminist ethic of care that contrasts with the virtue of individual achievement featured elsewhere in the program. Karrin Vasby Anderson argues that *P&R* is an alternative to other more biting television satires about women in political office because it emphasizes collaboration and concern for the welfare of others irrespective of their political differences. Anderson concludes that the program is an "exemplar of deliberative feminist citizenship."[47]

Although the program reflects a feminist care ethic, the program's earnest and positive portrayal of Leslie's commitment to others detracts from its concerns over neoliberalism's encroachment on public life. The model of care embodied by Leslie amplifies the cultural expectations for women's unpaid labor in support of others. Leslie's best friend Ann laments that she just cannot "compete" with Leslie's spectacular gestures of friendship.[48] That Leslie's commitment to other women is characterized in terms of competition highlights how Leslie's social value rests upon her labor in relationship to others who are less productive. When she cannot secure state or federal funds for city cleanup projects, she simply does the work herself. In this regard, the program celebrates the unpaid labor that neoliberal economics has both ignored and depended on, as it has facilitated the reduction of entitlement programs and state services.

Leslie's friends and family are drawn to her work ethic. Ben first hints at his attraction to Leslie in season 3 when he tells her, "I've never met anyone who works as hard as you. You're like the Energizer Bunny of city government."[49] That Ben admires Leslie for her work ethic foregrounds the program's attachments to neoliberal subjectivity in which an individual's most redeeming quality is that they work constantly. During her campaign for city council in season 5, Leslie tells her supporters, "If we work hard, never sleep, and shirk all of the responsibilities in our lives, there's nothing we can't do!"[50] The punchline to this and other quips about Leslie's tirelessness is that the success she is striving for is physically impossible, but it rarely rises to the level of concern that suggests she should do otherwise. Even if she cannot possibly manage her commitments to her career and her community, the program suggests that this should not deter the impossible woman.

P&R's construction of Leslie's likability undercuts its potential to offer critical commentary about the impossible woman because Leslie's likability helped suture viewers' affective attachments to her plucky resilience. Indeed, some viewers *like* Leslie so much that they wish to *be more like* her. In a focus group study, Robyn Stacia Swink found that viewers expressed positive identification with Leslie due to her positivity and the program's "feel good" tone.[51] One respondent commented, "I would love to hang out with Leslie Knope. And I wouldn't mind being more like her, it's aspirational."[52] Viewers' responses suggest that Leslie's likability is based on the dispositions of neoliberal feminism. Likable characters who routinely and cheerfully encounter sexism position viewers to anticipate that they or others should spectacularly overcome such damage rather than engage politically to prevent it from occurring in the first place. The irony of respondents' desire to emulate a character who encounters sexism routinely points to the porous boundary between satire and daily life; viewers wish they could be more like a fictional character who believes that she can achieve the physically impossible rather than view the constraints she faces as a sign that she should shift her approach to her work. Viewers' enthusiasm for Leslie highlights how self-delusion has become a feminist virtue under neoliberalism.

P&R's satiric edge is also blunted by its endearing portrayal of unlikely friendships and feminist men. The program invites viewers' sentimental attachment to main characters and their social bonds, bridging critical distance from characters' flaws and foibles. The storyline about Leslie's career development is supplemented by narratives about characters' close relationships. Because she cares for the welfare of others, Leslie finds community in her friends and romantic partners. As the Galentine's Day episode highlights, Leslie affirms supportive relationships with other women, including her best friend, Ann. She and Ron are confidants on matters of workplace and relationship conflict even though they vehemently disagree on the purpose of government.

Leslie's friendship with Ron presents a utopian vision of a democratic community in which people work together amicably despite their political differences. This portrayal of political friendship offers a model for civic engagement based on the recognition of the shared humanity of others. Given the increasing hostility, distrust, and dehumanizing rhetoric about people with different political beliefs in U.S. electoral politics, it makes sense that many critics have celebrated this dimension of *P&R*. However, I find that the loving depiction of Ron avoids a deeper interrogation of the ways in which structural inequities are often subordinated in favor of individualized understandings of political conflict. After all, Ron cares for Leslie, but he supports her only insofar as he *owes her* many favors, and he gleefully undermines her initiatives when they violate his libertarian principles. Ron's friendship is a salve for Leslie's feminist losses, which obscures the harms caused by the libertarian policies Ron endorses. Kindness and collegiality make for a better workplace, but it is not an adequate substitute for public policy on behalf of the people Leslie aims to serve.

As the portrayal of Leslie and Ron's cross-party friendship illustrates, one hallmark of the program's feminism is its portrayal of men who support one another and value Leslie. These men stand in stark contrast to the more offensive, patriarchal figures on the show. A scene featuring Leslie's wedding ceremony to Ben is memorable for their mutual wedding vows: "I love you and I like you."[53] The humor of the understatement places the couple's friendship at the center of their romance. Throughout their courtship and marriage, Ben never wavers from his support for Leslie's career in public service. As the series progresses, it features intimacy and connection over personal accomplishment as the means for achieving a fulfilling and successful life (see fig. 1.3).

The show's heartwarming portrayal of friendship is less an indictment of individual striving than a balm for the cruelty of life under neoliberalism. For

FIG. 1.3 Leslie's and Ben's wedding vows, "I love you and I like you," convey the themes of friendship and care present throughout *Parks and Recreation*. *Parks and Recreation*, season 5, episode 14, "Leslie and Ben," written by Michael Schur and Alan Yang, original airdate February 21, 2013, NBC.

example, an episode featuring Jamm's efforts to undermine Leslie is crosscut with a narrative about City Manager Chris Traeger's (Rob Lowe) search for love. He turns Malwae-Tweep's eye after she covers a bachelor party he organized for his friends. The episode concludes as Malwae-Tweep tells the camera, "Good friends, doing nice things for each other. That's what's important in life."[54] Several similar subplots foreground the virtues of kindness and empathy for others. The scenes temper the program's biting portrayals of crass sexism and corporate indifference to the needs of others.

Leslie's intimate relationships present earnest commentary about the values of personal integrity, friendship, and loyalty; but they do not resolve the problems she encounters. These characters seem to expect if not accept sexual harassment and neoliberal economic policy. Councilman Milton faces no repercussions for asking Leslie to kiss him in front of one of her coworkers even though he engaged in quid pro quo sexual harassment. Councilman Dexhart is never reprimanded even when he smacks Malwae-Tweep's bottom in city hall. Jamm's appeals to "tearing a chick" apart only result in an extended conversation about April's flaws in the Parks Department. Ron happily treats Leslie to waffles at her favorite diner, but he never rolls back his efforts to privatize the city parks' concession stands. The program also suggests that the city's only option to manage its financial constraints is to become more neoliberal. In season 3, the Parks Department must cut its budget rather than seek additional funds. When a high-tech computer company seeks to outbid Leslie for land she hopes to commit to the parks service during the final season, she begins to think like a neoliberal herself. She identifies a cheaper space for the tech company to purchase, making the land she wishes to purchase affordable for the state.

P&R's attention to personal relationships as the primary source of support and care presents an exemplar of feminist citizenship that enables neoliberalism and the attendant sexism to flourish in spite of the damage it causes. Although several episodes draw explicit attention to structural inequality, the program predominantly depicts feminism as a celebration of friendship, delinked from its broader associations with organized social change. Conservative viewers might find some positive identification with Ron, who appears virtuous in his steadfast commitment to libertarian ideals but whose loyalty sustains his friends and family in moments of crisis. In the absence of an informed citizenry willing to engage public officials to support the common good, the show celebrates private associations grounded in work and family life as the substitution for robust government programs that might serve the entire community. Such citizenship grounded in personal relationships and private interests is limited in its capacity to provide strong advocacy for substantive change on behalf of the people most exploited by precarious workplace conditions and a minimal social safety net.

Persisting in Perpetuity

As a representative anecdote about the fate of women in politics, Leslie Knope's impossible tirelessness has implications for feminist politics and organizing. After all, "fictionalized representations of politics" have played a "central role in the definition of expression of political culture and political leaders."[55] Beyond responding to Hillary Clinton's political failures, *P&R* anticipated more recent political campaign discourse that primes audiences to expect sexual discrimination. *P&R*'s portrayal of Leslie was a narrative precursor to mainstream media coverage of Elizabeth Warren's presidential campaign in 2019. Prior to her run for the presidency, Warren garnered enthusiasm from a range of progressives for her lengthy speech opposing President Trump's nominee for attorney general, Senator Jeff Sessions. Her supporters seized upon Senate Majority Leader Mitch McConnell's disparaging remark "Nevertheless, she persisted" as a campaign slogan that foregrounded her determination to be heard.[56] Driven by concerns regarding unregulated markets and the banking industry, Warren's career in the Senate focused on promoting consumer protections and a social safety net for vulnerable populations. Thus, the press characterized her as a renegade, determined to "fight[...] corruption and chang[e] the rules of the game."[57] While fellow progressive candidate Bernie Sanders performed solidly during the primary campaign, Warren's poll numbers steadily declined that summer and led news coverage to ponder the "electability question." The question was not whether Warren was qualified to serve but whether it was even possible for a woman to win a general election. That June, an Ipsos poll for *The Daily Beast* found that "while 74 percent of respondents claimed they were personally comfortable with a female president, only 33 percent believed their neighbors would be comfortable with a woman in the Oval Office."[58]

As the electability question suggests, sexist realism involves a deferral of agency insofar as sexism is construed as an inescapable reality. Presumably, Warren's loss to Trump in the 2020 general election was certain. Many Democrats decided not to vote for her or to consider other women in the primary race for that reason. That Warren's gender was a factor for avowed feminist sympathizers voting in the election points to the ways in which sexist realism has influenced politics. In a reflection on the 2016 U.S. presidential election, Karrin Vasby Anderson argues that gender was a "foundational and formative constraint" to Hillary Clinton's election bids. She concludes that "every woman is the wrong woman" when it comes to presidential elections in the United States.[59] A political climate informed by sexist realism suggests that the constraints facing women may not be entirely driven by sexist resistance to qualified women in office but by voters who have come to expect sexism as a routine feature of social and political life. Cruel optimism has grounded contemporary discourse about women's political leadership. As a quote from *The New York Times* instructs, "Women should still run, even if they keep failing."[60]

P&R's emphasis on neoliberal politics suggests that women may not be disparaged solely because they are women but because their agendas threaten to destabilize systems of economic and social stratification. On one level, women seeking to expand the social safety net to provide any degree of protection for those most vulnerable to the ravages of unregulated capitalism are particularly subject to sexist scrutiny. But on a deeper level, even neoliberal feminists may be anathema to the broader neoliberal project. If, as Asen attests, "neoliberalism draws on inequality for its very existence," women's subordinate status sustains neoliberal imperatives of competition.[61] Thus, any woman's advancement is a threat that must be contained.

The intractable problems facing the impossible woman also underscore how neoliberal feminism's investments in individualism undermine the coalition building that has been paramount to feminist political organizing throughout history. Sexist realism does not implicate all women in equal measure. Instead, it both buttresses women's subjugation as a class and affirms social hierarchies and exclusions. *P&R* largely ignores conflicts over forms of discrimination that structure political and social life beyond considerations of gender. For instance, the character Tom Haverford is of Southeast Asian descent, and Donna Meagle is Black, but they both appear to be unencumbered by structural or individual racism. A rare depiction of contemporary white racism occurs in season 1, when Leslie makes several insensitive comments about Haverford's dark skin. In the pilot episode, she presumes that he is from Libya even though he states he was born in South Carolina. Her remarks satirize white feminism's ignorance regarding race, but the program never depicts Leslie in the process of learning or reflecting upon her contribution to racial discrimination in the workplace.

P&R's shallow effort to satirize racism illustrates Colpean and Tully's observations about "weak reflexive feminist comedy," in which white feminists "joke about their whiteness without critically examining it, ultimately reproducing dominant racial ideologies rather than working to dismantle them."[62] Likely part of the writers' effort to make Leslie more approachable,[63] the program does not present her making racist comments after season 1; nor does it attend to racial discrimination as a problem of city government. Instead, the program disregards issues of racial discrimination. By focusing on white masculinity as the source of damage, the program ignores how white femininity also bears responsibility for conferring damage upon communities of color. With the exception of references to the lack of Indigenous sovereignty in Pawnee, the program avoids conversations about other routine forms of discrimination, portraying a vision of community in which inequities driven by disability, sexuality, gender identity, and so on seem to have little bearing on life in the town. The program's emphasis on the difficulties of relatively well-off white women who do not recognize the problems of less entitled groups normalizes the exclusions embedded in much of liberal white feminist organizing. In this regard, the program exemplifies the limitations of liberal feminism's pursuit of inclusion within extant institutions dominated by white men.

Intersectional politics is also obviated by the program's emphasis on perfection as the price of entry into male-dominated spheres. Ostensibly, the impossible woman deserves inclusion in male-dominated spheres because her exceptional talent distinguishes her from other women. As Dow remarks of the sitcom *Murphy Brown*, a focus on "exceptional women whose lives are cushioned by privileges of education, race, and class . . . overlook[s] the profound inequalities that burden women who are *not* like Murphy Brown (a category that, in fact, includes most women)" but specifically pertains to women who are poor, Black women, and Latinx women.[64] A feminist politics premised on the value of the exceptional woman downplays feminist commitments to justice for all groups subordinated within the dominant social order, including BIPOC and LGBTQ+ communities. While the impossible woman suggests that neoliberal feminist individualism may not be viable, it fails to present diverse coalitional politics as an alternative. This shortcoming is not unique to *P&R*. A variety of programs released subsequently featured resilient female characters who were hamstrung by competing goals of self-advancement and concern for others' well-being yet determined to prove themselves to mediocre men nonetheless.

2

Improbably Cheerful

The *Unbreakable Kimmy Schmidt*

In 2015, Netflix released the sitcom *Unbreakable Kimmy Schmidt* (hereafter *UKS*), a series about the titular character's efforts to rebuild her life after being rescued from an underground bunker where she had lived for fifteen years following her abduction by a charming but callous psychopath at the age of fourteen. An unlikely premise for a comedy series, *UKS* caricatures the cultural misogyny that foments sexual abuse and violence against women and girls. Kimmy Schmidt (Ellie Kemper) is funny because she is a survivor who does not want to be recognized for her resilience. She manages to live independently despite her traumatic past, and she goes to extraordinary lengths to hold her abuser accountable for his crimes. The series mocks the media fascination surrounding abductions and sexual assaults as Kimmy's backstory resonates with details surrounding highly publicized abductions of women and girls. A fan of the series, *New Yorker* TV critic Emily Nussbaum speculates that *UKS* might have been inspired by one of Ariel Castro's victims, Michelle Knight, who wrote a memoir about her eleven-year ordeal before her rescue in 2013: "Like Kimmy, . . . she has not merely survived the abuse—she's resilient and downright giggly, a fan of karaoke and dancing, angels and affirmations. It's a powerfully girlish model of human toughness."[1]

Nussbaum's commentary helps explain the series' popularity at a time in which mediated celebrations of "girl power" intermingle with popular culture's fascination with dead girls.[2] Kimmy remains cheerful and determined even though her victories pale in comparison to the overwhelming force of patriarchy that conditions her life. Kimmy's character is a variation of the impossible woman epitomized by Leslie Knope. Unlike Leslie, Kimmy is not a striver: she is a survivor. Lacking the support of middle-class parents and advanced education, Kimmy is on her own. The show mocks her unbridled optimism in the face of dire socioeconomic conditions and a dearth of public services. The series' emphasis on virulent misogyny as the basis for each new problem that Kimmy must address amplifies the message that feminist resistance is both laudable and laughable. In this storyworld, rape culture is a mundane feature of women's everyday lives within a neoliberal dystopia governed by private corporations designed to privilege white men. *UKS* shifts cultural meanings of survivorship to articulate it to a general condition of living as a woman or girl. As it portrays sexual harassment and gendered discrimination with a mixture of levity and satire, it depicts conditions of cultural misogyny in ways that invite viewers to both empathize with and laugh at central characters who are determined to overcome patriarchy. The series' overwhelming message is that, despite Kimmy's best efforts to crack it, cultural misogyny is unbreakable.[3]

Whereas *Parks and Recreation*'s exaggerated portrayal of Leslie foregrounds the folly of white middle-class women's investments in the promise of liberal feminism and its grounding in the presumption of social mobility based in meritocracy, *UKS*'s characterization of Kimmy lampoons survivor discourses that foreground overcoming obstacles as the path toward self-fulfillment and cultural recognition.[4] It offers a jarring satire of resilience narratives by illustrating how mainstream discourse celebrates women overcoming sexual abuse and other forms of virulent misogyny so long as they present an overarching positive attitude. And yet, the series' commitment to satire impedes its ability to offer an alternative to these conditions. The show is more invested in maintaining the dialectic between misogyny and popular feminism than in upending this dynamic. As I consider in the conclusion, one explanation for the series' sexist realism may be that white liberal feminism is yoked to patriarchy's imbrications with racial order, such that stories that draw on white liberal feminist frameworks—even those that question the merits of individualistic striving—necessarily advance narratives of failure.

Resilient Kimmy, Unbreakable Misogyny

UKS presents an absurd refraction of the social and economic realities that leave people of color, immigrants, women, and queer people vulnerable to exploitation by wealthy white men. Much of the humor revolves around Kimmy's naive and ill-informed understanding of her circumstances. She moves

FIG. 2.1 *Unbreakable Kimmy Schmidt* foregrounds the titular character's sunny disposition within the first five minutes of the pilot episode. *Unbreakable Kimmy Schmidt*, season 1, episode 1, "Kimmy Goes Outside!," written by Tina Fey and Robert Carlock, released March 6, 2015, Netflix Original.

to New York City to avoid the stigma associated with victims of interpersonal violence. After she is robbed of what little money she has, she resorts to sharing a desolate garden-level apartment with queer, Black, would-be actor Titus Andromedon (Tituss Burgess) and works as a personal assistant for a wealthy socialite, Jacqueline Voorhees (Jane Krakowski). With the maturity of a fourteen-year-old, her age at the time of her abduction, Kimmy wears bright, saturated tones reminiscent of a child's wardrobe, considers her purple JanSport backpack a close friend, and aspires to a career as a crossing guard. Because everyone around her is a narcissist, they routinely fail to appreciate how Kimmy's traumatic past has impacted her, even after they learn that she was one of the "Indiana mole women."

The series' title directly references its overarching theme of women's resilience to cultural misogyny. Kimmy is "unbreakable" because she manages to live independently despite having experienced years of abuse. This message is introduced early by the series' theme song and title sequence. A play on videos circulated by the musical web series *Songify the News*, the sequence presents a montage of images of women and girls, including clips from a news report about Kimmy and her fellow abductees' rescue. The images cut to a local Black resident who declares, "They alive, dammit. These females are strong as hell." That each episode opens with this parody of *Songify* is itself a commentary upon a cultural fascination with sexual violence. The parody is a direct reference to "Dead Giveaway," a video that remixed local news coverage of Charles Ramsey's interview with Cleveland reporters about his 2013 rescue of the women Castro had abducted—Amanda Berry, Gina DeJesus, and Michelle Knight; however, the show's viewers are likely to have been more familiar with a remix released three years earlier. In 2010, *Songify* (then known as *Auto-Tune the News*) gained popularity with its "Bed Intruder Song" video that set electronic musical accompaniment to a report about a man who broke into a Black woman's apartment and attempted to assault her until her brother, Antoine Dodson, intervened. The "Bed Intruder" video digitally manipulated Dodson's voice as he delivered a warning to viewers: "Hide your kids, hide your wife, . . . 'cause they're raping everybody out there," turning the earnest report into a humorous refraction of Dodson's comments.[5] Borrowing from the style of this music video, the opening to *UKS* positions Kimmy's background as another instance in which sexual assault has made national headlines for public entertainment; however, in this series, female victims of sexual violence are extraordinary by virtue of their survival.

The series repeatedly reminds viewers of Kimmy's fortitude. During the pilot episode, Kimmy dismisses Titus's despair over living in poverty. Recalling how she resisted her abductor's efforts to control her, she declares, "We're the strong ones and you can't break us!"[6] Her toughness equips her to cheerfully pursue a series of jobs in the service sector and part-time gigs despite low pay and degrading work conditions. Kimmy coaches others to be resilient as well. She tells Jacqueline to endure her husband's negligence: "You can take anything ten seconds at a time";[7] instructs Jacqueline's stepdaughter Zan (Dylan Gelula) to stick it out in college: "I know if you don't give up and think positive, things will work out";[8] and persuades fellow former mole woman Gretchen (Lauren Adams) to start her own cult rather than follow unscrupulous men: "We are strong independent women!"[9] By continually taking matters into her own hands, Kimmy is a figural illustration of the "amazing bounce-backable woman" called forth by women's magazines and self-help literature that instruct women to embrace challenges by adapting resilient attitudes.[10]

UKS satirizes how cruelty has become a resource for generating such responsibilized female subjects, as it portrays Kimmy's determination as a response to years of seclusion and sexual abuse.[11] In this way, the series presents misogyny as the precondition for women's social value. It is not simply that women victims must demonstrate their moral competence and risk avoidance efforts to receive public sympathy after experiencing abuse; it is their ability to withstand abuse itself that marks them as valuable subjects. Throughout the series, flashbacks to Kimmy's time in the bunker illustrate how she learned resourcefulness out of necessity. For instance, episode 2 flashes back to the time she knitted a scarf for a fellow abductee out of her own hair.[12] These flashbacks illustrate how resilience itself is a response to dehumanizing conditions, such that the level of a woman's strength is a measure of the degree of suffering she has faced. "I'm a survivor," she tells Jacqueline during season 1, "That's what women do."[13]

The series amplifies its dark take on resilience by foregrounding a broader culture of misogyny and sexual violence that thrives beyond her underground bunker. Like other women-centered series released in the early-to-mid aughts, the series contextualizes specific instances of violence against women as part of a broader system of heteropatriarchy that informs a wide range of social practices.[14] While the series involves both episodic and serial storylines, its serial narrative revolves around Kimmy's ongoing conflict with her former abductor, "Reverend" Richard Wayne Gary Wayne (Jon Hamm).[15] Kimmy's problems are grounded not in Wayne's assault but in the culture that enabled him. Even though he is known to have abused multiple women, the "Reverend" charms others with his handsome face and trite appeals to conservative values. Season 1 concludes with a double episode about Wayne's criminal trial in which he convinces almost everyone, including the two prosecuting attorneys and Titus, of his innocence (see fig. 2.2). The two attorneys, portrayed by Tina Fey and Jerry Minor, are named Marcia Cross and Chris Darden, a direct reference to the prosecuting attorneys who were unable to convince juries to convict O. J. Simpson of criminal homicide in the deaths of his wife Nicole Brown Simpson and her friend Ronald Goldman despite the strong evidence against him. The reference to the infamous case amplifies the series' attention to patriarchal conditions that enable abusers to avoid accountability. After her fellow abductees fail to persuade the jury of Wayne's wrongdoing, Kimmy takes extraordinary measures to present incontrovertible evidence disproving Wayne's testimony. That the mole women's eyewitness testimonies had little impact in the courtroom foregrounds one overarching lesson of the series: People do not believe women. Thus, women must figure out how to take matters into their own hands.

Kimmy continues to battle Wayne in subsequent seasons as several supporting characters continue to believe his version of events. In a season 4 parody of a true crime documentary, man's rights activist Fran Dodd (Bobby Moynihan) purports to prove Wayne's innocence. The episode's aesthetic cues invite comparisons to popular true crime documentary series such as *Making a Murderer* and *The Staircase* that questioned the evidence used to convict white men of murdering women. In doing so, the series obliquely comments upon the subgenre's propensity to erase women victims from stories about men's violent crimes. Natalia Vedric and Janine Little argue that such documentaries deny women's "subjective agency."[16] Kimmy is horrified when she learns that Dodd's case is based on the filmmaker's conclusion that Kimmy is decidedly "NOT CUTE." The episode manipulates clips of Donald Trump telling audiences "She would not be my first choice" to suggest that the former president also supported "the Reverend."[17] The degrading logic used to defend Wayne within the familiar documentary format points to the ways that streaming media have capitalized upon cultural investments in white men's innocence.

FIG. 2.2 The Reverend taunts Kimmy after nearly convincing a jury to acquit him of charges that he abducted her and three other women. *Unbreakable Kimmy Schmidt*, season 1, episode 1, "Kimmy Goes to Court!," written by Emily Altman and Jack Burditt, released March 6, 2015, Netflix Original.

By positioning viewers to experience Dodd's documentary from Kimmy's vantage point, the series reasserts women's subjectivity over the forms of privileged masculinity featured in most true crime dramas and points to the sexism that underlies popular fascination with the genre. As part of a broader story arc in which Kimmy continually pushes back against others' efforts to valorize Wayne, the episode reminds viewers that Wayne is not an extraordinary figure. Instead, he is mundane, part of the broader culture in which men violate women with impunity.

The program's portrayal of abuse against women and girls as a mundane feature of social life is reinforced by brief moments of dialogue in which characters make offhand references to sexual assault and murder for comedic effect. During season 2, Jacqueline seeks vengeance against her ex-husband, who took most of the couple's wealth and immediately began dating a younger woman after their divorce. The advice from one of her ex's business associates is that she should kill herself in her ex's office. "I always hate that," he shrugs.[18] To help Jacqueline identify a new career path the next season, Kimmy refers her to a career aptitude test that covers all careers from "architect to Zodiac killer." In that moment, Jacqueline realizes that her aptitude for work as a "guidance counselor bather" was "not based on a real test."[19] In the fourth season, Lillian poses as a Russian stripper to gain access to an exclusive, men's only event and tells the bouncer, "I'm OK with you kill me."[20] Three episodes later, a high school principal invites Titus to direct the school's next play because the theater teacher got "several girls" pregnant.[21] That each of these remarks has little connection to any storyline amplifies the series' overarching lesson that misogyny has become so entrenched in U.S. society that it doesn't merit serious or sustained attention.

The series' final episode suggests that the program might have been canceled because sexism is too mundane to warrant audience interest. In this episode, Jacqueline discourages Kimmy from writing a memoir about her experience: "Look, pretty much every woman in America has been kidnapped or MeToo'd since you. Nobody wants to read about that stuff anymore."[22] Expressed in the first minutes of the series finale, the same comment could be applied to the series itself. It also suggests that what's really unbreakable is the culture of misogyny that exploits and disregards figures like Kimmy, who remain resolutely determined to break the cycle of violence despite its omnipresence. The final episode's final moments sow some doubt regarding the certainty of Jacqueline's outlook, a point I'll address in the conclusion of this chapter; however, the vast majority of the show's humor revolves around a worldview in which women must continually withstand sexism and endure sexual violence.

Neoliberal Dystopia

Similar to *Parks and Recreation*'s depiction of corporate greed as a motive for sexual harassment within city government, *UKS* draws attention to the interconnectedness between cultural misogyny and neoliberalism. However, this series offers a far bleaker outlook for women's opportunities in a world governed by wealthy white men eager to hoard their wealth. Kimmy has no illusions about her opportunities for upward mobility. Within her storyworld, there is no government agency capable of intervening against corporate abuse or a social safety net for people whose bad luck subjects them to poverty, housing insecurity, and preventable disease. Kimmy, Titus, and their landlady, Lillian Kaushtupper (Carol Kane), live in poverty while others, like Jacqueline, are part of New York's wealthy elite. In the absence of any discernible commitment to the public good, the series presents a comically nightmarish realization of neoliberal governance. It spotlights a world in which people exercise freedom "without concern for social context or consequences, without care for society, civility, or social bonds, and above all without concern for the political cultivation of a common good."[23]

The show takes aim at public education during season 1, when Kimmy earns her GED solely due to her pluck and determination. Her instructor has no interest in teaching. "I can't get fired," he informs a distraught Kimmy. "I've got tenure."[24] The school administrative assistant offers to sell her a GED instead, but Kimmy declines the offer. Since budget cuts have left the school with limited funds, Kimmy resorts to teaching herself. In the process, she develops a friendship with fellow student Dong Nguyen (Ki Hong Lee), an undocumented immigrant tirelessly working to make ends meet. By foregrounding how public education has failed the students, the episode emphasizes that public institutions are ill-equipped to provide resources to those who need them the most.

Subsequent episodes satirize market-driven approaches to education by attributing the decline of affordable college education to corporate influence. After earning her GED, Kimmy's college options are limited to schools with a direct commercial tie-in: "Famous Ray's Original College"; a space unfit for humans: "SUNY The Sewer"; or a crime scene: "Hudson University."[25] The cover of Hudson University's brochure reads, "as seen on *Law & Order* SVU" and features stills of presumably murdered women lying prone in awkward poses, surrounded by yellow police tape. Kimmy is too naive and traumatized to feel discouraged. "These places all look great!" she tells Lillian.[26] Kimmy's affective response to the situation invokes comedic irony. Cáit Neylon compares Kimmy's affective response to the "irrational exuberance" of those who have unfounded optimism about economic markets.[27] Reading Kimmy's optimism as a mechanism for coping with repressed anger and unresolved psychological trauma, Neylon argues that the character's performance of cuteness is a strategic response to ongoing demands for women's resilience. In exposing the dysfunction that gives rise to her sunny disposition, the series points to growing cultural disenchantment with postfeminist gender scripts.

Kimmy is an exaggerated form of the neoliberal feminist subject who is irrepressibly cheerful as she struggles to exist in a culture that profits from her exploitation. The series' disenchantment with neoliberal imperatives is amplified by the series' dark humor. To help her choose a career, Lillian advises her to "work backward" and asks her, "How do you want to die"?[28] The exchange reinforces the series' overarching lesson that institutions don't work for people unless they are private corporations designed to serve privileged white men. In a later scene, a career counselor recommends jobs that offer limited or no pay: mannequin, FBI informant, and crossing guard. Kimmy's enthusiastic pursuit of a career as a crossing guard in season 3—a position that she is ultimately unqualified for because she is technically married to Wayne, a convicted sexual abuser—makes a mockery of neoliberal striving. Not only is Kimmy unqualified, but her primary competition for the job is a robot (see fig. 2.3). The series' cynical take on the promises of upward mobility for poor and undocumented people satirizes optimistic faith in the American Dream by foregrounding how the depletion of financial support for public services reinforces racial and economic stratification.

The narcissism of the other characters who compose Kimmy's world extends the series' cynicism. Titus and Jacqueline are too self-absorbed to recognize that Kimmy's problems far outweigh their own struggles. The subplots

FIG. 2.3 Kimmy competes with a robot for a position as a school crossing guard. *Unbreakable Kimmy Schmidt*, season 3, episode 2, "Kimmy's Roommate Lemonades!," written by Tina Fey and Sam Means, released May 19, 2017, Netflix Original.ç

about Titus revolve around his dismal acting career. Season 3 depicts him as a would-be sociopath who is so narcissistic that he mistakenly believes he has eaten Dionne Warwick after a jealous attempt to replace her as the main entertainment on a cruise ship leaves him shipwrecked and delusional. He and Jacqueline repeatedly attempt to curry favor with privileged white men who hold the key to their potential success only to be exploited, demeaned, and abused. As characters with a narcissistic attachment to a world in which they have no controlling share, Titus and Jacqueline act out what Lauren Berlant characterizes as the "fantasy of meritocracy." Despite precarious employment and abusive conditions, they continue to seek proximity to "the good life promised by capitalism" that remains out of their reach until the series' conclusion.[29] Although Jacqueline's character evolves over the course of the four seasons, her inability to appreciate the depths of Kimmy's suffering is an ongoing point of the show's humor. The supporting characters' absurd attempts to gain class and social status illustrate the subjectifying force of neoliberalism by foregrounding how immersion into a world bereft of any notion of the public good invites adherence to a cold and calculating neoliberal order.

The series' resignation to this state of affairs is pronounced in Jacqueline's storyline, as she strives and fails to disrupt structures of whiteness. Over the course of the first three seasons, Jacqueline tries to honor her Lakota Sioux ancestry by raising charity for Indigenous people, but she quickly learns that New York's high society of wealthy white men has no interest in supporting charitable causes that do not directly pertain to their interests.[30] After concluding that the only way to advocate for Indigenous rights is by appealing to white men's greed, Jacqueline convinces the owners of the Washington Redskins to change the team's mascot to the "Gunslingers" because it would appeal to a wider fanbase.[31] The episode is an indictment of neoliberal antiracism, as the team's owners are comically shallow and craven. Rahul Rao draws from Catherine Rottenberg's critique of neoliberal feminism to conceptualize neoliberal antiracism in terms of a variety of initiatives in higher education that purport to address racial inequities through mechanisms rooted in the very "structures of racism and whiteness that they purport to attack."[32] In a similar vein, Jacqueline's only means of challenging white settler colonialism is through securing whiteness's claims to wealth and corporate ownership of dominant cultural images and enterprises. The series' jaundiced portrayal of Jacqueline's efforts suggests that the only way to achieve modest advancements for people of color is to leverage one's own personal power to create interest convergence with the white, wealthy men who are disinclined to enact meaningful social change.

This cynical view of white masculine privilege is punctuated by the conclusion to the subplot revolving around Jacqueline's second marriage to Russ Snyder (David Cross). Jacqueline's efforts to change the sports team's mascot begin once she meets Russ, the estranged son of the family that owns the team who has dedicated his life to social justice causes. After a nearly fatal car accident forces him to undergo facial reconstruction surgery, Russ is transformed into a strikingly handsome lothario (Billy Magnussen). Thrilled that he has gone from "dud to stud," he abandons his commitment to helping others and regains his father's respect.[33] His transformation prompts a turning point in Jacqueline's character, as she decides that she would rather live on her own than return to a world of shallow rich men "who only care about beautiful things."[34]

Jacqueline's encounters with selfish men prompt her to become a better neoliberal subject. Abandoning social justice causes in the final season, she pursues her own lucrative career path. A season 4 episode inspired by Ticketmaster's price gouging practices suggests that Jacqueline's transformation has largely served to help her become a savvy, yet underhanded, entrepreneur. In this episode, she and Lillian conspire to make money by buying up all of the tickets for a high school play, driving up the ticket prices, and creating artificial demand for seats. Rather than just learning how to beat exploitative corporations at their own game, Jacqueline figures out how to play the game for herself and becomes more firmly entrenched in neoliberal striving in the process.

Kimmy is the only character that espouses ongoing commitments to the well-being of others. Part of the series' humor is that Kimmy's isolation from the rest of society during her adolescence enabled her to enter adulthood with a stronger moral compass than the other New Yorkers around her. Kimmy's traumatic past enables her to see beyond superficial appearances, recognize injustice, and find virtue in others. Her resilience born out of trauma equips her with a moral compass that characters like Jacqueline can barely access.

Since few other characters suffered the extreme deprivation and abuse that Kimmy endured, they are unprepared to withstand everyday forms of maltreatment and exploitation without Kimmy's help. Her friendship and support prompts Jacqueline to distance herself from the wealthy white men who have taken advantage of her. Kimmy's positive influence on other characters' lives amplifies the idea that ideal subjectivity is born from tremendous hardship. Thus, Kimmy becomes central to the welfare of her community because she can teach them how to cope.

The series unites its emphasis on Kimmy's resilience with its underlying critique of neoliberalism insofar as everything including survivorship is subjected to economic calculus. For Kimmy, being a survivor consists of moving on in a nation controlled by the depraved interests of the privileged elite. This portrayal diverges from dominant notions of what it means to be a survivor in feminist discourse and popular culture. Since the second wave, feminists' efforts to recast victims as survivors were part of a broader effort to politicize interpersonal gender violence that was largely ignored or hidden from public view. However, talk shows and other media depoliticized survivor discourse by framing the survivor as someone who overcomes suffering "through a process of self-exploration and styles of self-management."[35] Attending to the survivor as a discourse formation, Shani Orgad roots this shift in discourses of neoliberalism that deflect social responsibility toward those who have experienced abuse by foregrounding the "individual strength, bravery, self-sufficiency, and determination" of individuals who have suffered rather than attend to their traumatic experiences.[36] The series satirizes this discourse formation as "unbreakable" Kimmy continually runs up against structures of exploitation despite her best efforts to manage her own suffering.

As the series invites audiences to appreciate Kimmy's resilience with bemusement, *UKS* wrestles with the cultural value attached to trauma survivors. While Kimmy is a responsibilized subject, the form of survivorship that Kimmy represents is a permutation of the "psychotherapeutic idea of the survivor as a moral mission."[37] The series lampoons television talk shows' popularization of survivor narratives that have valorized the act of speaking out publicly as a means of overcoming victimhood. Across multiple episodes, media producers appear more career-driven than sincere when they invite Kimmy to discuss her trauma. In a parody of the show *Dr. Phil*, Kimmy finds herself on the *Dr. Dave* show to support former bunker mate Cyndee Pokorny (Sara Chase). Skeptical of the therapeutic value of the show, Kimmy consults Titus, who favorably describes the show as a form of "therapeutainment."[38] But Kimmy thinks that Dr. Dave is a "creep." Nonetheless, Dr. Dave (Jeff Goldblum) manipulates Kimmy to appear on the show with Cyndee and provokes a fight between the two women during the taping. "Ladies, please! Let's not do something that could go viral, #MoleFight," he gleefully jeers to the camera.[39] By foregrounding the crass commercialism that drives Dr. Dave, the episode suggests that televised survivor narratives primarily function as another mechanism for white men to profit from the suffering of others.

Paradoxically, the series draws attention to the ubiquity of sexual assault narratives in popular culture because it forgoes the details surrounding her abuse that viewers might expect to find in a program premised around a sexual abuse survivor. Kimmy consistently refuses to talk about her experience, and the series never reveals precisely what happened to her. By foregrounding Kimmy's struggles *after* leaving the bunker, the series transforms the meaning of the survivor from one who has overcome a uniquely traumatic experience to a more generalized definition of one who is living as a woman or girl in a deeply misogynist world. In Kimmy's storyworld, survival is a mundane act. As she states, being a survivor "is what women do." Because suffering is quotidian, the act of speaking about the most extreme instances of abuse is not curative; it is just another mechanism by which women are exploited. The series also subverts the genre of the survivor story by constructing Kimmy as someone who does not want to be recognized on the basis of her suffering. During season 3, she cancels plans to appear on Zan's college radio show because she resents Zan's description of her as "a symbol that people can overcome anything."[40]

The series mocks survivor discourse in other ways, as other episodes foreground Kimmy's private therapy sessions, where she learns that it's OK to be angry and that "happy places" can become violent very quickly.[41] These episodes poke fun at popular feminist demands for women to regulate not only how they behave but how they feel and think about themselves.[42] The drive for perfection entails heightened forms of self-regulation that entail upbeat self-expression.[43] Rosalind Gill observes that popular feminism is "resolutely *not* angry."[44] Akane Kanai explains that "upbeat" feminism is the product of women's labor in a neoliberal economy that calls for women to perform "resilience, strength, and individuality" and defuses the perception that women may be impacted by negative feelings of weakness or shame.[45] The imperatives of upbeat feminism pertain to politics as well as economics. Rebecca Traister argues that anger has been a "productive or catalytic force" within feminist social movements throughout U.S. history, yet women's anger is regularly maligned in mainstream culture.[46] Traister adds that the consequences of women's anger are uneven, as white women have received rewards and privileges for regulating their anger that are unavailable to women of color, especially Black women.[47] Brittney Cooper states the issue more pointedly: It is dangerous for Black women to express their rage because white fears of Black people can be lethal.[48]

While ignoring the racialized dynamics of women's emotional responses to their exploitation and abuse, episodes featuring Kimmy's therapy poke fun at resilience narratives that valorize women's positive dispositions as a condition of their social value.[49] There is some irony here, as these episodes point to the problematic lessons of the series' overarching portrayal of Kimmy. After all, Kimmy is exceptional, in part, because she does not want to be regarded as exceptional. Kimmy's refusal to serve as a symbol of resilience points to the series' ambivalence about the value of a survivor as a cultural formation.

As the following discussion explains, the series is rife with contradictions that muddy its underlying politics. Nonetheless, it routinely pairs its references to sexual violence with portrayals of neoliberalism run amok. The world presented in *UKS* is driven by forces of greed that invariably outmatch forces for social justice. *UKS* is fatalistic in its attempt to imagine anything better for people exploited by patriarchal neoliberalism. It features a darkly satiric take on New York City society in which anyone who hasn't been locked in a bunker for twenty years is unable to envision commitment to the welfare of a community. In this world, individualist striving is the only pursuit possible, even though such striving is almost certainly bound to fail for everyone except the wealthy white men who have controlling shares of the nation's most profitable business ventures. Until the series' final episode, it does not offer viewers any visions for a more hopeful future. Even as Kimmy maintains a commitment to making the world a better place, she seems to have learned the lesson that the only way to get ahead is by manipulating the structures of exploitation that were established to exploit her. In the series' final episode, she blackmails a publisher into publishing her children's book. As neoliberal forces appear unmovable, even Kimmy's commitment to doing the right thing must accommodate them.

Pseudosatire's Antipolitics

Although it maintains its dark satiric edge more consistently than *Parks and Recreation*, *UKS* is not necessarily more subversive than its predecessor. Whereas *Parks and Recreation*'s satiric edge is blunted by its endearing portrayal of "likable Leslie" and her unlikely friendships, *UKS* cuts both ways, as it expresses underlying cynicism toward both progressive and regressive politics. The series is overrun by ambivalence and contradiction. In addition to mocking cultural misogyny and neoliberalism, the series takes aim at progressive causes, including advocacy for more complex representations of Asian Americans on television and efforts to teach college students to critically interrogate white privilege.

The series' subversive potential is also undercut by its casual racism. Tina Fey and her cowriters received strong media criticism for *UKS*'s season 1 subplot surrounding Jacqueline's Lakota Sioux ancestry because it depended on offensive stereotypes and trivialized the concerns of Native peoples.[50] Season 2, episode 3, is a thinly veiled rebuke of the show's critics, as it portrays an Asian

American advocacy group protesting Titus's one-man performance as a "gang that cancels shows."[51] The episode suggests that the group's knee-jerk reaction to Titus's appearance as a geisha failed to appreciate the broader context of the performance. David Oh describes the episode as an example of white feminism: a discursive strategy that advances "White feminism's investments in White privilege" by discounting anti-racist critique.[52] He adds that the episode's conclusion marks the series' emphasis on pseudosatire, which undercuts its purported satire of cultural appropriation. Christopher Medjesky defines pseudosatire in terms of comedic performances involving dual-layered meanings that are devoid of critical commentary, which enable audiences "to laugh at the ills of the world without really doing anything about it, or, worse, perpetuating problematic notions."[53] Although this concept depends on an arguable assumption that true satire must counter hegemonic politics, it is useful for distinguishing the aesthetics of satire from its various rhetorical functions. That is, the presence of hyperbole, understatement, and irony in a text doesn't necessarily provide direct or obvious critical commentary. As Oh concludes, *UKS*'s treatment of anti-racist dissent does not satirically mock cultural appropriation. Instead, it pseudosatirically mocks the critic.[54]

I largely agree with Oh's analysis but would revise his reading of the series' characters. Oh interprets Lillian as a "metonym for anti-racist White women progressives,"[55] but the series routinely portrays her as deeply conflicted over her own racism and sexism. Several episodes recount how she shot and killed her husband because he was Black and she mistook him for an intruder, and she frequently makes racist and sexist remarks. Jacqueline also makes racist remarks when she is compelled to return a painting that she won in her divorce settlement because it had been previously stolen from a Jewish family by Nazis. Rather than grapple with her privilege, she is indignant: "The Jews took my painting!" she tells Kimmy.[56] Perhaps the series' casually racist commentary is intended to reveal the irony of white privilege by featuring white people's failures to recognize the contradictions in their worldviews. But such casual remarks never face scrutiny or consequence. Instead, the jokes appear to be weakly satiric, disavowing any serious political or social justice commitments.

The series also undercuts its feminist themes by obfuscating the distinction between its antagonists and protagonists. Although the series foregrounds the moral failings of Kimmy's closest associates—Titus, Jacqueline, and Lillian—it also features the positive attributes of some of its most violent characters. These characters are inspired, both directly and indirectly, by recent historical figures. Season 3 opens with an episodic storyline about Lillian's love affair with Robert Durst (Fred Armisen). The previous year, the real Robert Durst drew extensive media attention after the HBO documentary *The Jinx* recounted evidence linking him to the unsolved disappearance of his wife Kathie and the murder of his friend Susan Berman, including what appears to be a confession, muttered under his breath when he thought his mic was turned off. Toward the conclusion of the *UKS* episode, Armisen's Durst decides to leave Lillian because he knows he is not good for her. The episode depends on audience familiarity with the horrific case, drawing humor from an ironic violation of viewers' expectations by making Durst appear more laughable than monstrous and more capable of responsible decision-making than Lillian. Other recurring characters including men's rights activist Fran Dodd and Kimmy's abductor Richard Wayne Gary Wayne appear more buffoonish than malicious. Through such characterizations, the series' most virulent misogynists are not distinctly pernicious in comparison to other main characters who are openly racist and insensitive to the needs of others. Each of the show's main characters contributes to a culture of violence and exploitation.

Even Kimmy engages in behavior that promotes sexual violence in episodes with storylines about abusive women. In season 3, Kimmy counsels Gretchen after her failed attempt to lead a cult of adolescent boys. As she is being arrested, Kimmy tells Gretchen to never give up.[57] This leads Gretchen to become a cult leader from inside a woman's prison, where she finds that women are far more pliable than unruly teenage boys. The episode's triumphant conclusion is ironically detached from the realities of gendered forms of abuse that drive the rest of the series' narrative. Paralleling the series' ambivalence about Kimmy's resilience, it positions viewers to both appreciate and mock Kimmy's efforts to support her misbegotten friend.

During season 4, even Kimmy finds that she is a perpetrator of abuse. As a newly hired human resources manager at a software development company, Kimmy unwittingly sexually harasses a coworker in the process of firing him. At the end of the episode, she regrets that she made "nerds feel scared and powerless," just like Wayne made her feel when she was in the bunker.[58] The episode's humor is grounded in the gendered reversal of dominant relations of sexual violation throughout #MeToo discourse. The reversal speaks to the series' shallow engagement with feminist politics. By inviting a comparison between Kimmy's behavior and her abductor's, the conclusion frames workplace sexual harassment more as a problem of ignorance than a structural problem embedded within dominant sociopolitical institutions. As Sarah Kornfield and Hannah Jones note, the episode undermines #MeToo activism by portraying sexual violence as an issue that can be resolved by changes to individual behavior.[59] One of the series' showrunners, Robert Carlock, explains that the writers felt obligated to address #MeToo but chose to make Kimmy the perpetrator because a story about Kimmy saving victims of harassment would not be "particularly fun."[60] "I mean, we've certainly plumbed that in her story a lot."[61] That Carlock does not believe a recurring portrayal of women successfully protecting others from abuse would be enjoyable highlights the show's (or at least Carlock's) misogynist orientation. After all, the series routinely cracks jokes about men's routine violations of women. Yet the series never actually depicts Kimmy rescuing others from abusive situations until the interactive special, *Kimmy vs. the Reverend*, was released a year after the series ended.[62] Sexual violence, it would seem, is endlessly entertaining, whereas women's ability to prevent it is not.

Perhaps the program's overarching portrayal of Kimmy's bubbly personality ironically reinforces the series' cynicism. Kimmy is likable because she is virtuous, but she is also a "dummy," as her landlady affectionately describes her.[63] In foregrounding her naivete and stunted development as the primary reasons for her sunny disposition, goodwill toward others, and occasional perpetuation of abuse against other people more vulnerable than her, the show invites viewers to laugh at her as much if not more than laugh with her. In celebrating the extraordinary effort that is required for women to resist cultural misogyny, *UKS* invites viewers to both appreciate and mock the impossible woman's resilience. In short, the series has no clear telos underlying its critique because everything, including feminist activism, is subject to scrutiny.

My criticism is adjacent to Dana Cloud's concerns about "the irony bribe" in the reality TV show *The Bachelor*.[64] Cloud extrapolates from the reality series' capacity to simultaneously elicit genuine emotional investment and ironic suspicion of its reality to conceptualize the irony bribe as a relationship between the viewer and a mediated text that licenses "the enjoyment of that which one is critiquing."[65] Through this relationship, viewers might identify with TV figures' strategies for managing gendered power dynamics and internalize them as "common sense rules" even as they recognize the artifice of these gendered dynamics. A similar case may be made for satires of impossibly striving women. *UKS* invites viewers' investments in a positive outcome for Kimmy and her friends, yet it also elicits detached enjoyment in witnessing these characters' flaws and foibles. By mocking every character who espouses a deep commitment to a social cause, the series cultivates audience indifference to real-world appeals for accountability even though they directly inspired many of the series' episodes.

Admittedly, this analysis does not take the series' final episode into account. The closing scenes reveal that Kimmy wrote a popular children's book loved by boys and girls alike. In what is perhaps the most heartfelt moment of the series, a young boy approaches Kimmy to tell her, "Your books make me feel safe." This conclusion points to the possibility of feminism in the not-too-distant future, one that is markedly different from the world in which Kimmy has lived throughout the series.[66] While this ending is rather satisfying, few scenes prior to this final episode help readers anticipate this outcome. This surprise ending reveals that audiences may want the impossible woman to succeed yet may not be entertained by a narrative after she has done so.

The program's consistently satiric edge prior to this final episode overwhelms this earnest conclusion. Fans of the series would have likely watched its previous fifty episodes, which consistently feature the pernicious and omnipresent threat of sexual violence against women in a world marked by greed and selfishness. The series offers few resources for imagining how adults might help realize a feminist future. After all, part of Kimmy's ability to reach children is due to her own underdevelopment. Overarchingly, the series suggests that mature adults must ultimately accept the realities of neoliberal economics and its concomitant exploitation of women and their suffering. Furthermore, the series' subplots repeatedly amplify sexist realist themes.

The lack of imagination for a more feminist future that underlies the impossible woman is the hallmark of sexist realism, which reinforces the expectation that all those who are not white, able-bodied, cisgender men should expect discriminatory treatment. Of course, this has troubling implications. Sexist realism positions viewers to expect suffering as an inevitable condition of social life under neoliberalism for everyone but the most privileged white men. This lesson is particularly pernicious for women who may not see themselves mirrored by Kimmy's white, thin, and sunny visage. While television series that amplify sexist realist themes tend to foreground white women's pain, they obscure a deeper structural understanding of the conditions and impacts of sexual violence that disproportionately impact women of color.

The series' investments in whiteness might provide some insights to explain the sexist realism that drives this and other series' emphasis on misogyny as the unbreakable precondition for feminist agency. Television studio's predominantly white male writers and producers in the United States and Western Europe who are driving the production of feminist content are less invested in a feminist politic than they are in solidifying and expanding their international, upscale markets. Thus, they have less incentive to advance any of the intersectional awareness that is needed for feminist groups to challenge neoliberal patriarchy, as such awareness would attend to misogyny's inextricable connections to white supremacy, settler colonialism, and Western imperialism. A truly feminist imagination cannot flourish without recognizing these intersections. And yet, sexist realist narratives portray women who survive without it. Consequently, what Havas and Horeck refer to as "Netflix feminism" may more aptly be understood as a cynical effort to appeal to white feminism's alienation from neoliberalism while keeping structures of exploitation firmly in place.[67]

3

Exquisitely Lonely

The Marvelous Mrs. Maisel and *The Queen's Gambit*'s Beth Harmon

While impossible women appear across a range of television genres, the period drama is particularly invested in the figure of the exceptionally talented, resilient woman. AMC's widely praised series *Mad Men* featured women's struggles for autonomy and career achievement in the years just prior to the feminist second wave. Erin Levy, a writer and producer of *Mad Men*, reflected that Peggy was the series' central character because her ability to succeed in the men's world of advertising was nothing short of "amazing": "She's going through a period of time when there was a lot of turmoil for women, where it was really hard to do what she did. To go from a secretary, to becoming a copywriter, to being copy chief—it was almost unheard of."[1] Reflecting on the success of *Mad Men* and *Downton Abbey* in 2015, *Variety* magazine's Malina Saval remarked that shows set in previous eras make women characters more interesting than men because their life choices were more constrained economically, culturally, and socially. By Saval's account, period dramas are animated by an interest in historic conditions of patriarchy because ongoing forms of sexism ostensibly do not continue to limit women's opportunities and mobility.[2] Two years later, the fervor surrounding #MeToo would challenge this assumption (although it does not explain why Saval would not already understand this, given her decades of experience working inside

Hollywood). Presumably, watching women confront sexism makes them worth viewing, but in the context of a seemingly distant past.

Likely inspired by *Mad Men*'s success and renewed concerns about sexism within male-dominated fields in response to #MeToo, streaming television released several series featuring trailblazing women living in the years just prior to the second wave, including *The Marvelous Mrs. Maisel*, *Pan Am*, *Good Girls Revolt*, *The Playboy Club*, and the limited series *The Queen's Gambit*. These programs replicate many narrative and aesthetic elements of *Mad Men*, which offered an ambivalent yet stylish portrayal of the regressive gender norms within the burgeoning advertising industry during the postwar era in the United States. Across these series, uniquely gifted and talented white women strive to overcome obstacles caused by patriarchal family structures and gendered forms of discrimination. Much of the popular discourse regarding the merits of these programs has foregrounded their aesthetic choices, particularly regarding the costuming of the lead characters in period fashion. The enthusiasm for the series' ultrafeminine, expertly tailored clothing points to a vexing tension in trailblazer period pieces, as narratives of women's resistance to patriarchal gender norms revel in the semiotics of pre-sixties modernity as if they were not part and parcel with these norms. If feminism is "popular again," what explains the appeal of these programs?

In this chapter, I explore how trailblazer television elicits conflicting affective orientations to white women's struggles for inclusion. In one direction, the shows invite our critical attention to the everyday humiliations of previous generations of young women. In the other, they invite viewers' objectifying gaze toward these same figures. These disparate orientations work together to guide viewers' positions toward neoliberal feminist politics. Recent trailblazer serials depart from earlier postfeminist melodramas by foregrounding, if not celebrating, women's choice to struggle at work rather than pursue happiness at home or through romance. Their beauty helps them get noticed, but they express little interest in long-term relationships. By featuring this choice, series revolving around women's struggles for career advancement before the second wave respond to the intensified demands for women's individual achievement and perfection. In other words, the prefeminist past envisioned by these programs conforms to the harsh realities of the neoliberal feminist present in which women must tirelessly strive to get ahead.

In what follows, I explain how the nostalgia evoked by the prefeminist trailblazer is structured by a series of unresolvable tensions that point to popular feminism's ambivalent and fraught relationship with neoliberal imperatives that demand women's cheerful participation in their own objectification as a prerequisite for their career success. To elaborate on this point, I focus on the character construction of two of streaming television's most prominent trailblazers in Amazon Prime's *The Marvelous Mrs. Maisel* (hereafter *TMMM*) and Netflix's *The Queen's Gambit* (hereafter *TQG*). *TMMM* follows the early career of Miriam "Midge" Maisel (Rachel Brosnahan), a well-off, twentysomething mother of two who helps break the glass ceiling of New York's stand-up comedy scene after her husband abruptly leaves her for his secretary. Widely recognized for her role as the showrunner of the widely popular TV show *Gilmore Girls*, the series creator Amy Sherman-Palladino explains that she wrote *TMMM* to challenge male bias within comedy. She laments, "People still don't fucking think women are funny."[3] Although Sherman-Palladino credits her late father Don Sherman and comedian Joan Rivers as her inspirations,[4] Midge more closely resembles Jean Carroll, a Jewish female pioneer of stand-up comedy. As Jeremy Shere notes, Carroll drew laughs by evoking the image of a "refined, assimilated Jewish woman" who "talked trash" about her family members, "puncturing the idealized image of the loving mother."[5] Like Carroll, Maisel challenges the assumption that beautiful women cannot be funny.

After its release in 2017, *TMMM* quickly gained favorable attention from critics and fans. Its first season received eight Emmys, including awards for Outstanding Comedy Series and Outstanding Lead Actress for Rachel Brosnahan's portrayal of Midge. It was also the first streaming show to win the Outstanding Comedy Series Emmy. Over the course of the series' five-season run, it received twenty Emmys, five Screen Actors Guild awards, three Golden Globes, and six Critics Choice awards.[6] A variety of media outlets hailed the series as a counterpart to #TimesUp's critique of sexism in Hollywood. *Vogue*'s Emily Farra declared the first season a "feminist hit" with a galvanizing story for young women.[7]

Netflix released *TQG* in 2020, ten months after *TMMM*'s most popular and third season. *TQG* presents a fictional coming-of-age story about a young chess prodigy. Based on a 1983 novel by Walter Tevis, the story revolves around character Elizabeth Harmon's (Anya Taylor-Joy) journey to become the first woman to win the prestigious world chess championship in Moscow. The limited series received an outpouring of favorable commentary upon its release in October 2020. According to Netflix, sixty-two million households viewed it in its first month.[8] The following month, the streaming service declared that the show was its most-watched scripted limited series and ranked it within its top ten streaming programs in ninety-two countries, reaching the number one spot in sixty-three countries, including the United Kingdom, Argentina, Israel, and South Africa.[9] In addition to its popularity, the program received strong critical attention, winning two Golden Globes and eleven Primetime Emmy awards, including an Emmy for Outstanding Limited or Anthology Series. In the months following the series' release, sales of chess-related products skyrocketed.[10] According to *The New York Times*, the program inspired a new generation of women to play the game.[11] The resurgence in chess enthusiasm among young women illustrates how entertainment television continues to serve as a "persuasive and potent source of rhetoric" about women's social roles, opportunities, and permissible activities.[12]

Set during the decade that preceded the failed fight for the Equal Rights Amendment, the feminist critique of women's sexual objectification, and attention to the personal politics of heteronormative households, both series emphasize the characters' prodigious talents and beauty. Midge and Beth break glass ceilings in the fields of comedy and chess (respectively) by virtue of their charm, good looks, and virtuosity. The storylines about trailblazer beauty contribute to our understanding of white, middle-class women's achievements in the context of postrecessionary neoliberalism, growing austerity, a precarious labor market, and a resurgence in feminist activism marked by #MeToo, #TimesUp, and women's protests in response to Donald Trump's 2016 presidential election. Reflecting the impossible demands placed upon women to manage competing imperatives, these series are structured by multiple sets of contradictions: Period sexism is and is not a central constraint driving the characters' storylines; women trailblazers are both subjects for white women's identification and objects of visual pleasure; and neoliberal aspirationalism is both the cause for and solution to characters' problems. Collectively, these contradictory messages illustrate the contemporary crisis of neoliberal feminism in which women's advancement often depends on their debasement. They can neither have nor eat their cake, but they can look good coming out of one. Notably, these tensions are exacerbated by the racialized dimensions of trailblazer narratives, as both series suggest that white women's upward mobility is buttressed by structural racism and homophobia. It is not only their own debasement but the exploitation of more vulnerable populations that enables white women's trailblazing achievements.

The Ir/Relevance of Period Sexism

Both series contextualize the trailblazers' struggles within the gender politics of postwar America that valued white women primarily for their roles as daughters, wives, and mothers. This context provides some source of tension for the women as they strive to break barriers and gain access to male-dominated institutions. The pilot episode of *TMMM* introduces Midge as an industrious housewife whose chief occupations are maintaining her figure and supporting her husband Joel's (Michael Zegen) fledgling comedy career. Midge literally caters to her husband's aspirations by bringing brisket to the owner of a downtown comedy club, The Gaslight, in return for a decent slot on open mic night. She represents the idealized image of the white, upper-middle-class housewife that Betty Friedan famously challenged in *The Feminine Mystique*. Both Friedan and Midge are Jewish, Bryn Mawr–educated women whose talents are stifled by the expectation that they seek fulfillment solely through marriage and family life. Drawing from the image of the unfulfilled housewife that helped define the liberal strand of second-wave feminism, *TMMM* depicts sexual politics and women's enduring battles for workplace advancement.

Midge begins to seek fulfillment from beyond the private sphere once Joel leaves her. His decision is prompted after Midge catches Joel stealing other people's acts. Humiliated after he bombs on stage when he attempts to perform original material, he declares he can no longer stay with her. His abrupt departure throws Midge's life into crisis. After her ex-father-in-law evicts her from her apartment, she is forced to move herself and her two children back in with her parents. Her situation illustrates liberal feminist critiques of women's legal and economic subordination to their husbands and fathers in the postwar era. However, the pilot episode of *TMMM* reverses the gendered dynamics that Betty Friedan famously referred to as "the feminine mystique."[13] It is Joel who is unsatisfied with nuclear family life and his job as an executive in the plastics industry. Paradoxically, his unfulfillment is the catalyst for the trailblazer; his abandonment propels Midge into a male-dominated workplace.

The program's emphasis on Joel's unhappiness sets up the narrative arc in which sexism is ultimately not the primary obstacle to Midge's success. In fact, it facilitates her growth even as patriarchal norms threaten to hold her back. The context of economic precarity brought about by a man's need for validation enables Midge's brilliance to shine. Drunk and despondent, Midge returns to The Gaslight and delivers a raunchy impromptu act to rousing applause. The club's booker Susie Meyerson (Alex Bornstein) is enthralled by Midge's performance and convinces her to pursue a professional career in stand-up comedy. Under Susie's management, Midge begins to envision a new life for herself beyond that of a devoted wife and mother (see fig. 3.1).

Over the course of the five-season series, Midge uses her sharp wit to endure the suffocating sexism of her parents, low-entry workplaces, and fellow comics via impromptu stand-up routines that deride patriarchal norms. The series draws upon some Jewish stereotypes to depict Midge's parents and former in-laws, and Midge often pokes gentle fun at them in her acts. However, Midge's Jewish identity is portrayed largely in terms of her obligations to observe religious holidays. Her status as a woman is the distinguishing feature of her comedy. Most of my enjoyment of watching the show derived from watching Midge ridicule the sexism that conditioned those around her to wish she would return to her former role as a domestic caretaker. Although Midge's career opportunities ebb and flow over the course of the series, it is not until the last episode of the fifth and final season that Midge gets her big break. Working as a writer for a late-night talk show modeled after *The Tonight Show*, Midge finally convinces the show's host, Gordon Ford (Reid Scott), to allow

FIG. 3.1 Midge is a model of white, middle-upper-class female domesticity until her husband leaves her for his secretary. Here, she wears a stunning red dress because her mother believes it will be attractive to her soon-to-be-ex-husband. *The Marvelous Mrs. Maisel*, season 1, episode 2, "Ya Shivu v Bolshom Dome Na Kholme," written by Amy Sherman-Palladino, released November 28, 2017, Amazon Prime Video Original.

her to perform her act on air. Presumably, her career soars thereafter. A series of flash-forwards throughout the final season portray Midge as a comedy legend by the age of sixty, living a luxurious yet lonely life in a large, fully staffed house. Throughout the series, viewers are reminded that Midge's high-profile career is set in motion, not because Midge had long-standing aspirations to be more than a wife and mother, but because Joel could not bear to live with a woman who was funnier and more talented than he was.

Men's unfulfillment also serves as a catalyst in *TQG*. Beth's interest in chess begins as a mental escape from her traumatic childhood that left her orphaned at a young age. The first episode depicts her mother's mental illness and Beth's placement in an orphanage that is ill-equipped to care for its many bereft girls. Beth's chess hobby becomes her career at the end of episode 2 after her adoptive father, Allston Wheatley (Patrick Kennedy), abandons her and her adoptive mother, Alma Wheatley (Marielle Heller), leaving them penniless. After Alma realizes that competitive chess involves large cash prizes for the winners, she encourages Beth to pursue competitive tournaments. Beth's prodigious talent enables them to get along without a man in the house as she wins increasingly prestigious and lucrative chess tournaments.

Allston's callous disregard for Beth punctuates the stakes of her involvement in these tournaments as the series progresses. When Alma dies suddenly in episode 4, he refuses to make any arrangements for the funeral. "I don't want any part of this; I got problems enough," he grumbles.[14] In the second-to-last episode, Beth is thrown into crisis after he denies having any paternal relationship with Beth and attempts to evict her from her childhood home, which he still owns. Beth perseveres nonetheless and wins the title of Grandmaster in the final episode. By presenting male abandonment as a catalyst for the trailblazer, both series evoke feminist issues regarding employment and opportunity without featuring openly feminist characters.

While the postwar period situates Midge's and Beth's struggles as feminist issues, patriarchy is not an overbearing condition that structures these women's lives. On the contrary, depictions of chauvinistic men spotlight the main characters' remarkable talent because they break into male-dominated fields with relative ease. Both series elicit audience investment in the exceptional qualities of their characters, as the narrative development, scoring, and dialogue solicit viewer identification with their achievements. Each series provides the thrill of watching gifted women easily disprove the dismissive assumptions of the people around them.

Midge pushes her way into the male-dominated comedy scene because she is marvelous. She can construct jokes for different crowds at a moment's notice, and her audiences respond with uproarious laughter almost every time. In the final episode of season 2, she is offered her first television appearance for a telethon but is given an undesirable late-night slot. To build audience interest, she jokes that she makes no money as a comic and that her whole career was really a "ruse" to hold "the world's most unlikely stickup," as her only witnesses are "some drunk cameramen, three sailors on leave and fourteen people half asleep in front of their TVs." The producers chuckle and admit that "She's good!" "She's a natural!" Susie grins in response: "She's all that." Midge then answers phones with wisecracks. The camera cuts to one of Midge's coworkers at her daytime job at a department store who recognizes her on TV and gasps, "She answers telephones and tells jokes. What can't she do?"[15] Part of the humor is that women have been held to such a low standard that any woman's ability to do two things well might come as a surprise. Nonetheless, the scene amplifies Midge's natural gifts, which enable her to eventually overcome people's resistance to taking a woman comic seriously.

TQG similarly depicts people's astonishment at Beth's prodigious talent. Beth quickly disabuses her male competitor's assumptions that women cannot compete with them. During the first episode, a school janitor, William Shaibel (Bill Camp), introduces Beth to the game after she observes him playing by himself in the basement of the orphanage. He initially rebuffs her when she asks him to teach her the game: "Girls do not play chess."[16] She convinces him once she has demonstrated she has already begun to understand the game by merely watching him for a few moments. It is not long before she is able to defeat him. Handing her an advanced guidebook to the game, he remarks, "To tell you the truth of it, child, you're astounding."[17]

Reviewers of both series have described the characters as "superheroes." Rachel Syme of the *New Yorker* compared *TQG* to "the origin story of a wizard, or a superheroine." Rather than be held back by family trauma, "we see her decimate her opponents, easily winning tournaments against men twice her age."[18] A *New York Times* review similarly characterized *TMMM* as "a superhero story. Only this time, the protagonist's object is not to save the world but to find a place in it: to stand up for herself by doing standup for herself."[19] The superhero label signals the sexist realism underlying period dramas featuring strong women characters. What makes these trailblazers incredible is not that they can achieve goals that are humanly impossible but that, as women, they are more capable than most men of succeeding in their chosen professions. The superheroine's quest is simply to have the same opportunities as mediocre white men. By describing these as superhero stories, reviews suggest that this goal is a fantasy requiring exceptional talent.

In both series, the men who share the trailblazers' career aspirations are rarely put off. Instead, they are enthralled. Although individual episodes in *TMMM* portray sexist behavior within the entertainment industry and the family, the men closest to Midge, including her ex-husband Joel, go out of their way to help her succeed. Even though Joel concludes he can never return to Midge because he could not endure being the subject of her comedy, he agrees to be the primary caretaker of their two young children so that Midge can take her show on the road during season 3. In the final season, Joel sacrifices his business and personal freedom to protect Midge from her agent's corrupt business partners who have ties to organized crime.

Midge's talent and charm also win over her fellow male comics. At the end of season 3, several of them invite her to sit with them after show hours and praise her for being a tough competitor.[20] Throughout the series, Lenny Bruce (Luke Kirby) mentors Midge. Bruce is the only recurring character with a direct historical referent, and the series draws upon the actual comic's reputation as a tortured artist to create a fictional character who anticipates Midge's struggles. *TMMM*'s fictionalized Bruce is Midge's most ardent devotee. Remarking that he finds her "sensational," he helps her locate gigs throughout the city and offers career advice.[21] Bruce appears in the last episode of each season to punctuate major moments in Midge's transition from a devoted wife and mother to a successful comic. In the last episode of season 4, Bruce lectures Midge for turning down a gig that he arranged for her. Before walking away, he gives her a warning: "If you blow this Midge, I swear. You will break my fucking heart."[22] It is one of the last on-screen conversations between the two of them. Following the conversation, Midge realizes her next goal, leading to her big break. Bruce's character amplifies the role of men as helpmates for the striving trailblazer, obscuring the structural challenges that women face in their efforts to break into male-dominated fields.

TQG features a similar set of relational dynamics. After a national magazine article features Beth's early success, boys at her high school flock to her for her autograph. Many of her competitors fawn over her after she trounces them. Two teenage boys who dismissed her in episode 2 become approving fans by episode 3. Smiling, they remark that they won't compete in tournaments with her because they can't afford to lose. In subsequent episodes, they eagerly supply her with information about her opponents to help her succeed. Even unexceptional players view her as a leader. Greeting a player that Beth previously defeated, she shrugs and says, "Sorry." His response is incredible: "Don't be. After I finished weeping in my room, I replayed the game. I learned a lot from it, so thank you."[23] Several competitors remark on her exceptional talent with scene-closing one-liners. Her friend D. L. Townes (Jacob Fortune-Lloyd) repeatedly tells her, "You really are something, you know that?"[24] Even renowned Russian player Luchenko (Marcus Loges) approves after she defeats him: "You are a marvel, my dear."[25] Because they are so enamored by her guileless talent, a variety of men are eager to teach Beth how to play at increasingly advanced levels. Through their guidance and generosity, Beth becomes a Grandmaster (see fig. 3.2).

The storyline is delightful because it is so improbable, even by contemporary standards, that a woman would be welcomed into such a geeky, male-dominated

FIG. 3.2 Formidable chess Grandmaster Vasily Borgov grasps Beth's hand before giving her a warm embrace to congratulate her for defeating him to earn the title of Grandmaster at the Moscow Invitational tournament. *The Queen's Gambit*, episode 7, "End Game," written by Scott Frank, released October 23, 2020, Netflix Original.

field. Beth's welcome reception at the chess table is a sharp contrast to the violent misogyny that has been leveled at women in the gaming industry in the past decade. Beginning in 2014, the harassment campaign dubbed "Gamergate" involved thousands of self-proclaimed male gamers targeting women game developers with rape and death threats, doxing, and (sometimes successful) campaigns to have women fired from their places of employment.[26] Gamergate illuminates toxic geek masculinity's investments in patriarchy. As Sarah Banet-Weiser notes, the issue was not just that these women sought inclusion into the white-male-dominated gaming community but that these women publicly critiqued misogyny within games and gaming culture. Banet-Weiser understands Gamergate as a response to women's encroachment upon "economic territories" to which men in the gaming industry feel entitled and a reaction to geek culture's own marginality within hegemonic masculine culture.[27] *TQG* imagines a geek culture that eschews male entitlement. Instead of provoking death threats, television's female trailblazers produce male enlightenment. Eliding the broader systems of oppression that contribute to women's exclusion and marginalization from male-dominated fields, *TQG* portrays gendered exclusions more simply as the effect of men's lack of imagination that trailblazers may easily satisfy through charm and talent.

Ultimately, both series portray period sexism as a consequence of collective male blindness and naivete. *TMMM* highlights this explanation for sexism via a monologue delivered by Midge's father, Abe (Tony Shalhoub), to his male coworkers in the series' penultimate episode. During the previous episode, Abe discovers that Midge's daughter is intellectually gifted. Until that moment, he had assumed that it was the men in his family who were destined for greatness. In his last extended speaking role, Abe reflects on how his own sexism has harmed his family. The uncharacteristic close-up shot of his face and slow pace of his delivery punctuate the scene's significance: "My daughter was dumped by her husband, out of nowhere. . . . Instead of collapsing from the weight, she emerged stronger, a new person, so I thought. But now I think that was who she was all along. I never really took her seriously. . . . She's doing it on her own. With no help from me or her mother. . . . What could she have been if I had helped her and not ignored her? . . . My daughter is a remarkable person, and I don't think I've ever said that to her."[28]

The scene is unusual given the series' characteristically fast-paced dialogue and medium-to-long shots. With Amazon Prime's decision to end the series, the writers wrap up its story by announcing its overarching lesson: Women's abilities should be cultivated because women have the potential for extraordinary achievement. The scene suggests that extraordinary women and girls have the potential to undo patriarchy by forcing men to confront their chauvinism. In providing these lessons, the series ignores the deeper material and psychic investments in women's exclusion that have historically structured patriarchy and continue to do so at present.

By foregrounding men's transformations in the face of extraordinary women, both series give televisual, narrative form to the myth of the gifted woman (my term), which has been a long-standing rationale for women's inclusion in public life since the mid-nineteenth century. The myth of the gifted woman draws from the commonsense assumption of women's general inferiority to men, warranting women's rights in the potential for a few unique women to rise above their station. In *The Subjection of Women*, John Stuart Mill grounded his rationale for women's equality in the goal of providing opportunities for the exceptional woman. Barriers to women's entry into male-dominated spheres must be removed, he argued, to create room for "the minority of exceptional cases in which presumptions of biological determined qualifications do not hold. . . . If only once in a dozen years the conditions of eligibility exclude a fit person, there is a real loss."[29]

The myth of the gifted woman affirms a liberal progress narrative in which women's inclusion is a matter of meritocracy and masculine enlightenment. Mill appeals not to the inherent unjustness of women's subordination but to the potential for a few women to prove themselves worthy of inclusion within a male-dominated society. For Mill, society should let women pursue their "natural inclination" toward certain activities because competition with men suffices as a mechanism for deciding which activities are proper for women.[30] Such reasoning presumes men's entitlement to the benefits provided by women's emotional and physical labor as it suggests that women may compete with men so long as they do so on white men's terms. The period trailblazer reveals how neoliberal feminism is embedded within a longer feminist struggle that has always been entangled with cultural misogyny.

By featuring individual women's talents and the men who admire them, attention to gifted women obviates alternative narratives about gendered transformations in public life brought about by collective advocacy and mutual support among women who challenged the laws and practices that have buttressed male entitlement in policy, the workplace, and the home. By extending the myth of the gifted woman into contemporary popular television, *TMMM* and *TQG* contribute to what I have described elsewhere as selective amnesia of leftist activism during the late sixties. Hollywood film and television routinely "trivialize and negate the contributions of late sixties activists to politics and society."[31] Mainstream media also contribute to selective amnesia in narratives about the late sixties by excluding activist movements that defied "seamless narratives of national progress and unity."[32]

Narratives of men's enthusiasm for women trailblazers contribute to selective amnesia by proffering a memory of women's progress that renders women's organized responses to sexism unnecessary. Both series evoke critical consciousness about sexism without identifying the structural conditions that explain its origins or suggesting that any meaningful action should be taken in response to it—other than allowing exceptional women to shine. The series invert the postwar period's historical associations with sexism and misogyny by crafting a prefeminist history in which structural barriers never existed at all. Lynn Spigel understands period pieces such as *Mad Men* as emblematic of "postfeminist nostalgia," or the longing for a "nascent feminist consciousness . . . when middle-class women wanted more from life than an unromantic marriage . . . but did not yet want feminism."[33] She explains, "Nostalgia for the *Mad Men* era is all about imagining a future where feminism never happened, but where somehow miraculously, without political struggle, everyone gets a great job, great clothes and great mixed drinks."[34]

I largely agree with Spigel's assessment, yet postfeminist nostalgia does not fully explain the dissonances that structure the trailblazer series that followed *Mad Men*. After all, the show's periodization in the decade before the second wave is a precondition for viewers to appreciate the trailblazers' struggles and achievements. This periodization elicits the vicarious thrill of watching women overcome workplace sexism and restrictive gendered familial structures. As Saval's quote in the introduction to this chapter suggests, part of viewers' enjoyment depends on their historical distance from the events portrayed on screen. At the same time, viewers may identify with characters' resistance to restrictive gender norms. By understanding the fifties and sixties as a uniquely perilous period for single, career-minded women, viewers are positioned to see themselves within a broader historical narrative arc of women's overcoming patriarchal repression. Of course, viewers are also invited to celebrate the trailblazers' achievements. By making them exceptionally talented, the shows also provide some relief from the threat of patriarchal control over women's lives. As the women are gifted beyond belief, the writing is on the wall. These women will overcome well before Virginia Slims cigarettes could remind women, "You've come a long way, baby." These programs stage a conflict with patriarchy that feels good to watch because the happy ending seems predetermined. As the prefeminist period establishes a context for viewers to appreciate watching women overcome patriarchy, it marks the contemporary moment's ambivalent relationship with sexism. It is both objectionable and the basis for viewers' entertainment. This ambivalence is amplified by the series' investments in the aesthetics of postwar sexism.

Trailblazer Beauty

Although viewers might take pleasure in watching women overcome sexism, this is not the only or even the primary pleasure elicited by these programs because the series encourage viewers to take pleasure in looking at these women, period. Sexist realism evoked in period dramas about impossibly talented women is punctuated by television's investments in what I am labeling as "trailblazer beauty," or the cultural practices of looking and the visual pleasures they provide that have become sutured to our frameworks for recognizing women's achievements. Through the interplay between character development and costume choices, period programs attach the pleasure of witnessing trailblazers' overcoming to the pleasures of our gaze. Trailblazer beauty is marked by gorgeous sets and conventionally attractive women characters. In *TMMM* and *TQG*, the camera invites us to appreciate the aesthetics of the late fifties and early-to-mid sixties, when white women were expected to embody a distinctly feminine style before the second wave challenged the assumption that women should be valued for their to-be-looked-at-ness. Consequently, trailblazer beauty marks the ways in which viewing pleasure has become deeply connected to increasingly impossible expectations for women.

Sherman-Palladino suggests that the contrast between the beauty of *TMMM*'s aesthetics and its darker portrayal of postwar sexism is not coincidental. She explained to Vulture reporter Willa Paskin that she wanted *TMMM*'s visual style to give the program's feminist themes a "light touch" to avoid creating an overly serious drama. Paskin concludes, "Mrs. Maisel's aesthetic lodestar isn't realism so much as *The Pajama Game*. When you watch it, you're supposed to feel good."[35] Sherman-Palladino's remarks disassociate her series from the figure of the feminist killjoy that has attributed unhappiness to feminists themselves, avoiding deeper recognition of sexist conditions that prompt feminist critique.[36] The contrast between feminist realism and "feel good" television implies a confluence between pleasure and patriarchy insofar as pleasure is *not* to be found in watching women resist sexism; instead it is to be found in consuming the aesthetics of a period before feminism, when viewers didn't have to feel bad about objectifying women. Through their aesthetic choices, the series and its creator contribute to popular feminism's imperatives that women remain "upbeat" and "decidedly not angry."[37] *New York Times* writer Alexis Soloski described *TMMM* as a "midcentury fever dream in candy coating."[38] Attention to the sweetness of the show illustrates how even trailblazing women must provide the requisite eye candy needed for viewers to take them seriously.

Both series' eye candy is served up by the series' periodization via midcentury fashion and design. The locations, sets, and clothing provide a glamorous backdrop for trailblazing women's efforts, making their struggles appear as exquisite as they are. Midge tromps through New York's Upper West Side and Greenwich Village neighborhoods in hundreds of stunning outfits that *New York Times* style writer Rhonda Garelick describes as a "vast confectionary of . . . vibrant 1950s-style fashions."[39] *TMMM*'s costume designer Donna Zakowska received Emmy nominations for Outstanding Period Costumes for each of the show's seasons and won the award in 2019 (see fig. 3.3). The Smithsonian's National Museum of American History acquired two of her costumes

FIG. 3.3 Midge thanks her audience at the end of her breakthrough performance on the Gordon Ford Show during the series finale. Much of the episode's dialogue discussed her dress. *The Marvelous Mrs. Maisel*, season 5, episode 9, "Four Minutes," written by Amy Sherman-Palladino, released May 26, 2023, Amazon Prime Video Original.

from the first season, including the dress Midge wore in the final episode.[40] Zakowska's team painstakingly constructed their sets with period artifacts. The costume department pulled items from over 2,270 vintage shops, built intricate props including period-specific video cameras when originals could not be found, and designed over 320 separate costumes for Midge alone.[41] "We leaned into the vibrancy of the time," Sherman-Palladino explains. "The cars were beautiful. The [expletive] toasters were gorgeous. People really did dress like that."[42]

The backdrop for Beth's story is equally gorgeous. Beth wears expertly tailored dresses inspired by couture designers André Courrèges and Pierre Cardin as she defeats her chess opponents in swanky hotels across the globe, from Mexico City to Paris and Moscow.[43] *TQG*'s costume designer Gabriele Binder received the Emmy for Outstanding Period Costumes in 2021, and the series also won an Emmy for Outstanding Production Design that year. Shot almost entirely in Berlin, the stunning architecture and meticulously crafted sets evoke mid-century modernity. Set directors transformed a variety of German buildings into a postwar suburban American home and stylish hotels in Cincinnati, Las Vegas, Paris, and Mexico City using vintage wall coverings, fabrics, and mid-century style furniture. Although director Uli Hanisch explains that the exaggerated use of florals, stripes, and plaids used to construct Beth's adoptive parents' house were chosen to reflect "the façade of a happy home that was not a reality," a variety of websites offer advice for how viewers might achieve "that 60s look at home."[44] *TQG*'s cynical portrait of nuclear family life was clearly lost on these style guides. Now you, too, can mask your unhappiness with delightful patterns and colors!

Commentary about both series suggests that the pleasures of trailblazer beauty are grounded in an unproblematic attraction to and desire for white femininity that is shaped by a nostalgic attachment to pre-sixties-era beauty norms. Midge and Beth function equally as subjects and objects in the series: Their great clothes and flawless complexions carry as much importance in the series as their efforts to be recognized for more than their looks. Several popular press and fashion magazine articles suggest that each program's significance rests in the visual appeal of the characters and the worlds in which they struggled. For *Vogue* writer Julia Felsenthal, "The pleasures of *The Marvelous Mrs. Maisel* lie less in the stand-up . . . than in the mise-en-scène of Midge's life."[45]

While *TQG* generated some controversy regarding its lack of historical veracity in portraying women's participation in competitive chess,[46] its most favorable commentary emphasized the glamour that the program attached to the game, particularly via Anya Taylor-Joy's appearance (see fig. 3.4). As staff writer for *The New Yorker* Rachel Syme approvingly remarks, "The game of chess, in 'The Queen's Gambit,' sheds its schlubbiness and reveals a bewitching (and, it must be said sometimes erotic) elegance."[47] In the title of her *New York Times* style essay, Danielle Braff praised that *TQG* costumes "Make Us Want to Toss Our Leggings."[48] *People* magazine similarly notes that Harmon's clothes "are nearly as exciting as the chess games."[49] These and other comments about the program suggest that viewers care about Beth and her success because they take great pleasure in looking at her. The attention to Midge and Beth's beauty and clothing highlights how television remains deeply invested in gendered aesthetics that are invariably connected to the status of women as objects of visual pleasure. Thus, even stories about women seeking to improve their status are designed to provide aesthetic enjoyment.

Commentary from fashion magazines also foregrounds trailblazers' function as a platform for promoting the beauty and fashion industries. Numerous style articles rank Midge and Beth's best outfits using stills from the series featuring Brosnahan and Taylor-Joy in a variety of expertly tailored dresses, hats, and coats.[50] In articles that position vertical stills of actors in medium-long shots, the actors are akin to paper dolls that have historically reflected society's idealized version of womanhood.[51] Multiple news dailies and fashion magazines invite viewers to emulate the styles evoked by the shows, provide tutorials for how viewers might recreate Brosnahan's and Taylor-Joy's on-screen looks, identify the brands of lipstick the lead actors wore on set, and describe the actors' skincare routines.[52] In October 2019, the New York City department store Bergdorf Goodman featured *TMMM*'s fashions in its Fifth Avenue windows. That month, Zakowska also created a coat inspired by

FIG. 3.4 The styling of Anya Taylor-Joy's hair, makeup, and wardrobe gives the game of chess a glamorous makeover. *The Queen's Gambit*, episode 6, "Adjournment," written by Scott Frank, released October 23, 2020, Netflix Original.

the series for an auction event to benefit the Council of Fashion Designers of America's Fashion Manufacturing Initiative.[53] Zakowska's growing reputation as a celebrity designer illustrates how streaming television has maintained the broader television industry's investments in cultivating cross-promotional relationships with retail businesses that profit by cultivating women's obsession with physical perfection. According to *The New York Times*, thousands of the *TMMM*'s fans have recreated and photographed themselves in their favorite costumes from the series for social media.[54]

None of the aforementioned commentary acknowledges the contradiction between the series' emphasis on characters who desire to be valued for more than their looks and the celebration of characters' attractiveness. The omission is remarkable, in part, because second-wave feminists pointed to the confining undergarments required to achieve the A-line silhouettes featured in trailblazer fashion as illustrations of a sexist culture that prized women's shapeliness over their comfort and mobility. *TMMM* references this critique in its second episode. When Midge and her mother, Rose (Marin Hinkle), contemplate their first dinner with Joel and his parents after the separation, Rose instructs Midge to wear an alluring evening dress to show Joel "what he's missing." Midge retorts, "That is not what this dinner's for," but Rose coolly responds, "You're a single woman now. That's what every dinner's for." By emphasizing how women's desirability rests almost entirely on their looks, the scene foreshadows the uphill battle Midge will soon face in her effort to be taken seriously as a comic. The dinner ends in a heated argument, during which Midge learns that she and Joel are broke (see fig. 3.1). Midge reflects on her naivete on stage at The Gaslight in her second impromptu performance later that night. "How stupid am I?" she asks. Wearing the ruby red dress her mother recommended to lure Joel back into marriage, she jokes, "It's the bras, right? . . . And the . . . the girdles and the corsets, all designed to cut off the circulation to your brain, so you walk around on the verge of passing out, and you look at your husband, and he tells you things, and you just believe them."[55] Although Midge's comedy suggests that confining undergarments are a metaphor for the economic constraints facing married women, her shiny dress invites viewers to enjoy gazing at the very conditions of her hardship. In this regard, trailblazer beauty disassociates viewers from the subjects of feminist struggle.

Fetishizing the aesthetics of women struggling with the strictures of postwar sexism reverses the process Goldman et al. have identified as "commodity feminism." Playing off the Marxist idea of commodity fetishism, the authors note that advertising after the 1970s sought to make feminist ideas compatible with the fashion industry by portraying the female body as "the locus of freedom as well as sexual pleasure."[56] Across commercial media, women's liberation is routinely characterized in terms of their choice to be seen as sexual objects, reducing feminism to a signifier that can be bought and worn as a marker of novelty that affirms "ideologies of possessive individualism and free choice."[57] Fifty years later, trailblazer television spotlights the twisted logics by which advertising maintains beauty culture's viability. A paradoxical extension of commodity feminism, commodity sexism *depends on* consumers' recognition of the period's regressive gender norms, as it reduces women's postwar fashion to the status of a stylish signifier. Like a yarn that is twisted to the point that it begins to fold into itself, sexism itself has become intertwined with feminism to the point that the two have become almost indistinguishable. Commodity sexism illuminates Joe Tompkins's concerns regarding "promotional cynicism" in popular entertainment.[58] Promotional materials inviting audiences to emulate the styles associated with sexist norms in the postwar era encourage viewers' ironic attachment to beauty culture; viewers can acknowledge the culture's roots in patriarchy but embrace it anyway.

TMMM and *TQG* register the conflicted relationship between liberal feminism and the commercial beauty industry in scenes that emphasize trailblazers' fashion choices and beauty regimens. The first season of *TMMM* frequently pokes fun at sexist beauty and fashion norms by depicting the demeaning treatment Midge receives from men who solely regard her in terms of her attractive appearance. Midge's beauty poses some obstacles to her efforts to be taken seriously as a comic because she routinely endures unwanted sexual advances from men, including club managers, television producers, and corporate sponsors. Despite the jaundiced view of beauty culture presented during its first season, *TMMM* does more to promote fashion and cosmetics than critique it in subsequent seasons that portray sexual harassment rather playfully. Men's unwanted advances do not dissuade Midge from demanding recognition, nor does her refusal of them curtail her opportunities.

After season 1, *TMMM* depicts Midge's beauty regimen and wardrobe as something she wholeheartedly enjoys. Even after she loses her apartment and the handsome furniture it holds, she continues to embrace her love of fashion in scenes that humorously portray her overpacking for a summer vacation in the Catskills, lamenting the state of her leather heels after being caught in a blizzard, and coveting her mother's fine jewelry. Midge's desire to be seen in beautiful dresses is showcased during season 3 when she encounters a grand staircase at the famous Fontainebleau Hotel in Miami that leads to nowhere. Midge explains to a bewildered Susie that it solely exists "for ladies to walk down in their finest dresses and everyone can watch them."[59] Twenty-four hours later, she gracefully makes her way down the stairs in an elegant black, tiered satin dress while she smiles at the onlookers below her (see fig. 3.5). Throughout its multiple seasons, *TMMM* punctuates each of Midge's major career opportunities with scenes that depict Midge agonizing over her wardrobe choices. Viewers are encouraged to admire her wardrobe precisely because Midge takes great pride in her appearance.

FIG. 3.5 Midge takes a moment out of her performance schedule in Miami to walk down the Fontainebleau Hotel's famous "stairway to nowhere" so that onlookers can admire her dress. *The Marvelous Mrs. Maisel*, season 3, episode 5, "It's Comedy or Cabbage," written by Amy Sherman-Palladino, released December 6, 2019, Amazon Prime Video Original.

TQG's Beth is equally concerned with maintaining her appearance. She covets the saddle shoes and trendy dresses worn by the wealthier girls in her school. After winning her first cash prize at a tournament, Beth eagerly purchases a new dress. As the series develops, Beth revises her wardrobe, hair, and makeup continually, following the changing styles of the times. The chess community takes notice. After a shopping spree in Paris, a chess reporter asks her to respond to accusations that she is "too glamorous to be a serious chess player." Angrily, she replies, "It's easier to play chess without the burden of an Adam's apple."[60] By linking glamour to her gender, the scene sutures feminism to feminine style. Emphasis on Beth's attractiveness is unique to the series and not to Tevis's novel. *New Yorker* critic Sarah Miller notes that Tevis's novel describes Beth as decidedly "unattractive" until she learns to excel at chess. Beth's accomplishments in the chess world make her more attractive to others because that is what matters to her the most.[61] Netflix's adaptation obscures what Miller suggests is the central tension in the novel: the balance of individual goals and social expectations facing women in the postwar era. By featuring her beauty as a complement to her talent rather than as something she achieved by virtue of her professional accomplishments, *TQG* gives narrative form to commodity feminism's emphasis on beauty as an expression of personal freedom. As Goldman et al. observe, fashion magazines routinely instruct women readers that "the body is something you shape, control and dress to validate yourself as an autonomous being capable of will, power and discipline." In return, women establish their achievement and self-worth through the proper management of their bodies as though this itself is significant.[62]

Merging the feminism and sexism that is intrinsic to commodity culture, trailblazer beauty articulates a metonymic association between fashion and accomplishment that is bound up in heteronormative standards of desirability—and white femininity. The trailblazers' aesthetics are carefully scripted in the series. Costume directors for both series explained that the lead characters' hair, makeup, and clothing were specifically chosen to give meaning to their internal and economic statuses. For example, Zakowska tells *Women's Health* readers that she chose to make Midge's signature color, pink, increasingly bolder as her character became more confident over the course of the series' multiple seasons.[63] In *TQG*, the evolution of Beth's fashion style corresponds to her success. The series punctuates Beth's wretched conditions in early episodes by featuring her discomfort, as her clothing options are limited to ill-fitting garments found in secondhand stores. As she excels in increasingly competitive chess tournaments, her costumes become more refined. Both trailblazers appear in stunning white outfits at the end of each season. While Zakowska described Midge's white gowns as "palette cleansers,"[64] Binder explained that her intention behind Beth's chic, all-white outfit in the closing scene after she earns the title of Grandmaster in Moscow was to convey that "she is now the queen of the chessboard and the chessboard itself is the world" (see fig. 3.6).[65]

FIG. 3.6 Beth's white outfit in the closing scene of *The Queen's Gambit* conveys her new status as the "Queen of the Chessboard." *The Queen's Gambit*, episode 7, "End Game," written by Scott Frank, released October 23, 2020, Netflix Original.

By punctuating her achievements and financial success through characters' clothing, the programs illustrate Alex Bevan's point that "clothes can and do tell stories of their own that originate . . . in the material histories attached to the styles themselves."[66] Rather than emphasize fashion as an expression of individual character, Bevan points to the ways that "an article of clothing indexes the socially situated desires and constraints" of its makers, wearers, and spaces.[67] Reflecting on the series *Mad Men*, Bevan explains that nostalgia TV's emphasis on fashion and mid-century style "relies on the post-feminist re-embrace of fashion as a point of empowerment and self-exploration" even as it "denotes historical transitions in gender ideology."[68] Following *Mad Men*, *TMMM* and *TQG* use fashion to convey characters' constraints and self-determination.

Beyond using costumes to establish characters' achievements, costume directors and cinematographers sought to establish characters' sexual appeal through their hair, makeup, and lighting. During a Netflix short documentary on the making of *TQG*, Binder explains that the effort to make Beth appear "progressively sexier" also informed her choice in the use of three specific hairstyles to signal the character's developing age: "Baby Beth," "sexy kitten," and "glamour-puss."[69] As Binder intimates, women's sexuality is the crux of commodity feminism insofar as "meanings of choice and individual freedom become wed to images of sexuality in which women apparently choose to be seen as sexual objects because it suits their liberated interests."[70] Much of Midge's and Beth's professional success hinges on their sexual desirability, as their luminescent skin and thin frames motivate men to support, mentor, and hire them. Notably, the women are not entirely put off by male attention. In fact, they appear to relish it. By merging sex appeal with women's advancement, trailblazer beauty reinvigorates what Susan Douglas refers to as "enlightened sexism," or the message that women can enjoy power and respect through the "calculated deployment of their faces, bodies, attire, and sexuality."[71] Douglas points to a variety of media messages during the nineties and early aughts that have offered women fantasies of sexual power in which cultivating men's lust and women's envy is "more gratifying than political or economic power."[72] At the same time, these messages encourage women to embrace a feminist agenda of economic independence and professional achievement. Douglas concludes that it takes a "superwoman" to straddle the competing pull of feminism and femininity.[73]

Of course, both Midge and Beth model such superheroine ability. Aside from her relatives, almost all of *TMMM*'s male characters are enthralled by Midge's charm and beauty. During season 2, she wins the heart of Benjamin Ettenberg (Zachary Levi), a tall handsome doctor who never entertained the idea of marriage until he started dating Midge. During a night of art gallery and bar hopping, Midge stuns Ben by introducing herself to Declan Howell (Rufus Sewell), an acerbic and renowned artist. Howell takes one look at Midge and declares she is "extraordinary." He marvels at her complexion and declares, "It's like Vermeer painted you or you swallowed a lightbulb." The next scene suggests that Ben also finds her luminous. Contemplating their first intimate night together in front of his large Brownstone walk-up, Ben kisses her, looks into her eyes, and declares, "You are spectacular."[74] Even Lenny Bruce is captivated by her beauty. Although she rejects his invitation to join him in his hotel room in season 3, she takes him up on the offer at the end of season 4. The episode amplifies the series' efforts to disarticulate trailblazers' sexuality from the romance plot. Midge consents to having sex on condition that he continues to take her seriously as a comic afterward, and the two are never intimate again. The lesson at the end of the season is that women's sexuality is fully compatible with their career goals so long as women strategically direct their sexuality toward activities that advance their professional aspirations.

Beth's sexuality revolves around her career goals as well. Although her mother and female classmates prod her to talk about the boys who follow her around at tournaments, Beth expresses little interest in dating. Her only continuous sexual relationships are with fellow chess players Harry Beltik (Harry Melling) and Benny Watts (Thomas Brodie-Sangster), who eagerly help Beth win a world tournament in Russia. Despite their multiple suitors, neither Midge nor Beth are particularly interested in pursuing long-term romantic relationships. They leave men heartbroken when they reject their romantic overtures to focus on their professional aspirations. At the end of season 2, Midge breaks off her engagement to Ben once she realizes that her upcoming national tour would conflict with the expectations for marriage. Similarly, Harry is dismayed to find that Beth loves chess but does not love him. Their relationship ends after Harry concludes he has taught her everything he knows about the game. Beth is less dismissive of Benny, who is the most accomplished chess player among the variety of men who pursue her. In a reversal of her relationship dynamic with Harry, Benny is far more interested in advancing her career than in sleeping with her. Perhaps because of this dynamic, her relationship with Benny is more developed than it is with the other men who pursue her.

Trailblazer beauty illustrates a shifting dynamic within commodity feminism in the neoliberal period as it puts beauty in the service of professional achievement. To serve their professional ambitions, Midge and Beth spurn men's advances, have casual sexual affairs, and are more likely to wound men than to be wounded by a relationship's end. Both series intimate that Midge and Beth's sexual desirability contributes to their trailblazing successes but that they cannot pursue individual achievement and commit themselves to another person at the same time. Trailblazer beauties revive the enlightened sexism of previous decades as they gain power through their extraordinary talent and hyperfeminine physical traits, but their storylines resolve the tension between career achievement and femininity by putting the latter in the service of the former. That is, for the trailblazer beauty, male approval and love primarily function as means to achieve professional advancement.

The Costs of Trailblazing

If it's not sexism or relationships holding trailblazers back, what does constrain them? The central tension in both series revolves around the trailblazers themselves. Their stories affirm a neoliberal worldview in which obstacles to achievement are rooted in the individual. In this regard, trailblazer stories bear semblance to self-help literature such as Sheryl Sandberg's advice book *Lean In*, which tells women that the key to gender equality in the workplace is for women to learn how to attain a felicitous work-life balance.[75] Midge's and Beth's barriers are largely internal, rooted in their maladjustments to the traumatic circumstances that prompted their careers. The biggest obstacle to Midge's career advancement is her big mouth. While Midge uses humor to cope with her divorce and her parents' dismissal of her, she deploys this wit inappropriately, causing her to lose friends and alienate family members when she integrates jokes about their struggles into her act. Beth's biggest challenge is to learn to play chess without the soothing effects of drugs or alcohol, which she uses to manage her stress and to cope with experiences of parental loss and abandonment. The unique circumstances that contribute to their success threaten to undo them, and it is up to them to figure out how to negotiate this tension, which involves both careful self-management and considerable self-sacrifice.

By featuring main characters' impulsive reactions to difficult situations, *TMMM* and *TQG* portray idealized neoliberal feminists who achieve success through personal striving and embodied perfection. As Angela McRobbie explains, neoliberal feminism has replaced feminism's "collective ethos" with an "ethos of competitive individualism."[76] In this context, female success is equated with the idea of the perfect, or the demand that women perform excellence in life through constant improvement, successful management of career success, and a pleasing heteronormative feminine appearance. McRobbie describes "the perfect" as a category "driven by competition which operates to preserve privilege . . . while both describing and marking out a largely white and upper middle-class sector of women" as leaders of male-dominated corporate workplaces.[77]

Both characters portray commitments to embodied perfection. Midge literally worries about how well she measures up to others. The pilot episode reveals that she carefully measures each body part every day to ensure that she has maintained ideal proportions. She also has a competitive relationship with pioneering female comic Sophie Lennon (Jane Lynch), as each vie for coveted gigs and undermine each other. When she is not working on her career, Midge plans events for others: a wedding reception for a coworker, a birthday party for her son, a baby shower for her best friend, and numerous Jewish holiday gatherings for family members. Beth's meteoric rise in the international chess community epitomizes neoliberal subjectivity, as she performs with exceptional skill and unflagging determination to gain entry into an exclusive field organized around hierarchy and status. Her quest to prove she is superior to all other chess players foregrounds the virtues of competitive individualism. In accomplishing what no other woman had done before her, her ability to serve as a role model for others is premised upon her ability to set herself above and apart from them.

Although the characters illustrate neoliberal feminist dispositions, their storylines revolve around their imperfections. At first glance, Midge's hostess events seem perfect. However, events never go as planned; she makes inappropriate jokes during the Catholic wedding reception, she is hungover during her son's party, and she double-books the baby shower with an out-of-state gig. Consequently, Midge's parents deride her for being flaky and selfish. Midge also has some misgivings about what she must sacrifice in pursuit of her career. During her first out-of-state tour, she worries that her children will not recognize her when she returns home. Likewise, Beth's excessive drinking alienates her from friends and causes her to lose a crucial match against one of her most formidable opponents in the penultimate episode. Scenes featuring Midge's and Beth's foibles represent what McRobbie has termed "p-i-r," or "perfect-imperfect-resilience."[78] While the perfect continues to advance women's competitive individualism, popular appeals to the imperfect delineate the spheres where "flaws can be entertained."[79] McRobbie avers that the imperfect serves as a "corrective to the pressure that women put themselves under" while reconciling feminist resistance to demands for perfection with imperatives of consumer capitalism by deflecting attention from the capitalist structures driving these demands.[80]

Trailblazer narratives evoke the interplay between the perfect and the imperfect by pathologizing trailblazer's ambitions and foregrounding the costs of their pursuit of perfection. Both series portray their aspirationalism as a response to traumatic loss. Similar to other superhero stories, heartbreak gives them the motivation to pursue their unique talents and to live in isolation from others. However, trailblazers' heroism is found in their commitment to themselves rather than in saving others. In this way, the two series illustrate Robin James's point that neoliberal striving is premised on overcoming damage. James argues that neoliberalism replaced fragility with resilience as the "new feminine ideal" after 2000.[81] Because patriarchal conditions and the damage they inflict are presumed to be inevitable, the task for any female is to learn to overcome such injury. James remarks that "damage is *necessary* to health" insofar as it is an intrinsic part of growing up female in a seemingly intransigent patriarchal world.[82]

Trailblazer stories express some ambivalence about this dynamic. Midge and Beth are remarkable because they choose resilience over fragility at a time when ideal white upper-class, cisgender, able-bodied femininity "required the performance of fragility."[83] Yet their resilience does not inure them to the damage caused by male abandonment. While their trauma compels them to pursue their talents, it also prompts them to engage in dangerous or self-defeating behaviors. Because their talents and competitive individualism are born from traumatic loss, their achievements are won at the cost of their personal relationships and mental health.

Midge's resilience gives her the capacity for extraordinary achievement, but her talent also constrains her ability to maintain deep and lasting relationships when she uses her scathing wit to respond to personal affronts. Her talent poses obstacles to her career when she turns her wit on the very people she depends on for her career to flourish. As she achieves more success, she finds herself increasingly alone. The conclusion to every season of *TMMM* foregrounds Midge's isolation. During the final episode of season 1, Midge and her estranged husband, Joel, contemplate getting back together. However, Joel is taken aback when he surreptitiously observes her impromptu set at their favorite comedy club. Midge provides a hilarious routine about their relationship, joking that Joel's new girlfriend clearly had more rights to him than she had because she "had a teddy bear that he won for her at Coney Island while all I have is a wedding ring and two kids that call him 'Daddy.'" With tears in his eyes, he cries, "She's good! She's fucking good!" Even though he still loves her,

Joel cannot bear to resume their romance because he cannot allow their relationship to become fodder for her comedy.

The end of season 2 reverses the relational dynamics of season 1. In this season, Midge declines Ben's marriage proposal once she realizes that her upcoming national tour would conflict with the expectations for marriage. The final scene concludes with a despondent message about the prospects of Midge's personal life. She attends *The Steve Allen Show* backstage to watch Lenny Bruce perform a routine about the dissolution of his marriage amid rising career success. Accompanied by soft piano music, he ends his performance with a somber song. Frowning and looking at the floor, he sings, "All alone. I'll be rich but so all alone." The camera cuts to Midge's face as she listens to him. While it is Lenny's song, it is clearly about her. Despite Sherman-Palladino's "light touch," this conclusion reminds audiences that women's career striving does not always feel good. On the contrary, it often leads to heartbreak.

The conflicts between Midge's personal life and professional career dredge up the tired feminist backlash lesson that career success comes at the price of a fulfilling family life. Twenty years ago, Elsbeth Probyn observed that the postfeminist emphasis on choice renders women's career pursuits as an alternative to family, such that one pursuit precludes the other. As Probyn notes, the ideology of choice is not really a choice insofar as it presumes that women's fulfillment is ultimately found in the home. It presumes that women may never find the same kind of satisfaction experienced by their male peers.[84] While postfeminist narratives routinely celebrate women's return to the home, sexist realist storylines foreground impossible women who prefer personal losses over a return to family life. Reflecting on the "anti-romance narrative" of the political drama *The Good Wife*, Michaela Meyer concludes that the program conveys a fatalistic message that feminism may not serve its adherents because they will "end up unhappy and unfulfilled."[85] Although it is not clear that Midge is unfulfilled, *TMMM* also avoids a decidedly happy ending.

The final season reveals that Bruce's song accurately predicted Midge's life story. Through a series of flash-forwards, the final episode reveals that both Midge and her manager, Susie, became famously successful at the end of their careers. Yet Midge also became notorious for her numerous failed marriages. The final scene depicts the two women living by themselves, keeping one another company via nightly phone calls while they watch *Jeopardy!* in their pajamas. Commenting on the series finale for *The New York Times*, Sherman-Palladino remarks, "Life is a series of choices, and some of them are stupid choices and some great choices. . . . Part of what those flash-forwards did for us is show the consequences of the choices that she did make." In choosing to be significant, Midge chose to forgo loving relationships. *The New York Times*'s commentary on the final season indicates that this sacrifice is a direct outcome of Midge's neoliberal subjectivity. After quoting Rachel Brosnahan, who noted that she found Midge's "resilience inspiring and her courage to keep confronting change inspiring," the article asks, "But did that resilience and that courage come at some cost? This final season, however breezy, confirms that it did."[86]

That almost every season of this lighthearted and whimsical program ends on such a dour note would be incongruent with the program's emphasis were it not for its consonance with neoliberal feminist virtues. The conclusion reminds viewers that the neoliberal dispositions that affectively connect with viewers and invite them to identify with characters exist for their own sake, not for the sake of those who embody them. That is, the program invites viewers to feel good about feminist striving but infers that viewers should not expect too much in return. Sherman-Palladino explains she never intended for *The Marvelous Mrs. Maisel* to offer viewers a sense of optimism for the future. "I am such a cynic," she says. "I love a world where my lead characters are powering through it without that cynicism. I love the energy of female heroines tromping through life with their high heels and their great hair. Why not have some color in your fucking life?" she says. "You're going to be dead in like five minutes anyhow. Just enjoy it and wear a hat."[87]

Trauma is also a precondition for Beth's success, as her interest in chess begins while she adjusts to life in an orphanage after the tragic loss of her mother, who died by suicide when she was a child. The series suggests her commitment to chess is driven by a desire to repress family trauma. As she explains to Mr. Shaibel, the janitor who first taught her to play, winning at chess is the only thing that has ever made her feel good. Initial scenes of Beth's interest in chess are crosscut with images of administrators distributing tranquilizers to her and other girls at the orphanage. Beth imagines how to play the game while she is narcotized, and she concludes that she cannot effectively play when she is sober. In subsequent episodes, she seeks to defeat increasingly competitive players. Like the drugs she ingests to dull the pain of losing her mother, she is compelled to raise her chess profile in pursuit of greater self-gratification. By presenting her investments in chess as a response to trauma, the show presents her tragic backstory as her greatest asset; but because it is rooted in trauma, her achievement is a costly one.

By interlacing Beth's addiction alongside her achievements, the series figures trailblazing success as an abject condition bound up in loss and sacrifice. As the series director Scott Frank asserts, *TQG* is "about the cost of genius."[88] The script makes this point directly in episode 4. Before an important match in Mexico City, Beth reflects on advice Mr. Shaibel gave her during her time with him learning to play as a child: "People like you have a hard time," she recalls him telling her. "Two sides of the same coin. You've got your gift, and you've got what it costs."[89] As she reflects on his words, she buys a beer from a street vendor and begins to drink. This and subsequent scenes suggest that Beth's future hinges upon whether she can learn to control her addiction. The end of the episode reveals the gravity of Beth's addiction. She returns to her hotel room after losing the match to Grandmaster Borgov to find her mother has died, likely from hepatitis caused by alcohol poisoning. It is not until the final episode that Beth realizes she doesn't need to be inebriated to play well and is a more formidable opponent when she is sober.

TQG revolves around the dialectical interplay between suffering and success, in which depictions of loss and isolation share the screen alongside depictions of the trailblazer's competitive achievement. This dialectic contributes to sexist realism by foregrounding women's suffering as the precondition for appreciating their accomplishments. In discussing Beth, Taylor-Joy observes that the character suffers from "an emotional and intellectual loneliness" and notes that the miniseries establishes viewer empathy for her by depicting her "hard work" and "sacrifices."[90] Unlike upward mobility stories in which people contend with precarious circumstances, Beth's precarity is an internal state. The inner demons that drive her also make her vulnerable. Because she is smarter and more damaged than the other chess players who surround her, Beth spends most of her time alone. Presumably, other characters are unable to offer meaningful companionship. As is the case for Midge, Beth's isolation is a cost of trailblazing.

Midge and Beth's competitive individualism also obstructs their ability to support others, which compounds their isolation. Rarely, if ever, do these characters articulate a sense of solidarity with other women or express a desire to act on behalf of any cause that extends beyond their personal agendas. In this sense, the series amplify Rottenberg's point that work itself is the stakes of neoliberal feminism, not changing the conditions under which women labor.[91] Both series highlight how white women's mobility is situated within racist and homophobic structures by featuring Black and/or queer characters who empathize with the trailblazers' struggles yet recognize the trailblazers' privileged positionality. These characters appear briefly in both series to provide crucial resources and opportunities that facilitate trailblazers' successes. By depicting these characters as helpmates who facilitate white women's upward mobility, the series ostensibly reckon with the white privilege that lies at the heart of trailblazer stories without disrupting the fantasy of meritocracy that underlies both series' valorization of individual achievement.

TQG's sole character of color, Jolene (Moses Ingram), appears briefly in three episodes and largely serves the role of Beth's caretaker and confidante. A fellow orphan a few years older than Beth, Jolene tells Beth that she wants to change the world. Yet she is resentful when Beth is adopted before her because she knows racism has impacted her own adoption prospects. Despite her recognition of Beth's privilege, Jolene loans Beth three thousand dollars during the series finale so that Beth may compete in the prestigious Moscow Invitational. "What I want is what you got," Jolene tells Beth. "You've been the best at what you do for so long, you don't even know what it's like for the rest of us."[92] It is paradoxical, perhaps, that Beth serves as a role model for her friend based on the promise of gender meritocracy given that her whiteness facilitated her class mobility. The series' latent recognition of structural racism is submerged by its neoliberal feminist framework. By investing in Beth's success, Jolene's actions ascribe meaning to white trailblazing as a broader feminist achievement and displace her expressed desires for Black liberation.

TQG's brief attention to the racialized dynamics of trailblazing expresses what Casey Ryan Kelly has termed "white ambivalence."[93] According to Kelly, white ambivalence marks a contradictory divestment and investment in race, as it expresses the "desire to transcend race without abandoning the privileges afforded by white supremacy."[94] The narrative development of both series extends white ambivalent engagement with racialized dynamics of upward mobility in which women's achievements occur through the sacrifices of Black characters. Even though Black characters confront the trailblazers about their privilege, the trailblazers never express a sense of obligation toward those facing more precarious circumstances due to their race and sexuality. For Kelly, such dynamics "[attempt] to reconcile the tension between the insistence that the color line is obsolete and the refusal to forfeit the racial privileges it offers."[95] Here and elsewhere, appeals to race-neutrality bolster the idea that economic advancement is a matter of individual achievement, while race as a category of difference continues to position white people as most deserving of rights and recognition.

One subplot in *TMMM* during seasons 3 and 4 illustrates this tension. The subplot revolves around Midge's relationship with Shy Baldwin (Leroy McClain), a singer inspired by Black crooners like Harry Belafonte and Johnny Mathis. Recognizing her talent, Baldwin supports Midge's career by hiring her to be his opening act during his national tour. The opportunity represents a turning point in Midge's career. The series presents a variety of cues to signal that Shy is gay but seeks to conceal his sexual orientation from the public. Midge is oblivious until she finds him badly bruised and learns that his male date attacked him. She keeps his secret until she opens for him at the legendary Apollo Theater in New York City. Uncharacteristically nervous to appear on stage because she had never performed for a predominantly Black audience before, she talks about the one thing both she and the audience recognize: Shy. At first, Midge draws laughs by appealing to her whiteness: "It looks like you've just seen a ghost." After receiving applause, she proceeds to joke about Shy's effeminate appearance and about the men who fawn over him. "Shy comes home, he doesn't need a plane. . . . He just puts on his Judy Garland shoes, clicks his heels together three times and says, 'There's no place like Harlem.'" Although the audience breaks out in uproarious laughter, Shy drops her from the tour. He cannot risk the threat Midge poses to his career and his safety.[96]

Although the subplot foregrounds Shy's vulnerability and points to Midge's unwitting exploitation of his position, the series foregrounds the damage inflicted on Midge's career. Midge is devastated when she is dropped from the tour, and subsequent episodes foreground her financial struggles, as she was counting on the tour to pay her bills. Working The Gaslight with nowhere else to go, she tells the crowd, "Once again, a man fucked up my life."[97] Midge continues to frame her difficulties in terms of patriarchy. "It's a man's world," she laments when she cannot get credit to buy groceries.[98] Her remarks pit liberal feminism against anti-racism and gay rights, as though support for one agenda necessarily disadvantages the other.

The series continues to prioritize the concerns of white women at the expense of people of color, a practice that critics have referred to as white feminism.[99] As Meredith Neville-Shepard remarks, white feminism's appearance in television programs aimed toward a female audience "needs to be identified and understood as a form of anti-Black racism."[100] Midge takes little to no accountability for the damage she inflicted on Shy's career, even after she later learns that her act prompted Shy's record label to fire his manager and compelled him to marry a woman. When Midge does apologize to Shy, she approaches the issue in terms of her own victimization. Ambushing him during his wedding reception, she complains that she would have apologized to him earlier if he had let her. "I thought we were friends," she frowns before walking away from him (see fig. 3.7).[101]

FIG. 3.7 Midge confronts Shy Baldwin in the men's bathroom during his wedding reception regarding his decision to fire her from his tour. *The Marvelous Mrs. Maisel*, season 4, episode 5, "How to Chew Quietly and Influence People," written by Kate Fodor, released March 4, 2022, Amazon Prime Video Original.

Midge's response evokes a gendered and racialized politics of vulnerability in which her claims of victimization supersede those of people whom she has victimized, and in an ironic twist, enable criticisms of white, straight women's own complicity with whiteness and heteronormativity to be understood as "yet another way that white women are victimized within society."[102] By decrying Shy's violation of the norms of friendship, Midge engages in what Ruby Hamad describes as one of white feminism's "power moves," in which white women's "*appearance* of powerlessness" redirects attention from criticisms regarding their complicity with white supremacy.[103] The subplot concludes with a scene featuring a close-up of Midge as she looks back at Shy while he smokes a cigarette by himself, looking forlorn. While the scene conveys the sexual repression and homophobia of the early sixties, it continues to foreground the imperatives of white women's mobility. By demanding the moral high ground, Midge continues to evade accountability for destroying Shy's personal life and nearly ending his career. Putting Kelly in conversation with the work on white feminism, I see the scene as an articulation of white feminist ambivalence in which white women seek access to opportunities and resources historically afforded to white men without sacrificing white women's privileged position vis-à-vis others exploited by white supremacist heteropatriarchy. As the series frames Shy's story as a vignette in a larger story arc about Midge's career, *TMMM* illuminates how television in the streaming era has exploited images of Black suffering to give meaning to its strong white women. However, I'm not certain that the series invites viewers to celebrate this trailblazer.

While Midge is an apt illustration of white, neoliberal feminism, it is not clear to me that the series necessarily positions viewers to empathize with her or share her sense of righteous indignation after Shy fires her. Rather than viewing her as a heroine, several critics have described Midge as an antihero, more akin to *Mad Men*'s Don Draper than to classic TV feminists like Mary Tyler Moore.[104] If we look at Midge's character arc as the origin story of an antihero whose rising stardom makes her increasingly unable to express feminist commitments or take feminine care of others, the subplot about her relationship with Shy points to the limitations of both neoliberal feminism and postwar femininity; both Midge and Shy end up alone because their pursuit of wealth and stardom make intimate relationships impossible. Admittedly, Midge's cultural status—as a hero or an antihero—is a point of contestation among critics. In my conversations with fellow feminist critics who have watched *TMMM*, there is little consensus about whether the series invites viewers to admire Midge or view her skeptically. Disagreements about Midge's cultural status suggest that her character is ambivalent, refracting broader tensions about what sacrifices women must make to achieve professional or artistic success in a heterosexist, white supremacist culture.

Alternatively, *TQG* ends on a far more triumphant note. Rather than explore the future in store for Beth, the miniseries concludes moments after she has earned the title of Grandmaster. Refusing to return to the United States in the care of a public official charged with overseeing her time in the USSR, Beth approaches an outdoor chess table and invites a Soviet player to join her. The conclusion encourages viewers to celebrate Beth's determination to control her destiny by playing chess on her own terms. Here, Beth's personal journey trumps both geopolitical and identity politics. Moments earlier, however, brief shots of Jolene celebrating Beth's win by herself suggest that Beth's achievement is an accomplishment for them both. The conclusion foregrounds the postfeminist celebration of individualism as the ultimate expression of feminist agency that is only remotely concerned with hardships facing people who don't benefit from the privileges of white heteronormativity.

Beauty Must Suffer?

When I was a child, I learned to accept certain hair and beauty treatments with the knowledge that to look good, I had to endure a certain amount of pain. I am reminded of this lesson as I reflect on the misery that Midge and Beth endure to become truly great at their chosen professions. The contradictions that structure these trailblazer stories illustrate how neoliberal feminism is misogynist at heart because it ultimately affirms the status quo. *TMMM* and *TQG* replace familiar narratives of gender discrimination and workplace sexual harassment with a celebration of the current moment's intensified model of neoliberal subjectivity in which women's enterprising and competitive activities foreground their capacities to be self-responsible.[105] Both the ir/relevance of period sexism and trailblazer beauty exemplify neoliberal feminist imperatives. Beth's and Midge's stylish appearances point to the intensification of neoliberal dispositions of embodied perfection that are largely encoded by visual signifiers of women's faces, bodies, and consumer practices across streaming and social media content.

As they affirm the status quo, these stories also amplify the sexist practices that have enabled a small fraction of "exceptional" women to enter lucrative, male-dominated workplaces. As John Stuart Mill suggests, the gifted woman always exists as an extension of patriarchal arrangements. A psychoanalytic perspective on these series might explain the contradictions that structure these series as illustrations of how the feminine only has meaning by virtue of a male sign. Noting that embodied, physical attributes often define transmedia heroines, Aviva Dove-Viebahn asserts that "as long as women protagonists are an exception marked by feminine intuition or even empowered via symbolic gestures meant to signify how they are above average *women*, we will continue to define the feminine as opposed to the masculine reference."[106] Trailblazer beauty works alongside and with characters' exceptional talent because these characters do not challenge the gender order. Rather than represent feminist struggle, they invite white women viewers to champion themselves.

At the same time, trailblazer beauty also points to the limits of trailblazing as a means of personal advancement. Even when a career rather than a romantic heteronormative relationship is the goal, women must still look beautiful if they want to succeed. In featuring Midge's isolation at the end of her glamorous career, *TMMM*'s final season suggests that neoliberalism cannot provide a framework for imagining feminist futures. At best, the series implicitly invites viewers to seek other alternative visions in which people marginalized by white supremacist patriarchy do not end up alone and do not have to appeal to a hyperconsumerist culture to gain the respect and admiration of others. At worst, cultural affirmations of trailblazer beauty across television and elsewhere in our media landscape encourage women to not only accept but anticipate suffering and loss as the cost of greatness.

4

Insanely Gifted

Game of Thrones's Daenerys Targaryen

*Content note: The first major section of this chapter references a graphic depiction of sexual assault.

I have not oriented this book around the genres of fantasy and superheroes precisely because they are the most likely sites one might expect to find exceptionally empowered women figures. Who else besides superheroes, witches, and other magical women have resilience and talent that surpass the limitations of the human body? Who is more capable of withstanding patriarchal violence than a character who can time travel, fly, cast spells, or control minds? If the point of fantasy is to refract contemporary reality through a portrayal of an otherworldly figure, then, female characters' impossibility is the point. My goal in this book is to point to the variety of ways that expectations of women and feminist lives are impossible achievements according to the structures of television when generic conventions do not invite viewers to expect its characters to be magically gifted.

Although I do not centralize the fantasy genre throughout the book, I do so in this chapter to recognize that the themes running across this book also pertain to television's most extraordinary women. Several of scripted entertainment's super and magical women find that they can't defeat patriarchy without sacrificing themselves in the process. In *Chilling Adventures of Sabrina*, not even the daughter of Satan can defeat the misogynist and less-talented warlock Faustus Blackwood. Instead, the series' titular character must sacrifice her life in a bloodletting ceremony to save the world. The superhero genre similarly foregrounds female sacrifice. In *Avengers: Endgame*, Black Widow sacrifices herself so that a fellow male superhero can live. In this chapter, I focus on another character who dies despite her magical ability to thrive under conditions that no human person could survive: *Game of Thrones*'s Mother of Dragons: Daenerys Stormborn Targaryen.

A global phenomenon, HBO's hit series *Game of Thrones* (hereafter *GoT*) has been a subject of fascination and controversy since it premiered in 2011. Adapted from the literary saga *A Song of Ice and Fire* by American writer George R. R. Martin, the series attracted a record viewership on HBO and an active fan base, fulfilling TV's role as a cultural forum in a way few series have achieved since the proliferation of content and viewing platforms in the past decade. While many critics regard *GoT* as the best fantasy series ever made, others have claimed it to be the best television series ever made, period.[1] The series received numerous awards during its run from 2011–2019, including thirty-eight Emmys, more than any other prime-time scripted TV show in the Academy's history.[2] The series also elicited much commentary for its graphic depictions of gendered violence. While many condemned such portrayals as a crass and misogynist effort to captivate viewers, others praised the series' feminist undertones through its inclusion of numerous multidimensional female characters. The bar for reaching feminist credentials in Hollywood is low, of course. Throughout the series' seventy-three episodes, these female characters respond to varying forms of abuse—from threats of assault to actual rape—with fortitude and cunning.

Daenerys Targaryen (Emilia Clarke) stands out among them. She is the first major character to experience sexual assault. During the pilot episode, her brother Viserys (Harry Lloyd) sells her to the nomadic warlord Khal Drogo (Jason Momoa) in return for an army. The episode includes a horrific scene of Drogo raping Daenerys, the first among many of the series' vexing portrayals of gendered violence and gendered power dynamics. Daenerys (or Dany, as her closest associates affectionately call her) seems poised to become the series' righteous victor in the game of thrones. In her pursuit of glory, she defies chauvinistic men, empathizes with the downtrodden, and liberates slaves from the clutches of cruel masters.

Dany was one of the most talked about characters and the most vivid illustration of the irreconcilable tensions facing television's impossible woman on *GoT*. She is perhaps the most powerful character of the series, yet she is unable to achieve her goals. Unlike the women who gain power through their guile, stamina, and swordplay, she rises in stature by commanding fire-breathing dragons. Over the course of eight seasons, Daenerys deploys her dragons to vanquish a myriad of nefarious figures who seek to exploit her. Her power plays routinely disprove the assumptions of men who mistake her gender and small frame for weakness. As she conquers new territories and gains control of growing populations with each season, the series positions viewers to root for her ascendance. The series shocked audiences in the penultimate episode when, in a fit of madness or rage, Dany uses her dragon to burn down King's Landing, the seat of power in the series' storyworld. In the final episode, the remaining central hero of the story, Jon Snow (Kit Harrington), murders her for the sake of the realm.

Dany's fan community was outraged by the conclusion. By the third season, Dany was a feminist icon. Devoted fans created homespun merchandise dedicated to the "Mother of Dragons," named their daughters Khaleesi (her title once she married Drogo), held Khaleesi-themed weddings, and provided detailed instructions for how to recreate her intricate hairstyles.[3] Crediting her for demanding respect and using men's underestimation of her to her advantage, *Bustle* writer Tanya Ghahremani pronounced her "the baddest feminist bitch in all the land."[4] *Vox* writer Gaby Del Valle observed that, as the series set Dany up as an "unambiguously feminist hero," "Khaleesi became shorthand for a strong, empowered woman." A "warrior queen," she burned more than one man alive who got in her way.[5]

Before the show's conclusion, political figures and advocates turned Dany into an avatar for left-of-center politics. Hillary Clinton's supporters promoted her 2016 presidential run by circulating a since-deleted tweet referring to Clinton as "Hillary Stormborn" that featured an image of Clinton with a baby dragon on her shoulder.[6] The following year, images of Daenerys appeared online as a show of support for then-Senator Kamala Harris and others who questioned Jess Sessions during congressional hearings.[7] Around the same time, supporters of Spain's Podemos Party employed her image as a symbol of the movement's potential to challenge existing power structures.[8] Even Elizabeth Warren declared that Dany was her favorite *GoT* character for an op-ed in *The Cut*, noting that, unlike the rest of the series' characters, Dany espoused the "revolutionary idea" that rulers should "serve all mankind" rather than the "interests of the rich and powerful."[9]

Additional media commentary ensued after Dany became the series' primary villain. Was her demise the inevitable conclusion of her complicated character arc, or was it a lazy and sexist attempt by writers to wrap up the series before Martin's vision was fully realized? It depends on who you ask. Writing for *The Atlantic*, Parker Richards explained that viewers' anger was the outcome of poor writing because the final season lacked the nuanced dialogue and development that characterized the series' earlier seasons.[10] Others attributed viewers' outrage to HBO's inability to adapt Martin's complicated construction of Dany to the small screen. *Vox* writer Emily St. James noted that viewers who read Martin's books objected less to the TV show's conclusion than viewers who had not. James concluded that HBO's early framing of her as a feminist icon obscured her despotic tendencies, which were more evident in the books.[11]

Less commentary has addressed the racialized dimensions of Dany's character. Until the final season, Dany lives in exile in Essos, a region inspired by colonial stereotypes about the brutality of peoples from Asia, Africa, and the Americas prior to colonization. Several critics lamented her problematic white savior image, especially since the series accorded little agency or depth to characters of color.[12] Helen Young avers that Dany's relationship with former slaves provides an apt illustration of structural racism because her actions primarily serve her personal agenda. A Medievalist scholar, Young adds that the idea of Western Europe as lacking racial diversity during the Middle Ages stems more from modern ethno-nationalist discourse than from the historical record.[13] Racist stereotypes, not fidelity to the past, guided the series' portrayal of cultural difference. Given the whiteness at the heart of the series and Dany's character, the significance of her death cannot be understood solely by reference to the sloppiness of writers or by her fans' adoration of her; it must take her construction as a figure empowered by her relationship to the people of Essos into account. By constructing Dany as a feminist icon and imperialist with a white savior complex, *GoT* refracts the fraught status of white feminism.

Dany is an impossible woman because her white femininity prevents her from recognizing that her pursuit of monarchical power is incommensurate with her desire to liberate others from cultural backgrounds that are unfamiliar to her. But she is also an impossible woman because her commitment to liberation violates Western culture's demand for stories that confer power and authority to patriarchal white supremacy. Dany's storyline illustrates that white feminism is an anachronism because it cannot simultaneously advance a multiethnic feminist agenda and reap the benefits of white privilege. Drawing from Raka Shome and other postcolonial feminist scholars, this chapter explores how this character's impossible dream and the controversy surrounding the show's conclusion illustrates the "spectacularization of white femininity" that nearly replicates but then upsets the ways in which neoliberal formations of citizenship are expressed through portrayals of privileged white women.[14] In the rest of this chapter, I explore how Dany's position as a victim of sexual assault and her shifting position in relation to Western imperialism work together to explain viewers' attachments to the character and the writers' decision to give her a tragic ending. In the process, I detail how Dany enacts three personas across the series' eight seasons that convey her impossible situation: empowered survivor, failed global mother, and isolated madwoman. As the character's short-term achievements fail to lead to long-term success, her storyline illustrates how women's leadership within dominant power structures is incompatible with a decolonial feminist agenda. Women might be able to pursue power, but they should expect a tragic conclusion should they seek to dismantle colonial relations altogether.

Empowered Survivor

Dany's initial appearance illuminates how white feminism is imbricated with misogynist violence. The pilot episode introduces viewers to Dany as a girl who just wants to return to her home in Westeros but is forced into a marriage by a brother who sexually abuses her. Within the first minute of her initial appearance, Viserys takes off her top to appreciate that she has developed "a woman's body." Dany remains expressionless as the camera zooms in on Viserys's hand fondling her breast. The scene points to a broader pattern of his abuse toward her when he warns her that she must "be perfect" for him lest she "awaken the dragon." After Dany tells him she does not want to marry Khal Drogo, Viserys caresses her cheek and states, "I would let his whole tribe fuck you, all 40,000 men and their horses too."[15] Minutes later, Dany is seated uncomfortably before members of the Dothraki tribe engaging in a variety of ghastly wedding-day festivities. The scene revels in Orientalist tropes of native savagery, particularly once Drogo leads her away from the scene to consummate the marriage while Dany cries.[16]

Echoing plot developments of other series, including *Unbreakable Kimmy Schmidt* (chapter 2) and *Queen of the South* (chapter 5), Dany's status as an empowered feminist emerges out of her experience as a rape survivor. Sarah Hagelin and Gillian Silverman observe that we're drawn to Dany precisely because she offers a pleasurable fantasy about a downtrodden character who turns her victimhood into "an abashed show of triumph."[17] Indeed, *GoT* earned its feminist credentials largely on the basis of female characters' extraordinary ability to survive varying forms of sexual violence. Rape's function as a storytelling device points to writers' limited imaginations for giving women character depth, as screenwriters frequently use rape as a backstory to explain a female characters' motivations or hardened demeanor.[18] Sarah Projansky observes that thriller and horror films routinely incorporate rape or the threat of rape into the plot to "produce spectatorial anxiety" and then "resolve that anxiety through an independent woman character who triumphs in the end."[19] Over and over again, women characters' transformations from meek to powerful begin with their violation. I suppose if someone were to only understand gender relations from watching television, they might recommend sexual assault to any woman seeking advice for how they might more effectively "lean in."

Dany's violation and her objection to the rapes of other women also give her character feminist import. Tanya Horeck notes that rape has grounded feminist discourse at least since Susan Brownmiller's influential book *Against*

Our Will described rape as the "primal scene of culture" or the primary mechanism by which "all men keep all women in a state of fear."[20] Feminists have leveraged rape and the threat of rape as the basis for why publics should care about women and women's rights because this threat has contributed to a cultural imaginary that imagines women as victims, and thus as worthy of sympathy and care.[21] As Hagelin observes, it is not women in general but white women in particular who generate sympathy on the basis of their presumed vulnerability.[22] A broader implication of feminism's historic articulation with rape discourse is that patriarchal violence is the condition under which feminism gains currency in contemporary culture and that white women's cultural value is established through their ability to survive sexual assault. These implications are vividly illustrated in *GoT*, revealing how television paradoxically makes feminism meaningful by appealing to the misogyny and racism that underwrites it.

Orientalist tropes of the Dothraki as a violent and savage people amplify Dany's precarious situation by drawing upon white supremacist fantasies.[23] Dany's violation dredges up historic associations of dark-skinned men with threats to white women's purity and safety.[24] Her pale skin, blue eyes, and platinum hair mark her as a descendant of House Targaryen, a family that engaged in centuries of inbreeding to maintain pure bloodlines. Dany's Aryan beauty contrasts with Drogo's dark skin, large frame, and kohl-rimmed eyes. Her suffering and the Orientalist tropes that ground the portrayal of the Dothraki are designed to elicit viewers' simultaneous titillation and discomfort; these conflicting affects are resolved once Dany develops her own power and authority. As season 1 continues, Dany learns how to manipulate Drogo and forcefully resists her brother's physical abuse. She becomes more powerful once she becomes pregnant. Flipping the imperialist script in which white men enact colonial violence to protect white women, Dany falls in love with her abuser. After Viserys threatens the life of her unborn child, Dany approves Drogo's decision to kill him. Following through on his promise to give Viserys a "golden crown," Drogo melts gold into liquid and pours it over the sniveling, hapless man.[25] This scene, like others that follow, invites viewers to revel in Dany's emerging power, even as that power is necropolitical, dependent on her ability to determine who may live and who may die.[26]

Dany's love story is cut short when Drogo dies in the final episode of season 1, leaving her to fend for herself. By centralizing Dany in the storyline featuring Essos, *GoT* avoids what could otherwise be a story about a multiethnic power couple with dark origins. The season concludes with the revelation that Dany has the power to nurture and command dragons, which, up to that point in the narrative, were thought to be extinct. The specific circumstance in which Dany reveals herself gives added dimension to her status as a survivor. Drogo has died and rests upon his funeral pyre. Dany adds her prized dragon's eggs to

FIG. 4.1 Dany dreads the consummation of her marriage to the fierce warlord Khal Drogo. *Game of Thrones*, season 1, episode 1, "Winter Is Coming," written by David Benioff and D. B. Weiss, original airdate April 17, 2011, HBO Original.

the pyre before walking into the flames herself. The practice is loosely inspired by the Hindu rite of sati, or widow sacrifice. Postcolonial scholar Gayatri Spivak famously noted that the abolition of this practice by British colonizers came to be understood as a case of "white men saving brown women from brown men," leading her to ask whether it was even possible for the "subaltern (woman)" to speak at all.[27] Miraculously, Dany emerges from the ashes unburned, covered with three small dragon hatchlings. This gives Dany authority as Mother of Dragons and as a ruler in her own right.

The spectacle of Dany's survival is a counterpart to the scene of her violation. Without the latter the former would not elicit the same affective resonance or feminist meaning. As Menéndez and Morales observe, "There is a relationship of continuity and causality between the rape and the power the character acquires."[28] Before transforming into a leader, she is turned into a victim, "suggesting that only a woman who suffers can be successful."[29] The final scene of season 1 nearly parodies the fantasy genre's use of rape as backstory, or what Kathleen Murphey defines as "the phoenix moment": the "moment after a brutal and demeaning sexual assault or rape when the broken and brutalized female character snaps and rises, like a phoenix from her emotional and physical ashes, to become an avenging badass heroine."[30] Quite literally, Dany appears from the ashes to prove she cannot be burned. In emerging from the funeral pyre intact, Dany reinforces colonialist assumptions about the backwardness of non-Western cultures while simultaneously challenging the patriarchal norms that put decisions about women's bodies in the hands of men. Dany is poised to establish herself not as an object of protection from her own kind but as an agent uniquely capable of generating her own power from the resources of her victimization.

After the first season, Dany turns her focus toward gaining control of the Iron Throne, which she believes is her birthright. Her power grows as she amasses increasing numbers of followers in Essos who are willing to serve in her army to battle in King's Landing. Seasons 2 and 3 feature her struggles to overtake nefarious rulers in unfamiliar territories organized around a slave economy. In her ongoing cycle of suffering and striving, each achievement unlocks new experiences of degradation and dismissal from increasingly hostile foes. The series provides viewers with moments of vicarious thrill when Dany outsmarts and defeats guileless charlatans and witless tyrants. As her foes berate her with a slew of violent sexist remarks just before she dispatches her dragons against them, viewers are directed to understand her achievements in feminist terms.

One of the most celebrated scenes occurs in season 3, when Dany outwits an arrogant slave trader in the slave city of Astapor. Looking to build her army, she seeks to acquire the Unsullied, a group of elite warrior-eunuchs trained as slave-soldiers by the Good Masters of Astapor. Dany appears vulnerable to an unscrupulous trader as she hands off one of her beloved young dragons in exchange for the army of slaves. In previous episodes, captions translate the slaver's vile, sexist response to Dany's efforts to negotiate with him. Speaking in the ancient language of Valyrian, he remarks to fellow slavers, "The slut thinks she can flash her tits and make us give her whatever she wants." Because his translator frames his response in more diplomatic terms, viewers are led to believe Dany is unaware of the slaver's virulent misogyny. But when they make the trade, Dany reveals that she has understood him the entire time. Once the slaver hands her the whip, she turns toward the thousands of slaves assembled behind her and begins speaking to them in Valyrian. After she commands the slaves to murder their masters, she tells him, "I am Daenerys Stormborn of House Targaryen, of the blood of Old Valyria. Valyrian is my mother tongue." Declaring that "a dragon is not a slave," she orders her dragon to set fire to the bewildered slaver.[31] Hagelin and Silverman observe that the scene "is shot and edited to elicit delight in Daenerys's assumption of power and her commitment to freeing the disposed and protecting the innocent."[32]

After leaving Astapor, Dany and her army conquer the neighboring cities of Yunkai and Meereen. In the process, she gains new titles and monikers. She is Khaleesi (or Dothraki queen), Mother of Dragons, Breaker of Chains, and "mhysa" (or mother). Each new title signifies new achievements wrought by magic in her quest for the throne. Although seasons 4 and 5 foreground political problems that cannot be as easily resolved through dragon fire, season 6 renews the effort to code Dany in feminist terms. Dany is captured by the new leader of the Dothraki and is told she violated the cultural dictate that Khaleesi widows spend the rest of their lives among other widows in the

Temple of the Dosh Khaleen. When the Khal (or warlord) and his advisors argue over what to do with her, Dany defiantly declares that she is more fit to lead the Dothraki than they are. In response, the Khal details his plans to sexually assault her. Dany's lips turn upward as he talks. Then she sets the temple on fire, burning the men inside it. When she emerges from the temple—naked and unburned—the Dothraki kneel reverently and pledge their allegiance to her. Social media commentators praised the scene as "proof that Daenerys 'burnt down the patriarchy.'"[33] Hagelin and Silverman aptly describe the scene as a "near parody of empowerment or lean-in feminism—self-actualizing, body positive, confident, resilient, and luminous."[34]

As it toggles between scenes of her degradation and her triumphs, *GoT* elicits viewers' affective attachment to the Mother of Dragons. Scenes featuring Dany's resistance foreground misogyny as a precondition for feminist agency. For each scene of her overcoming, there are multiple episodes dedicated to watching her struggle. Dany continually faces threats of gendered violence and men's efforts to undermine her authority, illustrating how the affective lure of her story depends on her violation. If she is a "unique hero" and "model for . . . female agency and liberation," as film scholar Rikke Schubart believes her to be, then we need to wrestle with the conditions under which media culture enables viewers to imagine feminist liberation.[35] While these conditions are sexist, they are also deeply invested in whiteness.

Failed Global Mother

By locating Dany's resistance to tyrannical patriarchs in a region that is ostensibly an imagining of the Global South, the series sutures her feminism to her whiteness. It is through her position as a once vulnerable but now empowered white woman that viewers are meant to appreciate her desire to protect other women and liberate slaves. These secondary aims maintain narrative tension in the series; if she was solely driven by personal ambition, her three dragons alone would provide all the technological firepower needed to take the Iron Throne. But Dany wants to be more than just a powerful ruler: she wants to be regarded as a beloved and just queen. Her experiences in Essos are central to shaping her outlook. Exiled from the homeland of her birth, Dany develops an affinity with the downtrodden people of Essos. After all, it is where she falls in love, becomes the Mother of Dragons, and has thousands of devoted followers. Her title of "mhysa" is significant because much of her power and authority derives from her status as a mother—of a future son of a powerful Khal, to dragons, and then to the formerly enslaved.[36] Her titles confer her status as a "global mother" figure that draws upon the variety of stories and myths that have given exalted status to white women as symbols of "universal goodness, beauty, caring, and desire."[37] Analyzing media attention to Princess Diana, Shome explains that contemporary Anglo nations have rewritten "their modern and caring selves in the 21st century" through displays of white women's kinship, familiarity, and intimacy with people in the Global South.[38] The image of the global mother functions as a symbol of global togetherness, Shome notes, even as Western nations continue to perpetuate "geopolitical and economic violences that make true global harmony possible."[39]

Dany illustrates the contradictions underlying the global mother figure. At the same time as she wants to help people in Essos, Dany wants nothing more than to return "home" to Westeros. Feeling dislocated everywhere she goes, she claims ties to both Westeros and Essos. Her liminal status helps explain her conflicting regard for the Dothraki and former slaves as resources for building an army, as blood relations, and as people in need of saving and civilizing. Each of these positions replicates Western feminism's conflicted status vis-à-vis the Global South.

Dany's efforts to save and civilize the people of Essos begin in season 1 when she presumes to share common cause with the region's violated women, perhaps because she relates to their helplessness and vulnerability at the hands of Dothraki men. After the Dothraki raid Lhazar, a peaceful sheep herding community, Dany claims the Lhazareen women as her daughters to prevent Drogo's riders from raping them as "spoils of war."[40] Drogo's raiders are incensed. The scene draws from colonialist discourses that have articulated Western feminism to notions of "social progress on which modern colonialism is founded."[41] Although women experience sexual violence throughout the series' storyworld, *GoT* portrays the gendered violence that occurs in Westeros as a matter of individual pathology, the actions of sociopaths and power-hungry sadists. By contrast, sexual violence in Essos is attributed to culture, or to "the way it has always been," as Jorah Mormont describes Dothraki raiders' desires to rape their victims.[42] By depicting Eastern cultures as "sexually depraved" and "comparatively worse" than their Western counterparts, the series and the book upon which it is based tap into "Western literature's long history of Orientalism."[43]

The depiction of Dothraki as a savage people amplifies the stakes of Dany's story for white feminism as she assumes a civilizing mission for herself. Jenny Sharpe notes in her analysis of nineteenth-century British literature that English womanhood was an "important cultural signifier for articulating a colonial hierarchy of race" that helped justify ongoing colonial expansion.[44] The legacy of this signifier continues to shape the Western imagination. Shome explains that white female subjectivity continues to function as a "site of morality," as the figure of the white woman has reworked and restored colonial ideologies in recent decades.[45] Dany's insistence that she overrule her Khal affirms Western assumptions about the inherent immorality of Eastern cultures. In aiming to reform the Dothraki, Dany gives fantasy form to Sharpe's observation that Western European feminists "ground their own emancipation in the moral superiority of the British as an enlightened race, engaged in raising natives into humanity."[46] Notably, Dany does not speak to any of the women she speaks for. Her assumption of moral authority resembles the ways in which Western feminist subjectivity depended on the negation of the Indian woman during the modern colonial period. By foreclosing the possibility of Indian women's agency, "English women [could] appropriate the moral value of womanhood" for themselves "and transform it into a female form of moral agency."[47] In a similar vein, Dany's status as an empowered feminist depends on the absence of well-developed women characters outside of Westeros. By declaring the Lhazareen women as her daughters, Dany asserts her maternal authority in opposition to the patriarchal systems that govern both Westeros and Essos.

Dany continues her civilizing mission in subsequent seasons by liberating slaves in the cities of Astapor, Yunkai, and Meereen, an area the series refers to as Slaver's Bay. Dialogue between Dany and the people of Meereen during the final episode of season 3 portrays her as a uniquely enlightened figure in a feudal society that has no conceptualization of democracy or individual rights. After ousting the wealthy nobles from Meereen, Dany addresses the throng of liberated slaves, noting that she should not be credited for giving them their freedom. "Your freedom is not mine to give. It belongs to you and you alone. If you want it back, you must take it for yourselves. Each and every one of you."[48] Visibly moved, the group begins to raise their arms toward her, addressing her as "mhysa." In a gesture of closeness with them, Dany strolls through the crowd until two men lift her onto their shoulders. They carry her while the gathering moves in closer and the roar of "mhysa" grows louder. The episode ends as the camera pans out from an overhead shot, depicting Dany in a cerulean dress amid thousands of dark-skinned arms outstretched toward her. The visual coding of the scene confers moral goodness to Dany. The scene invites viewers to invest in Dany's storyline in subsequent seasons. Similar to photographs that depicted Princess Diana's visits to children in the Global South, Dany's ethos as a site of morality is "shored up by visual logics that represent her as an angelic figure."[49] Dany's radiant image is projected through visual techniques routinely used to depict white women as "pure, divine, angelic figures."[50] Glowing in the middle of a sea of brown bodies, Dany seems to float ethereally above the crowd. The high camera angles and scoring elicit awe and stature toward Dany's body while reducing the bodies of the formerly enslaved to an indistinguishable mass of heads, limbs, and torsos.

Despite the visual techniques that encode Dany as a global mother, plot developments and dialogue destabilize the image of Dany's moral goodness by foregrounding the egoistic aims that are at the heart of her desire for love and

FIG. 4.2 The newly freed people of Meereen embrace Dany as "mhysa" and carry her to the city gates. *Game of Thrones*, season 3, episode 10, "Mhysa," written by David Benioff and D. B. Weiss, original airdate June 9, 2013, HBO Original.

affirmation from the people of Essos. Dany did not travel to Essos on a civilizing mission, after all, and her liminal status raises questions about her motives and leadership ability. Just before the people of Meereen greet her, she reflects to Jorah that "perhaps they didn't want to be conquered." Jorah has to remind her, "You didn't conquer them. You liberated them."[51] As subsequent episodes suggest, the difference between conquering and liberating is not always very clear.

Dany's leadership falters as early as season 1. She doesn't anticipate the negative consequences of her decisions, even when people attempt to warn her of them. Her directive forbidding Dothraki men from raping women provokes a fight between Drogo and his lieutenant, Mago (Ivailo Dimitrov), which ends in Mago's death and Drogo being badly wounded. Dany is proven wrong yet again after a Lhazareen woman, Mirri Maz Durr (Mia Soteriou), introduces herself as the "godswife" of the Lhazareen temple and offers to treat Drogo's wound. Although Drogo's remaining lieutenant insists that Maz Durr is a witch, Dany insists on letting the woman provide a healing poultice to Drogo's wound. Drogo's condition only worsens, and Dany begs Maz Durr to use her blood magic to save her husband. Maz Durr's spell turns Drogo into an unresponsive shell of his former self and causes Dany to deliver a stillborn baby. Far from regarding Dany as her savior, Maz Durr already believed her life was bereft of meaning when the Dothraki murdered her friends and burned down her temple. When Dany confronts her, Maz Durr explains that her decision to give Dany a stillborn son was designed to prevent further destruction. "He would have been the Stallion Who Mounts the World. Now he will burn no cities. Now his khalazar will trample no nations into dust."[52]

The godswife's speech reveals that Dany gravely misunderstood the women she had claimed as family. While Dany believed her actions were liberatory, the Lhazareen woman correctly viewed her as a conqueror. Dany's mistake is emblematic of a white imperialist impulse that understands the needs of non-Western people through a hegemonically Western lens. As Lila Abu-Lughod remarks, the Western impulse to "save" brown women from brown men fails to recognize the unique and specific differences among women in the world and reproduces the very forms of global injustice that Western feminists purportedly seek to redress.[53] By failing to understand Maz Durr's motives, Dany made herself vulnerable to the older woman's manipulations. Dany's exchange with Maz Durr points to the problems that arise when Western feminists assume that all women share identical interests.[54] Maz Durr understood that Dany's humanism ultimately served her own agenda.

Subsequent seasons depict Dany as genuinely conflicted about her stake in Essos. While she fervently desires an army to fight her battle for the Iron Throne, she also appears genuinely concerned about the well-being of commoners in Essos. Her actions on behalf of women and slaves often hamper her efforts to amass an army to retake the Iron Throne. The issue is not that she is ill-intentioned; rather, she does not understand the full context in which power operates in Slaver's Bay, nor does she recognize that her desire to protect the vulnerable is incompatible with her quest for monarchical power. Seasons 4 and 5 foreground her failed effort to serve as a white savior. In mainstream cinema, the trope of the white savior foregrounds white agency and moral authority in stories about resistance to anti-Black and neocolonial violence. White saviorism also manifests in Western volunteer efforts to liberate or rescue people of color in Africa and other regions in the Global South. Jenna Hanchey observes from a psychoanalytic perspective that white saviorism is a fantasy structure that enables Western subjects to "find wholeness" in other countries by saving other people. For Hanchey, such wholeness covers over the contradictions between competing desires to ally with others in decolonial struggle and affirms a belief in Western exceptionalism.[55] Dany's efforts model a variant of white saviorism, or neocolonial white feminism, in which white women of privilege aim to disrupt Western imperialism by centering their own intrapersonal experiences. A mode of strategic whiteness, neocolonial white feminism responds to contemporary critiques of whiteness but ultimately serves structures of white supremacy.[56] In short, *GoT* depicts the ineffectiveness of white saviorism but keeps whiteness at the center of its story.

Ending slavery proves to be more difficult than Dany anticipated. Part of the problem is that liberation does not necessarily improve the living conditions of the formerly enslaved. When she first addresses the slaves of Meereen, she tells them she brings them "a choice": to welcome her or stand behind their masters.[57] Her appeal belies the limited options available to them, as those she freed in Astapor and Yunkai all stand behind her, serving in her army. After abolishing slavery in the city, one former slave asks her to let him return to his former life because it gave him a home and the respect of those he served. He tells Dany that all she has given him is "fear and squalor." In response, Dany allows the man to "sign a contract" with his former master. Afterward, Dany's most experienced advisor Ser Barristan Selmy (Ian McElhinney) warns her that "the masters will take advantage of the situation. They will be slaves in all but name."[58] The conversation and the events surrounding it resonate allegorically with Saidiya Hartman's analysis of the failures of Reconstruction in the United States. Explaining how the idea of freedom was "laden with the vestiges of slavery,"[59] Hartman explains that appeals to freedom justified new forms of violence and domination. "Self-possession [did not] liberate the former slave from his or her bonds, but rather sought to replace the whip with the compulsory contract and the collar with a guilty conscience."[60] By forbidding the practice of slavery, Dany attributed what Hartman calls "burdened individuality" onto the former slaves, leaving them with few resources to manage their precarious living conditions and holding them responsible for seeking contractual arrangements that continued to put their labor and bodies at the service of wealthy nobles.[61]

Other events cast doubt upon her leadership abilities as well. Dany loses the support of many people who once called her "mhysa" when she decides to execute one of her loyal subjects, a former slave, for murdering a member of an insurgent group, the Sons of the Harpy, without her permission. Dany also arouses people's ire when she forbids gladiatorial sports despite their popularity. She concedes only after her lover Daario Naharis (Michiel Huisman) explains that the pits helped him earn his freedom when he was destitute. Dany's refusal to grant mercy to those who defy her orders and her lack of respect for the long-standing traditions of Slaver's Bay opens herself up to increased scrutiny from the newly freed citizens of Meereen.

While former slaves do not necessarily find themselves better off under Dany's rule, former slavers pose ongoing challenges to her leadership. Wealthy slavers back the Sons of the Harpy, who launch coordinated attacks on the queen and her advisors. The insurgents murder Ser Barristan Selmy and cause her to flee from Slaver's Bay at the end of season 5. During season 6, the Sons of the Harpy set fire to every ship in Meereen's harbor. In Dany's absence, her hand, Tyrion Lannister (Peter Dinklage), attempts to negotiate with the slavers, only to have them break their peace treaty. It is not until Dany is able to return to Slaver's Bay with a dragon and an army of Dothraki raiders behind her that she is able to regain control of the region.

Seasons 5 and 6 obstruct viewers' ability to comfortably embrace Dany's white savior role because, ultimately, she's not very good at it. Dani's poor judgments obliquely point to criticisms about white feminism's unwillingness to learn from people whose social location differs from their own. In a conversation reminiscent of Dany's exchange with Maz Durr, the prostitute Vala explains that she conspired with the Sons of the Harpy because Dany is "a foreign queen" who brought foreign soldiers to "destroy our city and our history."[62] Dany's liberatory impulses were always grounded in assumptions of her moral superiority, drawn from her personal experiences as a white woman exiled to a region she never deeply understood. They're also driven by her firm belief that she is the rightful heir to the most powerful throne in the world. The series obliquely points to the problem at root in all stories featuring white saviors: racial inequities cannot be redressed by centering the experiences of white people, regardless of how well-meaning they might be.

Acting on her unquestioned assumptions, Dany refracts the conflict between neoliberal feminist goals of achieving upward mobility and decolonial feminist commitments to broader structural transformation. Beyond her inability to appreciate the cultural traditions and economic conditions that organize life in Slaver's Bay, Dany never seems to recognize that her goals of serving the greater good are incompatible with her efforts to win monarchical power. She cannot provide liberation for the masses in Essos *and* commit them to a bloody battle to restore her claim to the throne at the same time. As a Son of the Harpy tells military commanders who were born in Essos, "She doesn't belong here. And no matter how many of you traitors call her 'mhysa,' she will never be your mother."[63] While the Sons of the Harpy are a reactionary group invested in maintaining the social hierarchies and exploitative conditions that structured life in Slaver's Bay prior to Dany's arrival, the Son's comment also points to Dany's shallow investments in the region.

Dany seems perpetually uncertain about whether she should use Essos as a resource in her bid for supreme power over Westeros or whether she should fulfill a more moral mission by saving the commoners from enslavement. Dany's relationship with her dragons is a synecdoche for this conflict. The dragons are the basis for her power because they literally provide the superior firepower she needs to quash resistance to her reign and win the impending battle for King's Landing. Yet they keep eating the commoners and their livestock. In season 4, a commoner drops the charred bones of his young daughter at Dany's feet after one of her dragons attacked the girl. The fearsome creatures are symbols of imperialism, as they extract resources from the land that they helped conquer and terrify the native people into submission. To avoid future carnage, Dany confines her dragons to the catacombs below Meereen. She is brought to tears when she chains the dragons amid their cries. The scene illustrates that she cannot be the Mother of Dragons and "mhysa" at the same time.

In a subsequent episode, Daario reminds her that her decision also diminishes her authority: "A dragon queen with no dragons is not a queen."[64] In the following season, the dragons break out of their confinement during the slavers' second attack on Meereen. In doing so, they remind viewers that Dany is the Mother of Dragons above all else and that her endeavors in Meereen are ultimately a smaller part of her broader agenda for imperial power. At the end of season 6, Dany secures a fleet, and she and her army set sail to Westeros. Whether or not she is capable of becoming a beloved and prudent ruler remains to be seen.

Isolated Madwoman

Thus far I have described Dany as both an empowered woman and a failed global mother. These two contrasting positions appear together, side by side, creating a character who is both admirable and terrible depending on where she is in her storyline and what she is doing at any given moment. The final two seasons continue to portray her as someone viewers might equally fear and love, but they also present an important transition in her character. When she returns to Westeros, the people she comes "home" to do not regard her as a breaker of chains or as their "mhysa." Instead, most people regard her as a potential madwoman. Dialogue throughout the series explains that Dany's father, King Aerys II Targaryen, was a generous and wise ruler of the Seven Kingdoms until insanity caused him to become murderous and cruel. Known as the Mad King toward the end of his life, he was eventually deposed in a civil war. Dany strives to demonstrate that she is not her father's daughter. This task ultimately proves to be impossible.

Dany's incommensurate goals pull her in opposite directions: toward using violence on the one hand and behaving generously on the other. Despite her many faults, viewers are positioned to root for her until the final season because she is one of few characters who demonstrates empathy for commoners. Tyrion Lannister's arrival in Meereen is a key event during season 5, as it puts two of the most well-intentioned figures together for the first time. Tyrion initially seeks a meeting with Dany because his friend Lord Varys (Conleth Hill) has convinced him that she might be the "best last chance to build a better world."[65] Dany tells Tyrion that the royal families of Westeros are "all just spokes on a wheel." With disdain in her voice, she continues, "This one's on top, then that one's on top. And on and on it spins, crushing those on the ground." She concludes with one of the most quoted lines from the series, "I'm not going to stop the wheel. I'm going to break the wheel."[66] Moved by Dany's determination to protect the vulnerable, Tyrion maintains his support for Dany until the second-to-last episode, which contributes to the series' portrayal of her as a messianic figure.

Although Dany wants to make sure that "future generations will never be held hostage by a tyrant,"[67] several events leading up to the final episode suggest that her path to the throne will involve the very forms of violence that she deplores. After using dragonfire to destroy her rivals' army in her first battle in Westeros, she tells her potential ally Jon Snow that her actions were necessary: "We both want to help people. We can only help them from a position of strength. Sometimes strength is terrible."[68] Dany's commentary points to the fundamental contradiction of her character: She believes she can break the wheel and rule at the center of it at the same time. She imprudently believes in her own righteousness and moral authority above others. Thus, she does not consider the possibility that violence at her hands is no more righteous than the brutality displayed by the rulers who came before her. Yet she does continue to do good works for the people of Westeros, producing ongoing uncertainty about what her future holds—both for her and for the realm.

While Dany fails to reckon with her own shortcomings, she also faces bigotry from enemies, would-be allies in Westeros, and the series' writers. Whereas her whiteness shored up her sense of moral superiority in Essos, Dany's affinity for the people of Essos undermines her ability to gain allies in her native homeland. A variety of scenes point to Dany's connection to Essos as a liability. Cersei Lannister (Lena Headey), the queen Dany seeks to replace, frames her opposition to Dany in racialized terms, describing her army as "savages" and "heathens,"[69] but even Tyrion suggests that her affiliation with the Dothraki and the Unsullied are a problem for her. He remarks that she will need Westerosi soldiers, not soldiers from Essos, if she wants to reason with the people of King's Landing. In a marked shift from earlier seasons when Dany's resistance to the Dothraki encoded her with feminist agency, these scenes frame the Dothraki's support for her as dangerous for the white realm. The portrayal of her first victorious battle in Westeros marks the beginning of this shift. Somber scoring and editing techniques invite viewers to understand Dany's victory as a tragedy. When her dragon and the Dothraki slaughter Lannister's army, a Dothraki commander tells Tyrion, "Your men can't fight."[70] The emphasis on the Dothraki as uniquely violent points to the racism encoded by the series. Although the scene's aesthetic cues invite viewers to recoil from the Dothraki's ruthlessness, the violence is no less revolting than the myriad scenes that came before it depicting white soldiers warring with one another over the Seven Kingdoms. Presumably, what makes this scene disturbing within the context of the excessively violent storyworld is not that so many people meet a grisly end but that they meet their end at the hands of dark-skinned others. After all, the Dothraki were no more invested in expropriating resources from the less powerful than the Lannisters. The problem is that they are simply better at it. Fear of dark-skinned men helps to facilitate the series' effort to transform Dany's character from her position as the leading protagonist into a vexing antagonist.

At the same time the series begins to sharpen its portrayal of Dany, it subtly points to the white supremacist conditions that contribute to her downfall. The series illuminates the narrow-mindedness of her would-be allies in the North when Dany helps them defeat the White Walkers during the first half of the final season. The White Walkers, a horde of zombies intent on destroying humanity, would have succeeded had Dany not diverted her army and her dragons and brought them to Winterfell, the capital of the northernmost kingdom of Westeros. When everything seems hopeless, Dany bravely uses her dragons to incinerate the monsters. Dany's help is no small sacrifice. Dothraki riders succumb to the walkers after they charge into the dark field before any of the other soldiers venture forward to protect the realm. When the Northern soldiers retreat behind Winterfell's gates, the Unsullied remain outside to hold the horde back until the rest have time to regroup. In a reversal of the racial dynamics of earlier seasons, it is brown men who save white people from the White Walkers. Despite her and her army's heroism, Dany receives a lukewarm reception for her efforts. Her handmaiden Missandei receives a hostile reception from children who recoil from her when she greets them affably. The scene suggests that Dany is unlikable in Westeros because she is positioned in proximity to brownness. Her liminal status and Targaryen heritage are part of the problem. As Arya tells Jon, "She's not one of us."[71]

Dany's biggest challenge, one that she cannot overcome, is that she is a woman. By season 8, the people Dany must depend on to win the war over the throne align themselves with Jon Snow even though he has no interest in becoming king. Sexist double standards are highlighted during the celebratory feast after the White Walkers have been defeated. Amid the revelry, a Northern wilding, Tormund Giantsbane (Kristofer Hivju), delivers a blustery speech praising Jon for attributes that could also describe Dany: "Strong enough to befriend an enemy and get murdered for it! Most people get bloody murdered, they stay that way. Not this one. . . . He comes back and keeps fighting. . . . He climbed on a fucking dragon and fought. What kind of person climbs on a fucking dragon? A madman or a king!"[72] The crowd around him cheers while the camera zooms in on Dany, looking forlorn in the background. No one sings Dany's praises even though she had been riding dragons long before Jon Snow.

A subsequent scene makes the sexism underlying Westerosi politics explicit. Tyrion and Varys begin to rethink their support for Dany after she announces her plan to win the "final war" in King's Landing. Varys hones on the issue that she cannot control: her gender. For Varys, Jon Snow would be a better ruler because "he's a man, which makes him more appealing to the Lords of Westeros, whose support we are going to need." When Tyrion scoffs, Varys emphasizes the point: "He's an heir to the throne . . . because he's a man. Cocks are important, I'm afraid."[73] The scene articulates the assumptions underlying sexist realism directly. Even though both Jon and Dany have similar leadership credentials, gender remains the great *unequalizer*. Not even the Mother of Dragons can overcome the assumption that "every woman is the wrong woman" to hold the highest political office in the English-speaking world.[74]

For viewers drawn to the feminist portrait of Dany, the final episodes are heartbreaking. Dany faces a crushing blow in her first approach at King's Landing. Cersei's army manages to kill one of her dragons, and Cersei murders Missandei in front of her. Bereft, Dany is unsure of how to move forward. Missandei's last word is "dracarys," the command for dragons to breathe fire onto anything in front of them. Tyrion begs Dany to hold off on an attack to give time for the commoners to ring the city bells and raise the gates to announce their surrender. But after Cersei's army drops their swords and the commoners ring the bells, Dany proceeds with her plan to burn the city and its inhabitants. No longer known as the Mother of Dragons, Dany becomes the Queen of Ashes.

Although the series invites viewers to understand Dany's descent into madness as a genetic defect, a feminist interpretation of the events leading up to her final days might understand her madness as a consequence of white supremacist patriarchy. She relates her problem to Jon Snow the night before the attack: "I don't have love here. I only have fear."[75] She might have gone insane with rage, but she wasn't delusional when she concluded that people were conspiring against her. Realizing that she could never receive the same support as a white man whose central distinguishing qualification was his ability to fulfill patriarchal expectations of male leadership, Dany asserted her authority by drawing upon her most terrifying weapons.

The final episode evokes antipathy toward Dany's actions. In her penultimate scene, Dany delivers a rousing speech to her army of the Unsullied and Dothraki riders. Congratulating them for their success, she pledges to keep fighting until she and her soldiers "have liberated all the people of the world!"[76] Although the speech reinforces Dany's commitment to breaking the wheel, the orderly rows of soldiers and an enormous red and black flag evoke the imagery of fascist propaganda. Given that Mussolini's and Hitler's regimes were counterrevolutionary efforts to safeguard private property by excluding and scapegoating Jews and "inferior races" for broader economic crises, it would have made more sense to code Dany's detractors in Westeros as fascists.[77] Instead, the series relies on mainstream politics' tendency to paint all political perspectives critical of wealth accumulation and colonial exploitation with the same dark brush. Alongside ominous scoring, the staging aligns Dany and her army with some of the most violent and oppressive political regimes in the history of Western Europe. Presumably, the destruction Dany pledges to

FIG. 4.3 Dany's army lines up to listen to her victory speech after she has taken King's Landing in the series finale. The series' creators arranged the flag and orderly rows of soldiers to evoke the imagery of midcentury fascist propaganda. *Game of Thrones*, season 8, episode 6, "The Iron Throne," written by David Benioff and D. B. Weiss, original airdate May 19, 2019, HBO Original.

cause promises to be worse than the wheel that she aims to break. With limited cues to prepare viewers for the about-face, the scene suggests that Dany's goal to liberate the dispossessed poses a grave danger to the white characters the series has positioned viewers to love, like the Stark family of Winterfell. A different interpretation of the series might have depicted this event as a cause for celebration. After all, the Dothraki and Unsullied had spent their lives in relative squalor and had never been given a seat at any Westerosi table. But in HBO's vision, it is the savage violence of the wretched of the earth that must be stopped.

Realizing that Westeros as they know it would come to an end under Dany's control, Tyrion convinces Jon Snow to end the queen's short reign. In his final act of bravery, Snow approaches Dany in the now crumbling great hall that houses the Iron Throne, where Dany gleefully imagines her future. "It's not easy to see something that's never been before. A good world," she tells him.[78] But Snow balks at her suggestion that she alone can envision a just future. While kissing her in a tight embrace, he stabs her in the abdomen and watches as she dies in his arms. Depicting Jon Snow and Tyrion Lannister as the sole voices of reason in the final episode of the series affirms the sexist belief that white men are in a far better position to mete out justice (even if it involves tolerance for slavery and exploitation). This conclusion reaffirms the tired argument that women cannot be trusted in leadership roles because they lack the capacity for good judgment. Indeed, the series' final lesson is that women's power must be contained because they are ultimately guided by their dangerous and unruly passions.

HBO's White Masculine Vision

Dany is neither innately virtuous nor inherently evil, so the implications of her storyline cannot be neatly summarized. Just as white feminism remains a dominant ideological force yet accomplishes very little for people exploited by white supremacist heteropatriarchy, Dany is a liminal character, never belonging to any one place or people but driven by desires produced by her kinship relations in both the West and the East. Her desires appeal to a white feminist fantasy of empowered feminism, and yet her failed effort to "break the wheel" points to the limits of that fantasy. The series both represents and mocks neoliberal feminist appeals to white women's unbridled self-assurance because Dany's value and likability are grounded in her extraordinary ability to overcome sexism more than in what she accomplishes after she earned a measure of authority on her own. One dimension uniting the variety of observations one might make about Dany's story is that *GoT*'s writers could not imagine a story in which a well-intentioned but flawed woman could enact meaningful structural change in a world driven by exploitation and violence.

Daenerys Targaryen's character and *GoT*'s broader storyline are rife with contradictions. One contradiction revolves around the show's acknowledgment and perpetuation of sexist beliefs. The misogynist violence throughout the series' storyworld affirms the radical feminist assumption that patriarchy is a global phenomenon. Dany's struggle for recognition and authority acknowledges that sexism is a formative constraint to women's ability to attain political power. While the series teased viewers with nods to popular feminism, feminism was certainly not the show's politic. After all, an alternative ending might have detailed Dany's efforts to reconcile the tension between seeking power and liberating the dispossessed. That the writers did not pursue that angle despite Dany's popularity reveals the depths to which patriarchal culture structures the televisual imagination, and perhaps the political imagination as well. Dany's decision to lay waste to King's Landing in a fit of rage bears semblance to misogynist arguments, at least since Hillary Clinton ran for president of the United States, that women are unfit to hold the office of the presidency because they might instigate war during their menstrual cycles.[79] Rather than bring the series to a satisfying conclusion for viewers captivated by Dany's story, the series chose to turn these fans into chumps.

Likely an effort to appeal to HBO's target market of white, upper-class male viewers, the conclusion illuminates HBO's investments in affirming white supremacist patriarchy by amplifying hegemonic commonsense assumptions that a feminist agenda could only end tragically. Sarah Hagelin and Gillian

Silverman point to *GoT* as a vivid example of television's failure to "think outside the limits of masculinist culture. . . . Every attempt to posit women's liberation ends up being a meditation on the forces that she's rebelling against and that she can never fully defy. You can put a Khaleesi on a dragon, but apparently you can't stop her from freefalling."[80]

The series creates another perplexing set of contradictions as it references the politics of liberation. Indeed, the series provides both good and terrible reasons to critique certain investments in structural change. Dany's failure to liberate Slaver's Bay challenges neoliberal assumptions that putting women in power will necessarily lead to progress. Her mistakes interrupt uncritical Western enthusiasm for global white motherhood by indexing the problems that ensue when wealthy white women fail to listen to other women before they speak for them. Yet the series hardly invites critical reflection about its racial realism, taking for granted a viewership that is uncritical of Hollywood's investments in Western imperialism and white supremacy. Beyond its sexism, the series intimates that women are destined to fail when they ally with people of color. What marked Dany for death was her radical decolonial agenda, not her white savior complex. In a smart MA thesis, Abigail Kahler concludes that *GoT* ultimately supports "white imperialist feminism." She explains that although Dany "won a following with her charisma and idealism, she ultimately posed too significant a threat to the institutions of Westeros, and had to be destroyed, while her non-white followers disappeared, sailing away into the background."[81] This message corroborates the lessons of other series I have explored here (like *Parks and Recreation*) that women cannot rise through the ranks of already existing institutions and fight for disenfranchised and exploited classes at the same time. It's not their gender but their desire to fundamentally transform society that ultimately does them in. By depicting Dany's death as an inevitable and just conclusion to the series, *GoT* celebrates the status quo of a world in which slavery is tolerated because, presumably, it is the only future imaginable in a fantasy in which dragons can fly and zombies walk the earth.

5

Gangster Girlboss

The *Queen of the South*

*Content note: The first major section of this chapter references a graphic depiction of sexual assault.

"You built this business through sheer determination. This move is a building block for your future."[1] Foregrounding achievement and resilience, these lines address a subject who has made smart investments and is poised to receive promising returns in the years ahead. She is a responsibilized entrepreneur, the figure hailed by self-help books such as Ivanka Trump's *Women Who Work*, which urge women to cultivate networking and negotiating skills in order to make their marks in the world.[2] The character addressed by the prior quote shares much in common with other determined women characters featured in this book; she seeks challenges, takes risks, and pursues her goals with gusto. But she does not have the privilege of U.S. citizenship or whiteness to buttress her pursuit of economic advancement. To reach her full potential, she must literally destroy her competition.

This chapter focuses on the character development of Teresa Mendoza (Alice Braga) on the USA Network series *Queen of the South* (2016–2021). A poor woman from Sinaloa, Mexico, Teresa's mobility depends on her successful navigation of illegal narcotics trafficking. The speaker of the quote in the prior paragraph, James Valdez (Peter Gadiot), is a *sicario* (or drug cartel hitman) who has just murdered several men, and Mendoza is both his boss and his lover. James advises Teresa to pursue a risky venture with her primary adversary at the end of the series' third season, just as Teresa is poised to become a ruling aristocrat in the illicit drug trafficking world. By the end of the next episode, Mendoza completes her transformation from mule to *jefa*, earning her title as the "Queen of the South."

Queen of the South (hereafter *QotS*) is among a variety of television programs about the illicit drug trade, including Netflix's *Narcos*, AMC's *Breaking Bad*, the comically dark woman-driven Showtime series *Weeds*, and Netflix's miniseries *Griselda*. *QotS* draws most directly from Telemundo's telenovela *La Reina del Sur* and the novel that inspired the first series by Arturo Pérez-Reverte. As Javier Ramirez notes, the USA series shares a similar narrative trajectory to the Telemundo series but departs from it in significant ways.[3] Perhaps the biggest distinction between the two shows is that the *QotS* pits Teresa against another female drug queen, Camila Vargas (Veronica Falcón). In this regard, *QotS* shares much in common with the BBC America thriller *Killing Eve*, another series about impossible women immersed in an illicit gore economy. Both *QotS* and *Killing Eve* foreground women who refuse to be bound by the rule of law, strive for upward mobility via careers that involve violence and murder, easily outmaneuver their mediocre male counterparts, clash with formidable women foes, and struggle to extricate themselves from their professions once they become ensconced within them. These series also introduce viewers to central women characters in terms of their deaths, a point I will return to later. By featuring female rivalry, *QotS* and *Killing Eve* highlight television's effort to appeal to viewers with storylines featuring women who embrace competitive individualism. This chapter focuses on *QotS* to explore the possibilities for television's impossible women who are neither white nor U.S. citizens. By featuring a Latina character from a poor city in northern Mexico, the series highlights both the reach and the limit of neoliberal feminism for imagining Latinx women's economic advancement.

The crossover between Telemundo and USA foregrounds the networks' interests in cultivating a broader Latinx market using conventions associated with "prestige TV."[4] Ramirez observes that the series walks a "representational tightrope." Although it advances stereotypes of exotic Latinas and savage Latinos, *QotS*'s depiction of Teresa complicates conventional portrayals by following in the "prestige tradition of celebrating antiheroes" who transgress social norms.[5] The first season received mixed reviews from critics and a score of 68 percent on Rotten Tomatoes.[6] The program's reception was likely impacted by its target market and emphasis on a Latinx character. As Ramirez notes, while white men predominate among media reviewers, women critics tend to evaluate "minority-led and minority-dominant series more favorably than their White male counterparts."[7] Alongside Ramirez, I believe the series deserved more credit than it received for its complex storytelling devices and emphasis on a complicated female antihero. In particular, the series' use of feminist themes to expand upon the narco-crime-thriller subgenre exposes the limits of neoliberalism as a mode of women's empowerment. In this series, neoliberal striving is, quite literally, a dead end.

QotS contributes to the impossible woman trope by foregrounding an extraordinarily resilient female character who seeks upward mobility within an illicit market economy that operates via brutality and murder. Over the course of five seasons, the series portrays its leading character as a drug queenpin who becomes caught up in illegal narcotics trafficking in Sinaloa, Mexico, after local cartel boss, Epifanio Vargas (Joaquim de Almeida), catches her boyfriend, Guero Dávila (Jon-Michael William Ecker), running cocaine behind his back. Teresa manages to survive Epifanio's *sicarios* by rising up the ranks of his wife Camila's Dallas enterprise and outsmarting her to become the cartel boss at the end of season 3. She ascends to the position after winning the loyalty of a handful of men and women who aid her pursuit, but with each new episode, she faces unanticipated challenges from a variety of people who wish to see her dead. In featuring a Mexican woman who must continually navigate the U.S.-Mexico border within an illicit economy to survive, *QotS* illustrates how the brutal demands of global capitalism perpetuate structural inequities that disproportionately subject Mexican immigrants, women, and Black people to violent and exploitative working conditions.

Although a show revolving around a woman narco may seem like an outlier within the broader catalog of impossible women on television, it is not entirely surprising that scripted series featuring illicit criminal enterprises can accommodate stories about extraordinarily resilient women competing with one another under precarious circumstances. The drug trafficking business is an extension of neoliberal logics that reduce the value of human life to economic principles and cost-benefit calculations. As Sayak Valencia argues, persistent structural inequities, economic instability, and the celebration of hyperconsumerism in Mexico have propelled the illegal narcotics trafficking industry and are a consequence of broader economic conditions under neoliberal capitalism.[8] Valencia draws from Misha Glenny, who explains that the "liberalization of international financial markets" and the "dramatically uneven distribution of wealth" following the collapse of communism created conditions in which human life itself has been transformed into a commodity.[9] Valencia avers that contemporary capitalism empties life of its intrinsic value in "Third World" (Valencia's preferred term) nations that have a limited idea of the future. Faced with perpetual precarity and exploitative working conditions, many people working in illicit industries have come to regard life as "an object of monetary exchange in the market. . . . [T]he only measure of value is the ability to mete out death to others."[10]

Narcotrafficking's commensurability with dominant economic principles is not lost on the series' writers. During season 3, James poses as a stockbroker to manipulate the family members of a man he has been hired to kill. When asked what his job is like, he tells the wife of the ill-fated husband, "It's murder. Markets are volatile, and the competition's cutthroat." Crosscut with short clips from scenes of his grisly work as a *sicario* during season 2, James concludes, "At the end of the day, it's all down to supply and demand."[11] In telling the story of Teresa's incredible road to success and James's murderous efforts to support her, *QotS* highlights how neoliberal economics have shaped conditions of impossibility for poor Mexican women near the U.S.-Mexico border via what Valencia has identified as "gore capitalism," or the extreme and conspicuous forms of violence that have provided opportunities for precarious populations to achieve social mobility.[12]

Reading *QotS* through the lens of scholarship on gore capitalism and racial capitalism, I argue that the series contributes to the popularization of gore practices in mainstream U.S. media even as it encourages viewers to identify with figures struggling to resist the culture that such gore capitalism produces. In this regard, *QotS* contributes to the aporia that structures stories about women's neoliberal striving under impossibly difficult circumstances. Disenfranchised women may be forced to participate in a gore economy, but their effort to thrive within it is likely to get them killed. Beyond expanding the trope of the impossible woman, Teresa's story suggests that neoliberal feminism is no match for forces of gore, white supremacy, and misogyny, each of which thrive under global capitalism.

Impossibly Alive

Teresa is an impossible figure because she manages to stay alive when her death seems inescapable. Nearly every episode of this fast-paced thriller showcases Teresa's improbable survival as she contends with a variety of threats: numerous assassination attempts from rival cartels, a cocaine-producing death cult, and corrupt law enforcement officers. Teresa's astonishing endurance earns the respect of *sicarios* James and Pote Galvez (Hemky Madera), who decide to abandon Camila to work for her. As Pote tells her when she faces a daunting obstacle at the end of season 3, "Whenever you're down, you always come back stronger. . . . You're a survivor. You never stop fighting."[13] Teresa is the ultimate resilient subject, a TV action hero resembling MacGyver, Jack Bauer, or perhaps Buffy the Vampire Slayer; only this character's moral compass is compromised, and the series' pilot episode leads viewers to believe that her demise is certain.

Although each episode foregrounds Teresa's extraordinary survival skills, the pilot episode opens by depicting her murder by an unknown assailant. The first shot presents Teresa exiting a helicopter flanked by bodyguards as a voice-over tells viewers, "I ran the biggest drug empire in the Western hemisphere.

You could say I'm living proof that the American Dream is alive and well. And I'm good at it."[14] This portrayal of the lead character introduces viewers to the Queen. Wearing her characteristic white pantsuit and designer sunglasses and with her hair pulled back into a sleek bun, the Queen appears in the first three seasons solely as a projection of Teresa's imagination and a source of inspiration to propel Teresa's resilience and resourcefulness when her death seems imminent. This vision of Teresa's future self contrasts with her present wavy hair and the flannel shirts and blue jeans that she wears until season 4, foregrounding the wealth and status that she will accrue while she fights to stay alive.

As the voice-over continues during the opening scene, Teresa walks into the large bathroom of her opulent mansion and takes a bump of cocaine from a golden chest on her bathroom counter. "The trick is to stay alive long enough to enjoy the fruits of this labor."[15] As she finishes this sentence, the camera cuts to a close-up of a bullet piercing her bathroom window and shooting her in the forehead. Teresa falls backward, and the next shot is of blood trickling from her mouth as she lies dead on the white tile floor. "I knew this day would come."[16] The rest of the series is presented as a flashback to explain the events leading to the day of her death. While the mise-en-scène conveys the Queen's privileged status within a hyperconsumerist culture, the image of Teresa as a powerful figure is quickly undone when the bullet hole appears in her window. In featuring the Queen's violent death, the opening scene presents a jaundiced view of the American Dream. This Mexican woman's impossible American Dream is destined to become a nightmare.

FIG. 5.1 The opening scene of *Queen of the South* depicts Teresa's future self, the leader of a drug empire who lives a life of luxury thanks to her business acumen and command of ruthless *sicarios*. *Queen of the South*, season 1, episode 1, "Piloto," written by M. A. Fortin and Joshua John Miller, original airdate June 23, 2016, USA Network.

The graphic violence of the opening sequence primes viewers to expect a show in which women's resilience is yoked to an anticipation of violence. Although depictions of death and gore are central conventions of serials featuring narcotics trafficking, the shot of Teresa's lifeless head within the first minute of the series points to television's investments in representations of dead, violated women. That "prestige television" has often sought to attract viewers to woman-centered programs with the prospect of witnessing their violent deaths illuminates broader cultural ambivalence regarding strong woman figures. The title of *Killing Eve* alone presents the allure of femicide to draw viewers to its woman-driven crime thriller. By inviting viewers to anticipate women's deaths, both *QotS* and *Killing Eve* highlight how gendered violence underwrites sexist realism in products marketed toward diverse women viewers.

The rest of the pilot episode depicts sexual violence as a catalyst for Teresa's narrative arc as it takes viewers back to the day that Teresa first learns that her husband, Guero, has stolen money from his boss and that *sicarios* are intent on murdering her to exact their revenge. In a pivotal and graphic scene toward the end of the episode, one of Epifanio's *sicarios*, Gato (James Martinez), apprehends Teresa and begins to rape her, promising that he will murder her once he has finished. It is at this moment that the Queen first appears to Teresa. "A moment like this defines your future," the Queen tells her. "Go on, honey. You know what to do."[17] While Gato continues to assault her, Teresa pulls his gun from his holster, shoots him in the face, and escapes from his clutches.

By depicting Gato's assault as Teresa's "phoenix moment" (see chapter 4), *QotS* presents a macabre illustration of gendered resilience discourses that have accorded value to women's injury. *QotS* imagines Teresa's traumatic experience as transformational, enabling the at-risk woman to imagine herself as a take-charge woman of the future. The portrayal of degradation as a resource for becoming is reiterated three episodes later, when the Queen compares Teresa to a "flower that grows in the darkness. . . . It actually does better in the shade."[18] The graphic brutality Teresa experiences throughout the series illustrates how narco stories provide fitting vehicles for impossible women and the sexist realism at the heart of television's interest in strong women; as media culture has turned damage into a resource for women's achievements, drug cartels' extreme violence and terror is an apt platform for appreciating women's extraordinary perseverance under patriarchal conditions.

Teresa learns to exist within a system of gore capitalism wherein people victimized by drug cartels embrace violence to survive. She encounters a variety of figures who openly embrace murder and torture. The Colonel is one of the most horrific among them. A sadist, he manipulates both Epifanio and Camila in an effort to take control of Sinaloa's cartel. After the Colonel realizes that Epifanio has ordered Gato to kill him, Epifanio is treated to dinner at the Colonel's home to find Gato roasting on the spit. The Colonel exemplifies what Valencia describes as a "violence specialist": a person who "control(s) the means for inflicting damage on people or objects through the use of force and the mercilessly efficient techniques that aid them in maintaining or seizing power."[19] Like the violence specialists that Valencia describes, the Colonel is connected to government security forces and is particularly well-trained in the use of torture as a technique of governance.

Gore becomes Teresa's reality as she works alongside numerous narcos who regard murder as transactional and leverage the spectacle of extreme violence as a display of power. The first time she witnesses a man being murdered, Teresa is revolted and refuses to accept James's description of cartel violence as "an occupational hazard."[20] As Teresa becomes ensconced in Camila's operation, she becomes increasingly involved in its brutality. A pivotal moment in her evolution occurs during the season 1 finale when she shoots and kills a man known as El Limpiador (or The Cleaner), a narco tasked with the role of murdering people and storing dead bodies on his compound on the outskirts of Culiacán. The episode amplifies the financial stakes of gore as Teresa pursues El Limpiador because she erroneously believes he is a money launderer. To her horror, she realizes that the cartel was more invested in cleaning out its dead bodies, crucial assets in need of hiding from public officials. This and other scenes illustrate the extreme and ultraspecialized forms of violence that characterize gore capitalism. Valencia contends that as tremendous human loss has become an acceptable cost of unregulated markets, economies in the "Third World" harnessed violence as a resource for survival, "bringing together workplace precarity, existential precarity, and marginality with a new way of thinking of violence and crime as transnational businesses."[21] The series portrays this violence in ways that largely comport with Valencia's characterization of a form of "capitalism founded on the speculation of bodies-as-commodities."[22] Teresa's encounter with El Limpiador is the first among numerous grisly scenes featuring dead, mutilated, and brutalized bodies, victims of numerous cartels' efforts to traffic cocaine from Columbia, Bolivia, and Mexico into the United States. As the series progresses, Teresa increasingly relies on violence to protect her business interests.

The series establishes its relevance for the #MeToo era by illustrating how misogyny underwrites narco violence. During the pilot episode, Epifanio tells Teresa that he cannot allow her to live after he caught her husband stealing from him. "If they can't let the man get away, imagine letting a woman escape," he explains.[23] Subsequent scenes expand on the machismo within narco culture that depends on women's debasement. One subplot during the first two seasons revolves around Epifanio's tumultuous relationship with Camila. While he insists that she abandon the Dallas enterprise to support his political ambitions in Sinaloa, Camila refuses. She would rather be dead than be subservient to her husband. Consequently, Epifanio engages in multiple schemes to force her from her business.

Beyond their interactions with Epifanio, Camila and Teresa are subjected to routine forms of sexual harassment from fellow crime bosses, *sicarios*, and government officials who don't believe that women are capable of effectively leading a drug empire. Across its five seasons, men involved in criminal enterprises attempt to destroy Camila and Teresa, not just because they pose a threat to their business interests but because their success poses a threat to their masculinity. When cornered, their enemies often respond by making violently sexist remarks. During season 3, Teresa apprehends a local Phoenix cartel boss known only as Pecas (Armando Risco) who betrays her to maintain control over the Arizona market. Even though James's gun is pointed at his head, Pecas jokes about choking Teresa. Pecas continues just before James pulls the trigger: "I don't kneel to bitches."[24] The scene amplifies the masculinist logics underlying macho culture, which Valencia characterizes as Mexico's "national heritage."[25]

Because it pervades every aspect of their lives, both Camila and Teresa develop careful strategies for establishing control in an industry filled with sociopaths who would rather murder them than follow their orders. Following the logics of sexist realism, misogyny is a precondition for Teresa's and Camila's success insofar as men's underestimation of them makes them more resolute and cunning. "All my life men have underestimated me. I've grown used to it," Camila confides to James. "See, most men are very basic creatures. They can't seem to see beyond my legs. So, sometimes I use that to my advantage, and others, I just depend upon it."[26] Because she is not as exceptional as Teresa, Camila's approach backfires on her. Lacking Teresa's perceptiveness, she doesn't know how to distinguish between men who are genuinely attracted to her and men who feign interest to undermine her business. This facilitates Camila's undoing, which helps catapult Teresa's rise as cartel royalty. Insofar as she uses her femininity to her advantage, Teresa is the legacy of earlier action heroines of seventies-era television: *Charlie's Angels*. Aviva Dove-Viebahn reflects on how the Angels used their performances of femininity to gain control over situations. Because they are underestimated and exceptional, they can accomplish goals that men cannot.[27] Dove-Viebahn concludes that the underestimation of women is both a "blessing and a curse" for these characters because "any representation of a strong female character only embeds her in notions of gender norms, gendered expectations, and gendered exceptionalism."[28] Similarly, Teresa's femininity disarms her business partners, but this makes her achievements conditional on her ability to fuel their desires and affirm their masculinity. Teresa's careful balancing act—weighing her performances of femininity alongside masculine performances of strength—proves to be impossible, especially after Teresa begins to aspire to a leadership position in the cartel. In this regard, the series avoids a triumphant storyline about women's upward mobility. As the first scene of the series intimates, the entrepreneurial woman's story will end tragically.

An Impossible Dream

Finding that she can escape immediate death but cannot escape the cartel, Teresa learns to live within the world of narcotics trafficking. While Teresa is an impossible woman during season 1 simply by virtue of having survived a cartel boss's demand for her head, subsequent seasons foreground her impossible dream of gaining control over a lucrative international drug trafficking empire while maintaining a clear conscience. Once she learns that Camila has betrayed her at the end of season 2, she maneuvers to take control of Camila's business and find a "better way of doing business" that does not operate via violence and gore. "None of us has to die," she tells James when she invites him to work for her.[29] Her mission is precipitated by disagreements with Camila throughout season 2, as Camila insists that gore is the price a cartel boss must pay to stay on top. The first three seasons pit Teresa and Camila against one another, staging a conflict between necrofeminism and narcofeminism. While Ana Peluffo understands "necrofeminism" as a feminist response to the administration of necropolitics,[30] I think the term more aptly denotes the alignment of necropolitics with neoliberalism's emphasis on competitive individualism as the central means of women's empowerment. I also draw from Valencia's discussion of "necroempowerment," which refers to the ways in which narcotraffickers "illicitly enrich and perversely self-affirm themselves" through practices of murder and torture.[31] Camila is a model of necrofeminism as she and her *sicarios* murder many of her husband's associates to wrest control of the cartel. Handing Teresa a glass of tequila that costs two thousand dollars a bottle, Camila notes that a better life is possible for Teresa but that she must abandon her concern for the well-being of others if she wants to succeed as a businesswoman.[32] Teresa refuses to follow Camila's lead. She wants to have it all: a just cartel and a viable drug trafficking business.

When balancing her concern for others with her own ambitions, Teresa is a model of narcofeminism. Here, I use this portmanteau to signal the ambivalence that structures media portrayals of well-intended women immersed in illegal narcotics trafficking. An oxymoron evoked by the series' construction of Teresa, "narcofeminism" points to the contradictory subject position Teresa inhabits as she touts the virtue of compassion as a more principled means of managing an illicit drug empire. Teresa's narcofeminism is defined by her refusal to accept that gore is the price a woman must pay to earn respect and authority as a narco. Instead, she insists that an ethic of care can guide the cartel's decisions and practices. Her loyalty toward the people who work for her—refusing to sacrifice her *sicarios* for the sake of her own financial success—earns her admiration and respect from a variety of figures including Pote and James. As Pote tells her when he commits himself to work for her, "You're no Camila. . . . You've got a heart."[33] Teresa establishes control of the market by attracting willing business partners to her vision. The series makes Teresa more likable, a key consideration in TV writers' rooms where female characters are concerned, by foregrounding her compassion in a context in which having compassion for others is likely to get one killed.[34]

In addition to her performance as a narco with a heart of gold, Teresa proves she is capable of reigning over a male-dominated illegal drug economy because she is a brilliant strategist. Teresa's vision of leading a just cartel is grounded in her faith in market logic. Her code assumes *homo oeconomicus* drives narco politics. She uses savvy negotiating skills to establish partnerships with gun runners, cocaine manufacturers, local distributors, money launderers, and heads of crime families in South America, the United States, Malta, and Russia. She also demonstrates mastery of logistics by pursuing horizontal and vertical integration to take her business global. Teresa frequently appeals to potential partners by promising greater earnings with reduced risk. The first episode of season 2 illuminates her business acumen when she convinces a drug runner known as King George (Ryan O'Nan) to help her move her product from Bolivia to the United States. A notorious womanizer, King George is taken aback after Teresa informs him that he would achieve "10 percent more profit with 25 percent less risk." After letting out a whoop, "Ohh! Brains, balls, and booty!," he declares, "I might just make you my queen!"[35] The scene parallels developments in *The Marvelous Mrs. Maisel* in which Midge embraces her normative beauty to gain favorable attention from men who can help facilitate her goals. King George transforms into one of Teresa's most loyal employees, suggesting that neoliberal feminism is not necessarily incompatible with misogyny insofar as financial incentives appear to induce the crassest of chauvinists to appreciate extraordinary women.

Beyond her negotiating skills, Teresa demonstrates a knack for business by attaining access to the purest cocaine in the world, finding inventive means of distributing her supply, and—despite her high-minded ideals—literally killing off competitors who refuse to work with her. More than any other character discussed in this book, Teresa is an entrepreneurial feminist subject who optimizes her resources through "incessant calculation, personal initiative, and innovation."[36] During season 2, Teresa surpasses her male counterparts in Camila's cartel because she understands the logics of gore capitalism better than they do. She allows others to treat her as a commodity as she puts her own life up as collateral in risky business ventures, understanding that such risk-taking also provides opportunities for greater financial rewards. Teresa frequently justifies speculative deals with dangerous drug manufacturers and distributors via neoliberal feminist logics of choice. As she embraces high risks for high rewards, she gains the respect of the more enlightened narcotraffickers.

The series routinely attributes Teresa's intellect to her gender. In this storyworld, women routinely prove they are better than men at managing business. After Teresa and Camila part ways, Teresa colludes with a variety of criminal entrepreneurs who enthusiastically embrace her innovations. During season 4, she develops a partnership with Oksana Volkova (Vera Cherny), who approves of Teresa's plan to distribute pure cocaine in liquid form, disguising it as tequila. Oksana is particularly pleased to imagine that, once customers realize she has a superior product, demand will grow, enabling her to raise prices. In an episode entitled "Noche de las Chicas" (or Ladies Night), Oksana's associate Raul (Pêpê Rapazote) approves of the partnership, laughing and commenting, "Like I always say, *el futuro es feminino*."[37] The series winks at audiences by including the slogan in a plot about women's efforts to corner the illegal narcotics market in the eastern United States. A drug dealer who is hardly interested in women's rights or advancement, Raul is an unlikely person to repeat a second-wave feminist slogan popularized by Hillary Clinton in 2017.[38] Thus, the scene may more readily resonate with Clinton's detractors than her feminist-identifying supporters. At the same time, the disjointedness between the feminist sentiment and the women's aims points to neoliberal feminism's dependence on market-driven logics in which "competition and capital appreciation override all else."[39] As gore capitalism represents a distorted version of neoliberalism's tendency to translate all human experience in terms of economic value, Teresa's narcofeminism illustrates (or perhaps mocks) the ways in which popular culture has framed any effort a woman makes toward achieving a financial goal, no matter how suspect, as a feminist triumph.

After Teresa forces Camila out of the cartel, she grows her business by creating "a free market" in which she can earn maximum profits from distributors who might otherwise lower the value of her product.[40] A surprising amount of dialogue is dedicated to explaining market logics to viewers because much of the conflict of the series is driven by Teresa's efforts to gain monopolistic control over the cocaine supply in the United States, expand her profits, and limit her competition. Teresa convinces several lower-level distributors and *sicarios* to put their faith in her ability to subdue the most exploitative, brutal cartel bosses. During seasons 3 and 4, an Indigenous narcotrafficker in Arizona, Taza (Zahn McClarnon), and a Black gangster in New Orleans, Marcel Dumas (Alimi Ballard), ally with her because they believe she is the only person capable of fighting the virulently racist and corrupt white men who control the finances of the illegal drug trade in their communities.

Plotlines featuring racist crime bosses draw on the broader cultural conditions of contemporary public life, suggesting that the biggest problem within narcotics trafficking is that it is subject to the same forms of structural and individual racism that imperil all minority-owned businesses in the United States. The show infers that Teresa's background gives her a unique standpoint that enables her to empathize with other narcotraffickers who are subjected to racial exploitation and that this intersectional awareness enables her to fight for an equal playing field for all crime bosses regardless of their race or gender. While Teresa presumes, often correctly, that financial incentives can turn her competitors into willing business partners, her anti-racist agenda is driven by financial imperatives to build partnerships that will expand her profit margins. Teresa's efforts to run a just cartel evoke the tension within neoliberal feminism wherein progressive intent and individualism sit together uneasily, incompatible yet mutually confirming each other. By linking free markets to an anti-racist agenda, the series aligns Teresa's narcofeminism with a multicultural neoliberalist understanding that the pursuit of economic rights is the ultimate condition of freedom.[41]

Gore Capitalist Reality

Over the course of *QotS*'s five seasons, Teresa learns that her dream of leading a just international drug cartel is impossible and that she cannot take the gore out of the illegal drug economy. The series is structured by contradictory plot developments in which Teresa increasingly turns to gore while also aiming to avoid it. The first two seasons foreshadow her eventual embrace of violence as she participates in increasingly brutal schemes at Camila's behest. In the process, she learns that extreme violence is a valuable tool for economic advancement. Teresa's gradual acceptance of necroempowerment is overseen by the Queen, her future self, who assures Teresa that her survival depends on her ability to enact extreme violence against the people who would profit from her violation, defilement, and murder. As the series develops, the Queen becomes an embodiment of necrofeminism. By urging Teresa to transfer her precarity to others, the Queen takes it upon herself to decide who may live and who must die in Teresa's quest for advancement.

Foregrounding her superior knowledge and resilience over that of her less competent male peers, the series portrays Teresa's use of gore as a necrofeminist achievement. The Queen's white pantsuit (see fig. 5.1) extends the feminist themes of the series by evoking the outfit Hillary Clinton wore to accept her nomination as the presidential candidate for the Democratic Party in 2016 and anticipating Alexandria Ocasio-Cortez's iconic attire when she was sworn into Congress in 2019.[42] In articulating a liberal feminist agenda to Teresa's story, the series recodes the meaning of narco violence, disassociating it from masculine desires for power and authority. Indeed, *QotS* explains Teresa's necrofeminism as a response to a range of misogynist affronts that make the embrace of

FIG. 5.2 Over the course of five seasons, Teresa learns to embrace violence as a means of gaining power in the illicit drug trafficking industry. *Queen of the South*, season 2, episode 1, "El Cuerpo de Cristo," written by Natalie Chaidez, original airdate June 8, 2017, USA Network.

gore seem inescapable. Within the series' diegesis, Teresa's routine encounters with violent misogyny justify necrofeminism as an extension of the neoliberal feminist struggle. In other words, the TV show validates Teresa's participation in an illicit market that operates chiefly through the spectacle of masculine violence by framing her violent actions as a means for her own spectacular overcoming. She appears as a model of female empowerment even when she puts the lives of innocent people at risk.

As violence and brutality become her mundane reality, Teresa experiences the subjectifying force of gore capitalism. Teresa begins to envision herself not only surviving but thriving within an illicit market that depends on gore to maintain its stability. When her faithful *sicarios* question her, she justifies her decisions to engage in kidnapping and murder with the refrain that she had "no choice" to do otherwise. A key development in her transformation occurs during season 2 when she encounters a Bolivian cocaine supplier and cult leader known as El Santo who uses blood magic to torture his enemies. El Santo agrees to give her access to his product on the condition that she die and be reborn by ingesting a poisonous beetle. "Time for you to create yourself, Teresa Mendoza," El Santo declares before she becomes incapacitated.[43] In the following scene, Teresa finds that her rebirth has given her newfound resilience and the impossible strength to kill a Bolivian military official in hand-to-hand combat. She accomplishes what James could not: convince El Santo that she is pure of heart *and* bludgeon a military commander with her bare hands.

This and subsequent scenes mark Teresa's transformation into what Valencia has termed "an endriago subject." Drawing from a monstrous figure from medieval literature, Valencia explains that "*endriagos* embrace necroempowerment to establish themselves as valid subjects with the *possibility of belonging and ascending within society*."[44] The *endriago* subject turns to necro-practices of gore to attain value within the economic order they have been largely excluded from. In wielding influence over the intensity and ubiquity of violence within a criminal economy, *endriagos* "legitimate the processes of underground economies."[45] They are "entrepreneurs of gore capitalism" guided by economic imperatives in the absence of any other ethical guidelines, because for the *endriago* subject, justice is "focused on the pursuit of . . . wealth accumulation and victory over all competitors."[46] Ethics is determined by "the most radical dictates of the market."[47]

Teresa's transformation from idealistic narcofeminist to violently empowered necrofeminist occurs while she pursues increasingly ambitious deals with fellow narcotraffickers that establish her as the head of a transnational cocaine-trafficking empire. In addition to her gradual immersion within gore capitalist culture, Teresa struggles to manage personal relationships alongside her professional obligations as a *jefa*. This struggle contributes to her downfall. Teresa's impossible dream is connected to the more conventional tension evoked in popular depictions of women striving to maintain vibrant careers and fulfilling personal lives. Although Teresa refuses to choose the cartel over her loved ones, cartel life chooses for her. Both Camila's and Teresa's personal relationships suffer due to their career ambitions. Such suffering follows the logics of gore capitalism: a *jefa* cannot afford to have a family because murdering the loved ones of people involved in drug trafficking is routine business practice. As the Queen tells her in the first episode of season 2, "*No puede tener todo.* You can't have it all. . . . If you want to succeed in this business, someday you will have to choose between survival and your heart."[48] Both Camila and the Queen warn Teresa against pursuing men romantically. The issue becomes acute when Teresa learns that her husband, Guero, is alive. Demanding that she choose the cartel over Guero, Camila tells Teresa that Guero is a "little mosquito draining" her of her "spirit."[49] Camila's words prove to be prescient when Guero dies after Camila's men have tortured him. Distraught, Teresa loses herself in a fantasy of necroempowerment.

Teresa's loved ones become casualties in the life of the queenpin. As her best friend, husband, and godson die by *sicarios'* hands across multiple seasons of the series, the cartel becomes Teresa's only family. Her grief has profound impacts on her leadership and decision-making. Guero's death is a turning point that makes Teresa colder and more calculating. Driven by despair, the Queen reminds Teresa that "pain should be a weapon against your enemies, not yourself."[50] Taking the Queen's lesson to heart, Teresa begins to use innocent people to protect her and her business.

The body count at the hands of Teresa's *sicarios* rises in seasons 4 and 5 as Teresa approves the use of torture and bloodshed to contain her competitors and overcome the challenges posed by corrupt businessmen who stand in her way. During season 4, she abducts the girlfriend and son of a drug dealer who has been arrested to prevent him from testifying against one of her business partners. Her transformation nears completion after a corrupt New Orleans judge installs an explosive device in her car, accidentally killing her godson. Injured by the explosion, Teresa goes into a coma. When she wakes up, she is the Queen and announces to James, "We're going to kill them all."[51] In a subsequent episode, she pursues revenge against the people she suspects were involved in her godson's death. Episodes in the final season foreground the heart-wrenching consequences of her full transformation when she violates the very rule that won her the respect of her sicarios: She betrays her loyalty to Dumas by letting local police arrest him for a murder that he did not commit.

Teresa's metamorphosis from a narco with a heart of gold to a calculating *endriago* subject demonstrates how gore capitalism cannot accommodate any agenda that values humanity, let alone an explicitly feminist agenda. While the incompatibility between the two orientations is rather obvious, Teresa's transformation contributes to sexist realism in less recognizable ways by amplifying the message that it is impossible for precarious women in the Third World to achieve upward mobility without contributing to the economic conditions that produce gore. If *Parks and Recreation*'s Leslie Knope struggles to get ahead because she maintains her commitment to the public good, Teresa Mendoza gains momentum by abandoning her ethical commitments to others. Yet the series does not completely explain Teresa's failure as a personal one; instead, it foregrounds the broader conditions that have enabled gore capitalism to form a symbiotic relationship with licit economies and dominant political institutions.

Racial Realism at the U.S.-Mexico Border

By featuring a variety of U.S. public officials and law enforcement officers complicit in gore practices, *QotS* foregrounds how *endriago* subjects emerge from growing wealth disparity and U.S.-government-sponsored violence against Latinx immigrants. The last three seasons present new and unexpected challenges to Teresa's efforts to run a just cartel in Phoenix and New Orleans, where she attempts to establish new bases of operation. Teresa expresses faith in neoliberal economics as she sets up her base of operation in New Orleans. Distancing herself from the U.S.-Mexico border, the move evokes multiculturalist frameworks that regard Western nations, and the United States in particular, as true lands of opportunity unfettered by the presumed "monoculturalism or other historico-cultural deficiencies" of people struggling to survive in the Global South.[52] Conditions in the United States do not live up to her expectations, however. While gore becomes a subjectifying force central to her transformation from mule to *jefa*, racism and sexism thwart her ability to innovate and scale up her operations once she attains the status of narco royalty.

Teresa struggles, at least in part, because she fails to appreciate the threat she poses to the gendered social order upon which narco culture is built. For Valencia, the *endriago* subject is putatively masculine. The culture of violence produces a "phallocratic model of power in which macho breadwinners decide who lives and who dies."[53] Valencia explains that the Mexican concept of machismo ties notions of manliness to the authority of the state and denotes a "logic of defiance and the struggle for power."[54] Such machismo contributes to the criminal class's efforts to assume the "absolute right to commit violent acts."[55]

Teresa intervenes in this process by prohibiting her subordinates from committing acts of indiscriminate violence. While her most loyal *sicarios* respect her, her rivals-turned-partners from the Jimenez cartel regard her as soft and take it upon themselves to murder white public officials who treat them with disrespect. Beyond exuding macho authority, their brutal murder of a city commissioner illustrates what James Messerschmidt refers to as "dominating masculine necropolitics," or the exercise of power and control over matters of life and death without regard for the opinions of others.[56] Teresa does not suspect her *sicarios* when the commissioner goes missing and is later found dead. Her myopia leads to a chain of events that prevents her from building a criminal coalition that might work peacefully alongside corrupt political figures in New Orleans. The Jimenez cartel's actions exemplify Valencia's observation that the *endriago* subject is, in some cases, "a response to the fear of demasculinization that haunts many men as a consequence of rising workplace precarity and their own subsequent inability to legitimately take on the role of male provider."[57] Beyond her embodiment as a woman narco, Teresa's leadership threatens to remove the immaterial rewards of masculine authority and control that elicited the men's participation in the underground economy. One takeaway from this subplot is that gendered hierarchies are not ancillary but foundational to gore capitalism. Insofar as gore capitalism is an extension of neoliberalism, the series presents an exaggerated illustration of neoliberalism's incommensurability with even the most moderate feminist agenda.

The brutal misogyny underlying gore capitalism is amplified during season 3 when Teresa encounters a money launderer, Rocco de la Peña (Jordi Mollà), who promises to keep her money safe in his impenetrable vault in Malta. After she entrusts her money to him, Teresa discovers that the "technowizard" also runs a sex trafficking ring and carves his name onto the backs of the women he sells.[58] With MacGyver-like skills, Teresa manages to retrieve her money and rescue dozens of women from his clutches. Her newfound nemesis calls to taunt her during her flight back to the United States: "My

God Teresa, you could have been amazing. But now you're all alone fleeing for your life while Europe burns down behind you. . . . How does it feel, Teresa, to know that you were so close to greatness and you just let it slip through your fingers? Why, Teresa?" Teresa replies sternly, "Some things aren't for sale."[59]

Although Teresa upholds her moral convictions, her achievement disrupts the trafficking of women only briefly. As Teresa's plane flies into the sunset, Rocco reminds her that "girls" are an expendable and renewable resource and tells her that he already has a new shipment of young women available for sale the following day. By setting Teresa outside and apart from the women he abuses, Rocco illustrates the shifting configurations of systemic inequalities under multicultural neoliberalism. Unlike the women he has abducted, Teresa is one of neoliberalism's beneficiaries. She earns a place within the male-dominated drug trafficking industry but is accepted only insofar as she benefits the gore capitalist agenda. Her refusal to cast aside her allegiance to women who remain vulnerable to exploitation becomes a primary impediment to her ability to enter the European market. Cast out of the European criminal underworld, Teresa turns her efforts toward capturing the U.S. market.

Teresa fails to control local markets in the United States without bloodshed because she underestimates the racist motivations of corrupt public officials. The last three seasons resituate Teresa's struggles via conflict with male authority figures in the United States, including business leaders and corrupt law enforcement officers. Every institution Teresa works with in the United States is complicit with illegal drug trafficking, and every representative of these institutions—including local police officers, city commissioners, judges, real estate moguls, and CIA agents—intends to exploit and/or murder her. Her ongoing conflicts illustrate sexist realism's connection to racial realism, or the perspective that recognizes that racial inclusion hinges on advantages for whiteness.[60] Despite their potential to make money by working with her, Teresa's adversaries would rather go to war against her because she is a Latina immigrant who insists on treating Black and Native narcos equitably. Her rivals' racism and nativism illustrate how American conceptions of equality, freedom, and democracy are imbricated with the nation's founding in white supremacist and colonialist practices.[61] Teresa's oversight obliquely points to the larger project of whiteness that understands "racial domination as a practice of freedom."[62] As Cristina Beltrán argues, anti-immigrant sentiment owes its legacy to the broad history of Western European expansion in the Americas in which violent domination of Indigenous, Black, and Mexican populations became the condition for the rights and freedoms of white citizens. For Beltrán, this legacy explains why Donald Trump supporters' anti-immigration positions superseded economic considerations during the 2016 presidential election.

QotS references such border politics during season 3 as Teresa contends with a corrupt law enforcement officer, Sheriff Jed Mayo (A Martinez), who demands steep bribes from the Phoenix crime syndicate known as La Comisión. Mayo's character is a thinly veiled reference to the notoriously racist and criminal Maricopa County Sheriff Joe Arpaio. Among his violations, Arpaio routinely violated the rights of prisoners, created illegal posses to enforce immigration law, and arrested reporters for covering investigations into his office. *QotS*'s Sheriff Mayo is equally racist and perhaps more corrupt and violent, as he controls the illegal narcotics trade in Phoenix through intimidation and kills a journalist for reporting on his corruption. Mayo conspires with Pecas, a white narco, to kill Teresa and Taza, who turned to drug trafficking after his tribe's casino failed. Mayo and his real-world counterpart exemplify what Beltrán refers to as "Herrenvolk democracy" in America, a practice in which white citizens and Latinos who see themselves as white come to see racial domination as a practice of freedom and a civic good.[63] A Latino, Mayo tells Teresa that persecuting immigrants is his "cross to bear" because they have caused white Arizonans to discriminate against all Latinos.[64] Couching his violent intimidation of Latinx immigrants in terms of his commitment to law and order, Mayo's remarks illustrate Beltrán's point that "American conceptions of equality, freedom, and democracy have historically been constituted through white supremacy."[65]

Mayo and Pecas single Teresa out when she refuses to let them exploit the immigrant and Native American members of La Comisión. Unlike Taza, she is neither grateful nor deferential to Mayo. This provokes his wrath. Mayo's hostility toward Teresa and the character's resemblance to Arpaio's cruel immigration policies point to the legacy of the racialization of Mexican migrants in the United States. As Lisa Flores argues, the American public welcomed Mexican immigrants on the basis of their disposability and deportability, but once they entered the United States of their own accord, they were criminalized and dehumanized.[66] Finding that Teresa is not easily exploitable, Mayo resolves to destroy her. Although she prevails at the end of the season, dozens of people are killed in shootouts that she might have otherwise prevented.

The series foregrounds the racist motivations of other public figures who spew derogatory remarks about communities of color. In seasons 4 and 5, the conflict shifts from the U.S.-Mexico border to the plantation, another racial geography where white sovereignty is enacted. Teresa's main adversary is a local judge, Cecil Lafayette (David Andrews), who demands that Teresa give him a large percentage of her profits in exchange for his help in brokering deals with other crime bosses. Lafayette is eager to exploit Teresa's vulnerability, taking millions from her while privately vowing that he will never let Teresa turn "Bourbon Street into Tequila Street."[67] The series points to the judge's racism as a motivation behind much of his decision-making. He admonishes Teresa at the end of season 4 when she refuses to concede to his demands: "I've indulged you, Miss Mendoza. I've let you and all the riffraff in your organization walk around in my city like you belong here. And it appears my reward for not showing you my teeth is you forgetting your place, little lady."[68] Lafayette's paternalism carries with it the threat of deportation or, more likely, murder. Moments later, when Teresa is out of earshot, he remarks to the head of the local Black crime syndicate that "Mendoza is an invasive species." Metaphors of infestation and invasion are common anti-immigrant tropes marking immigrant bodies as sources of contagion in need of containment. As J. David Cisneros remarks, such metaphoric understandings of immigrants create "conceptual and social hierarchies" that naturalize stringent deportation efforts.[69] In extending the metaphor to Teresa, the series foregrounds the broader discursive frameworks that have limited geographic and financial mobility to predominantly white U.S.-born citizens, restricting Latinx immigrants' agency.

Acting as a paternal sovereign, Lafayette suggests that only he has the authority to decide what rules may be broken in "his city." The judge's performance exudes what Casey Kelly describes as "a plantation mentality" that continues to affirm white paternalistic control over people of color to ensure a steady supply of exploitable populations for white capitalist supremacy.[70] Drawing from psychoanalysis, Kelly argues that "plantation culture promulgates an array of fantasies of white invulnerability and self-mastery over the very racial threats that sprung from the white imaginary. But as a zone of exception, the plantation offers a reprieve from the taboos of race mixing and miscegenation so long as such indulgences do not threaten the racial order.... The plantation permits both cruelty and compassion—opposites unified insofar as they both organize white enjoyment."[71]

Teresa disrupts the racial order by trespassing into white territory without showing adequate deference to the corrupt white patriarch, leading to the judge's determination to destroy her after extracting as much profit as he can from her. Lafayette's nativism illustrates how multicultural neoliberalism has not overturned the social and cultural stratifications that legitimized the expropriation of slave labor and Indigenous lands in U.S. history. Rather, neoliberal capitalism depends on racialism to continually justify the practices of exploitation and resource extraction that bolster white supremacy.

Lafayette's investments in white supremacy are further highlighted when the corrupt judge schemes with a local contractor to build a private prison in return for kickbacks from prison officials. Lafeyette tells the contractor that the project will help him manage the rise of "illegals" flowing into New Orleans.[72] This exchange points to the way in which prison-industrial complexes have leveraged anti-immigrant fervor to generate profits in the past decade.[73] It is an unlikely coincidence that the series aired three years after Trump's first electoral victory, when the stock prices of several leading private prison and immigrant detention centers soared. William Robinson argues that "every phase in the war on immigrants has become a source of profit-making," giving investors in the private prison industry "a stake in immigrant repression."[74] When Teresa's *sicarios* learn that Lafayette has been greasing her to help fund the project, they are irate. Confronting the contractor, Pote laments that the people Lafayette has incarcerated are poor kids who "never had a chance!" before shooting him in the chest.[75] Here, the series reverses the dominant U.S. discourse that frames narcotrafficking as a major threat to public health by depicting the white-controlled criminal justice system as the largest threat to the civic good. A *sicario* who has murdered numerous people finds the private prison system to be outside the bounds of acceptable behavior! It is significant that the subplot foregrounds private prison contracts, as the series creates a storyworld not unlike those of *Parks and Recreation* and *Unbreakable Kimmy Schmidt* in which neoliberalism has transformed all public services into profit-making enterprises. *QotS* expands on themes in other impossible women series by foregrounding how this process depends on the expropriation and commodification of migrant bodies.

The series draws connections between white supremacist nativism and anti-Blackness when Lafayette attempts to compel Dumas to murder Teresa. "You people have a history of killing each other," Lafayette sneers. "When that levee breaks, I need to know I can count on you." Lafayette's comment points to the history of racial stratification in New Orleans that subjected poor Black communities to the worst of the impacts of the devastation wrought by Hurricane Katrina when levees broke, flooding the lower Ninth Ward. Lafayette fails to persuade Dumas, who believes his interests are aligned with Teresa. Teresa is incredulous that Lafayette would rather kill her than continue to exploit her business. "I just paid him 30 million dollars. Why would he make a move against me?"[76] While Teresa concludes that Lafayette's motives "must be personal,"[77] Lafayette's remarks imply that his deception is rooted in the racialized nature of capitalist society, which demands the construction of binaries that separate the (white) human deserving of rights and freedoms from the nonhuman available for expropriation.

Lafayette is deeply committed to racial capitalism. Through his relationship with Teresa, the series gives narrative form to the ways in which racialization contributes to broader processes of wealth accumulation.[78] Michael Dawson observes that the racial order reinforces capitalism by demonizing Blacks and Latinx immigrants. Drawing from Nancy Fraser, who describes expropriation as the accumulation of wealth by confiscating and conscripting the bodies and resources of Indigenous and racialized groups, Dawson observes that capitalism was founded on violent expropriation, theft, and murder and that the "distinction between superior and inferior humans—codified as race"—provided a necessary justification for "slavery, colonialism, the theft of lands in the Americas, and genocide."[79] For Dawson, the racial order that separates rights-bearing subjects from nonhumans is a "background condition" that continues to "produce the boundary struggles against expropriation."[80] Failing to understand this context, Teresa does not immediately recognize that the stigma attached to Latinas as subjects available for expropriation would imperil her dreams of running a just cartel and eventually heading a legitimate business operation.

By the end of the final season, Teresa's status as an expropriable subject overrides her value as a neoliberal entrepreneur. She realizes that the judge's death is part of a broader system of racial capitalism when she learns that she is just as exploitable and disposable to the CIA as she is to local law enforcement. Far from ending narcotrafficking, the CIA manipulates the industry behind the scenes to build relationships with narcotraffickers they believe are amendable to U.S. foreign relations. At the end of season 5, Teresa learns that the CIA intends to kill her after using her to help them foil a Russian diplomat with ties to organized crime. This development references the CIA's history of supporting guerrilla armies in Nicaragua and blocking law enforcement efforts to investigate illegal drug networks that helped fund its covert war in that country.[81] By foregrounding the CIA's duplicity, the series illustrates how the United States maintains its privileged position as a locus of freedom and multiculturalism while reasserting the Global South's subordinate relationship to Western nations. The series concludes after Teresa realizes she cannot survive as a key player in the global narcotics economy. Realizing that chasing power and influence is a morally bankrupt endeavor likely to get her killed, she conducts an elaborate scheme to fake her assassination so that she can extricate herself from the business and retire with her closest allies to a remote location in Belize. The final scene depicts Teresa living in domestic bliss, learning how to cook for James, Pote, and Pote's family in a large seaside estate (see fig. 5.3).

Beyond Neoliberal Multiculturalism?

Even though I draw heavily from Valencia's critique of gore capitalism, I'm not certain that she would approve of my analysis. As she notes, a wide range of mediated texts featuring violent crime have legitimated gore practices by numbing viewers to their real-world implications. For Valencia, these texts may not only entertain but instruct by teaching *endriago* subjects lessons for increasing their efficacy and using spectacles of violence to their advantage. *QotS*'s regular and graphic portrayals of murder and torture contribute to Hollywood's penchant for gore.

Yet my analysis also suggests that this series' lessons are inconsistent. Valencia's commentary about texts such as the video game *Grand Theft Auto* and the HBO series *The Sopranos* indicates that mediated texts featuring organized crime present a variety of messages about criminality and violence. *QotS* exists among the media products that present biting critiques of the relations

FIG. 5.3 Teresa evades those who wish to kill her by escaping with her boyfriend and best friends to a seaside estate on a secluded beach in Belize at the series' conclusion. *Queen of the South*, season 5, episode 10, "El Final," written by Benjamin Daniel Lobato and Dailyn Rodriguez, original airdate June 9, 2021, USA Network.

between state actors and the criminal underground. Teresa's decision to leave the cartel suggests that narcotraffickers' glamorous image is little more than a segue between a life of abject poverty and death at the hands of rivals. The series' conclusion reveals that the scene of her death was a ruse, but it also suggests that the image of her success was a mirage. The Queen was a fantasy that gave her the will to survive but was never a persona she could fully inhabit because wealth accumulation necessarily involves political corruption, fraudulent enterprise, and opportunism. In Teresa's world, violence is an indispensable and regrettable feature of contemporary capitalism beyond the gore economy.

Teresa's status as a strong woman informs the series' departure from portrayals of unscrupulous male narcotraffickers. Gendered expectations for likable female television characters demanded that Teresa fail at gore capitalism. Women are not supposed to be agents of gore; rather, their purpose is to be consumed by gore capitalism. If Hollywood functions as a "users manual for the practices of gore capitalism,"[82] then the lesson for women is that the instructions don't apply to them, even if they're far more skilled at handling the machinery.

While *QotS* is about narcotrafficking in its most literal sense, it also relates to the economic and sociopolitical conditions in which we as viewers might fantasize about the possibilities of narcoempowerment. For those of us who would never seriously consider a life of violent crime, the series provides lessons about neoliberal feminist striving under impossibly difficult circumstances by reminding viewers that adherence to market-driven principles alone cannot overcome people's investments in gendered hierarchies or racial capitalism. Teresa's story gives narrative form to Jodi Melamed's argument that race "continue[s] to permeate capitalism's economic and social processes, organizing the hyperextraction of surplus value from racialized bodies and naturalizing a system of capital accumulation that grossly favor[s] the global North over the global South."[83] That a USA series offers this lesson suggests that neoliberal multiculturalism's status as ideological common sense has diminished. That is, the series points to the development of a new racial order that does not abide by the logics of neoliberal multiculturalism but recognizes, for good or for ill, that neoliberalism remains a form of racial capitalism.

This is not necessarily a cause for celebration. The series offers no positive vision of what might emerge in place of multicultural neoliberalism to offset the ravages of racial capitalism. Although it celebrates Teresa's flight from forces of gore capitalism, white supremacy, and misogyny, the conclusion grounds the possibilities of flight within those same forces. Teresa's participation in economies that contribute to human misery provided the necessary resources that enabled her escape. Her transformation suggests that a capitalist logic that openly embraces the racialized and gendered dimensions of gore may be far more resonant to viewers than one that envisions multicultural inclusion as a locus of freedom and opportunity. Thus, her failure to create a just cartel gives the series a happy ending. But her new life is imagined not only as a flight from gore capitalism but as a flight from participation in public life altogether. Missing from the series is a vision of community that actively resists gore and neoliberal values of private wealth accumulation. It is important to recognize that those communities exist beyond television's purview. Héctor Parra García points to feminist and LGBT activism in Central and South America, as well as the Mexican municipality of Cherán as opportunities to imagine escape routes from gore capitalism. As García notes, it was women activists who "put community concerns at the center of politics."[84] These are the stories that might intervene in the sexist and racial realism of contemporary television entertainment, if only the industry would dare to draw from them.

Epilogue

The Impossible Woman highlights how a variety of television series featuring extraordinarily resilient and talented women have contributed to sexist realism, or the widespread assumption that it is now impossible to imagine an alternative to the patriarchal conditions that structure our lives. While television's emphasis on strong women characters signals a market for feminist storylines, the characters' stalled or failed efforts to achieve justice for themselves or others subordinated by white supremacist patriarchy indicates that television has a limited imagination for envisioning what justice might look like. Recurring themes across the variety of series explored throughout this book offer additional insights into feminism's status in contemporary social life.

An insight that is not all that surprising but is worth stating nonetheless is that television's enthusiasm for strong women is dependent upon a shallow understanding of feminism devoid of the movement's historic investments in broad structural transformation. For all their emphases on empowerment and fighting injustice, these series never depict the kinds of organizing efforts that feminist activists have historically undertaken to demand political recognition, access to resources, and legal protections. Relatedly, these series point out that the spectacle of popular misogyny is not isolated to the far right or to fringe spaces of online social networks; rather, the portrayal of virulent misogyny undergirds the U.S. television industry's fascination with strong women.

Two subthemes running through the chapters in this book amplify misogyny's stable home in scripted television. The first is that viewing pleasure remains deeply connected to expectations that women characters fulfill normative expectations for physical attractiveness. Although I elaborate on this point in chapter 3, a similar argument could be made of each of the impossible women featured in this book. Such norms also include expectations for whiteness; even *Queen of the South*'s Teresa conforms to the media industry's tendency to favor Latina actors with lighter skin.[1] That each series depicts these characters' sexual objectification while also inviting viewers to appreciate the actors' aesthetic beauty illustrates the influence of commodity sexism in the past decade.

A second subtheme regards the affective politics of television's impossible women: While TV shows often position viewers to identify with women characters who maintain overall positive demeanors (even when we know they have little to feel cheerful about), they continue to depict women's rage as a problem. While cheerful women make friends, angry women like Dany provoke men to dig their graves. The struggles facing television's impossible women illustrate how television paradoxically makes feminism meaningful by appealing to the misogyny that underwrites it. That television frequently kills off its strongest women characters, like Daenerys Targaryen or *Killing Eve*'s Villanelle, once they have vanquished their most formidable opponents illuminates how mainstream culture continues to regard powerful women as threats in need of containment.

My central argument, however, is not just that television's female characters experience sexism because they are women but that women characters experience misogynist treatment when they pose a threat to the broader structural forces that maintain structural hierarchies. That is, women's goals of achieving upward mobility are thwarted when their goals also include making the world better for others, such as when Leslie Knope tries to prevent corporations from selling unhealthy snacks at public parks, when Daenerys Targaryen announces her plan to break the wheel of monarchical violence in Westeros, or when Teresa Mendoza chooses to free abducted women rather than make a lucrative deal with a sex trafficker. Conversely, women's careers and economic conditions tend to improve when they are willing to exploit their relationships with less advantaged associates, such as when Midge Maisel nearly exposes Shy Baldwin's sexuality to a crowd of his biggest fans, or when Beth Harmon takes her best friend's hard-earned money to compete at a prestigious chess tournament. Women's opportunities also grow when they learn to embrace neoliberal principles, as Jacqueline Voorhees does when she inflates the value of tickets to a children's theater production on *Unbreakable Kimmy Schmidt*.

The tensions and contradictions in television series about impossibly capable women's losing battles with the forces that conspire against them illustrate the fundamental incompatibility between feminism's emphases on equality, justice, and public welfare and neoliberalism's emphases on individualism, privatization, and wealth accumulation. As I have suggested throughout this book, the emergence of the impossible woman in scripted television underscores the limits of individualist striving as a means of empowerment for historically exploited and subordinated groups. The programs featuring impossible women discussed in this book present cynical portrayals of such striving, illustrating how postfeminist portrayals have given way to content that is more directly critical of structural conditions that limit opportunities for women and minoritized populations. Unlike postfeminist programs from the late nineties and early aughts, such as *Sex and the City* and *Ally McBeal*, that celebrated professional white women's pursuit of heterosexual romance or neoliberal feminist self-help literature like Sheryl Sandberg's *Lean In* that encourages women to strive for upward mobility and a happy work-life balance, These series elicit an affective disinvestment from neoliberalism by depicting competitive individualism as a fruitless endeavor for all but the wealthiest people. So long as women inspired by Leslie Knope continue to seek advancement by appealing to the individuals who benefit from their dehumanization, they will never be empowered to change those institutions for the better. As long as women seek upward mobility within institutions that have historically depended on exploitation and violence, they will be forced to abandon feminist projects rooted in ending structures of domination, including imperialism and global capitalism. In some inchoate way, series featuring impossible women make bell hooks's point that feminism that focuses strictly on women's autonomy or equality of opportunity with men cannot "rid society of sexism and male domination."[2]

These series are part of a broader shift in television portrayals of women following the 2008 recession.[3] Amy Shields Dobson and Akane Kanai observe that comedic series like *Broad City*, *Insecure*, and *Crazy Ex-Girlfriend* foreground experiences of "disappointment, frustration, and dissatisfaction in working life," thereby challenging the "neoliberal mythologies of women's career 'success' as accessible, meritocratic, and 'chosen' by individuals" through cultivating feelings and performance of confidence, self-esteem, and empowerment.[4] Such programs stand in contrast to media forms present immediately following the recession that proffered "strained fantasies of rejuvenated individualist enterprise."[5] Subsequent postrecessionary television has responded to young women's worsening economic conditions and job prospects with portrayals of characters who defy neoliberal investments in women's positive, confident dispositions. Characters in programs such as *Broad City*, *Fleabag*, and *Girls* violate normative expectations for female behavior by embracing "imperfection and unruliness."[6] Meg Tully describes such characters as embodying what she refers to as "trainwreck feminism," a performance that reveals the contradictions and impossible standards for women in postfeminist culture.[7] Sarah Hagelin and Gillian Silverman reflect that such trainwrecks are "comedic antiheroes," who recognize that ambitious, politically minded women are bound to fail and reject the "achievement mandate" in favor of friendship and adventure. Rather than attempt to seize power, they refuse to play politics altogether.[8]

For all their cynicism, television's impossible women and trainwreck feminists suggest that late-stage neoliberalism has lost some of its status as ideological common sense. Declining living standards, climate change, the crisis of care labor, growing racial inequities, anti-Black violence, and other conditions reveal that entrepreneurialism and hard work are not adequate solutions to the problems that plague us. Given the violence that neoliberal economic policy has caused to people and natural environments throughout the world, the decline of neoliberal common sense might not be a bad thing. The crisis affords opportunities for new economic systems and cultural values to emerge in its place.

Tragically, what is emerging in place of what Jodi Melamed has termed "multicultural neoliberalism" does not advance a feminist agenda. Since I began writing this book, right-wing populism has flourished in the United States and elsewhere across the globe. While the movement has appealed to the victims of financialization and global capitalism, it is fueled by racist, sexist, transphobic, and anti-immigrant discourse. A new "new traditionalism" has developed alongside such populist appeals which tout "biblically based" definitions of family—including women's submission to her husband—and pledges to fight feminism's "emasculation of men."[9] Reflecting on the dismantling of abortion rights in the United States, the popularity of sex trafficker Andrew Tate, and a variety of ageist remarks about women celebrities and political figures, *Glamour* writer Hanna Lustig declared that misogyny was the biggest trend of 2023 and predicted (perhaps accurately) that 2024 would be particularly bleak. "Misogyny isn't just a psychological issue that lurks in the hearts and minds of bad men," Lustig concludes. "It's a system in which nearly everyone is culpable."[10] What we are seeing in place of the alignment of feminism and neoliberalism is a more blatant and direct form of white supremacist patriarchy that would remove women's participation from public culture altogether. Jilly Boyce Kay notes that an aggressive form of "reactionary feminism" has emerged that rejects both liberal individualism and misogyny but is profoundly hostile toward social justice organizing and is virulently transphobic.[11]

Sexist realism provides a framework for understanding the center-left's response to the current crisis, as it points to a broader culture of resignation toward the retrenchment of patriarchy. Up until Kamala Harris became the Democratic frontrunner for the 2024 U.S. presidential campaign, little even remotely resembling a feminist alternative to Donald Trump's agenda has gained traction in the mainstream press. But as my prior discussion intimates, feminist enthusiasm for Harris's run should be tempered with the recognition that one woman's aspirational effort to assume presidential office does not in and of itself achieve a feminist agenda rooted in intersectionality and economic justice. We should not applaud Harris's presidential run solely because she is a woman of color. Her foreign policy positions, stance on law and order, and support for fracking hardly reflect the kinds of feminist commitments I recommend here. But she also deserves credit for supporting expanded Medicaid coverage of postpregnancy care and renewing President Biden's failed effort to promote a broader care economy by expanding paid family leave, housing assistance, and childcare.[12]

Predictably, Trump and his supporters used racist and sexist insults to delegitimize her campaign almost immediately after Biden threw his support over to her. These remarks, rather than her agenda (which gets far less media attention), articulated Harris with a feminist project and amplify my point that popular feminism is underwritten by a deep-seated culture of misogyny. This manuscript was under review when the November 2024 presidential election results were announced. Although multiple factors contributed to her loss, I could not help but reflect on how Trump's recent election extended sexist realism from the small screen into politics. According to many Democratic pundits, Harris ran a flawless campaign in the truncated timeline she had been given.[13] Yet more voters were swayed to support a male candidate who has been convicted of sexual abuse; made numerous derogatory remarks about women, immigrants, and trans people; and failed to articulate a coherent or economically viable policy agenda on the campaign trail.

Meanwhile, television entertainment has embraced pessimism as a means of coping with the misogynist culture that surrounds us. As I argue throughout this book, sexist realism buttresses patriarchy, not because its adherents hate women per se, but because they presume that sexism is an unshakable dimension of society and politics. Nikki Glaser's 2024 comedy special is a case in point. The raunchy stand-up comedian who routinely rails against misogynist norms concluded the special by relating to the experiences of women porn stars in graphic detail, miming the experience of penetration from multiple sex partners at once. "Life is a gang bang," she tells the crowd just before ending the set. "The good news is someday you'll die."[14] The lack of imagination of a more feminist future that underlies the impossible woman is the hallmark of sexist realism, which reinforces the expectation that all those who are not white, able-bodied, cisgender men should expect abusive treatment. Like many television series about women experiencing sexual violence, Glaser's jest refracts broader anxieties over the seeming intractability of our misogynist times.

How might individuals committed to feminism avoid the trap of the impossible woman? One possibility is to reject the imperatives of individual striving in favor of collective organizing with people who exist beyond one's workplace or the home. An alternative to sexist realism lies in the pursuit of coalitional feminism and the full inclusion of Black, brown, trans, queer, and disabled women in movements that offers a capacious and inclusive vision for social justice. Such organizing requires new forms of resilience, marked not by the extraordinary labor of individuals but by the cooperation and everyday participation of all of us seeking a cleaner, safer, and equitable world. To return to bell hooks, we need to promote feminism for everyone.

Such a broad feminist movement needs to be able to imagine something beyond the aporias that structure narratives about impossible women. While their stories rarely appear on the small screen, strong networks of activists and feminist political organizations suggest cynicism is not universal or totalizing. Likewise, literature and cinema have provided alternative stories about female solidarity and activism. Take, for example, George Miller's thrilling reboot of the Mad Max franchise, *Mad Max: Fury Road*, in which the agent of change is not Max but Imperator Furiosa and her tribe of women warriors who liberate the region's water supply from a brutal warlord to care for not just themselves but people throughout the region. While it is fantasy fiction, the movie provides a rare portrayal of feminist success in the face of daunting odds. The British teen comedy series *Sex Education* offers a rare example of feminist content on the small screen. The series, which ran from 2019 to 2023 on Netflix, featured a diverse group of adolescents in the process of exploring how their varying social locations impact their sexuality. A season 2 subplot revolves around Aimee Gibbs's (Aimee Lou Wood) struggles in the aftermath of a sexual assault. Her classmates' determination to rally around her provides a particularly affecting example of television's capacity to depict feminist expressions of solidarity in the face of common experiences of sexual trauma and rape culture.

Alternatives to sexist realism also require that we exceed the limits of the white imagination that fuels much of the transnational television and film industries. Writing about the fantasy genre, Ebony Elizabeth Thomas laments the "imagination gap" that cannot envision a future that doesn't revolve around whiteness.[15] The whiteness that structures popular series about impossible women indicates that this aperture extends beyond fantasy. Scripted storytelling across genres needs to close this gap, not just by centralizing Black characters and other characters of color, but by foregrounding heroism through visions of collective struggle. Such transformational storytelling is akin to what Jenna Hanchey describes as "neocolonial dreamwork," a practice that calls for new kinds of impossible stories grounded in visions of a future developed outside of Western epistemologies.[16] For viewers not already deeply immersed in feminist communities and culture, television's lessons do little to direct a vision of inclusive feminism. We need to demand better stories from television's creators and circulate feminist narratives that are replete with possibilities for a livable and just future for everyone.

Acknowledgments

I am grateful for the advice, encouragement, and enthusiasm of the many friends, colleagues, and family members who helped me write this book. *The Impossible Woman* began with my intention to write a journal article about sexist realism. In the process of revising, I realized that I had much more to say than could fit in one essay. Many thanks to then-*Quarterly Journal of Speech* editor Karrin Vasby Anderson and the anonymous reviewers who encouraged me to pursue this project further, even as I persisted in critiquing Kari's most beloved television show. That article, an earlier draft of chapter 1, appears as "The Impossible Woman and Sexist Realism on NBC's *Parks and Recreation*" in the *Quarterly Journal of Speech* 107, no. 4 (2021): 373–397, © 2021 National Communication Association, reprinted by permission of Taylor & Francis, Ltd.

The Rhetoric Society of America's 2022 Career Retreat for Associate Professors connected me with a generous mentor, Letizia Guglielmo, and delightful writing group partners Sarah Kornfield and Alice Myatt, who helped me get this project off the ground after the official retreat ended. My department colleagues and graduate students in the Department of Communication Studies at the University of Nebraska–Lincoln provided constant encouragement throughout my writing process. I am fortunate to work with such a brilliant community of scholars. I could not have asked for a better research assistant than Katy Schneider, whose keen observations and detailed notes made writing chapter 4 possible.

I am also thankful for many individuals who offered thoughtful commentary at various stages of my writing. Sarah Kornfield and Meredith Neville-Shepard provided nuanced readings of earlier drafts of my book. Their incisive remarks have sharpened my writing and thinking about how feminism is encoded on television. Angela Aguayo, Rachel Dubrofsky, Sarah Hagelin, Leslie Harris, Julia Havas, Michael Lechuga, Marina Levina, Helen Morgan Parmett, Ryan Neville-Shepard, Rae Lynn Schwartz-DuPre, Gillian Silverman, and Graham Slater also provided helpful suggestions in conversation about this project. Nicole Solano and Rutgers University Press have been outstanding supporters of this book, as have anonymous reviewers who have read with the grain of this project without letting me off the hook for defending my arguments. I am also grateful for Hannah McGinnis and the rest of the team at Scribe for their close attention to the manuscript. I am tremendously proud that this book will appear in Rutgers University Press's catalog. I am also thankful for opportunities to present and discuss portions of this work to students and faculty at the University of Arkansas Department of Communication's Research Series, sponsored by the UA's Center for Communication Research, at the University of Illinois Urbana-Champaign Communication Studies Department colloquium series and at Southeast Missouri State University Department of Communication Studies' annual Low Lecture.

Finally, I thank my spouse, colleague, and TV-viewing partner, Casey Ryan Kelly, for his unflagging support, thoughtful insights, and vast library of knowledge regarding the horrors of white masculinity (which he studies but does not perpetuate). Casey is an excellent feminist companion and friend. If he didn't cook, we'd both starve.

My apologies to those of you who adore the television series that I might have ruined for you here. May feminist futures bring us new series that we can enjoy together.

Notes

Introduction

1 Sarah Banet-Weiser, *Empowered: Popular Feminism and Popular Misogyny* (Durham, N.C.: Duke University Press, 2018), 4.
2 Banet-Weiser, *Empowered*, 2.
3 Mark Fisher, *Capitalist Realism: Is There No Alternative?* (Winchester, U.K.: Zero, 2009), 2.
4 Banet-Weiser, *Empowered*, 3. Emphasis in original.
5 Sarah Sharma, *In the Meantime: Temporality and Cultural Politics* (Durham, N.C.: Duke University Press, 2014).
6 Series including Netflix's *Reprisal* in 2018 and Amazon Prime Video's *Paper Girls* in 2022 creatively avoided linear temporal narratives and portrayed women as capable of advancing justice for themselves and others. That these series were canceled after one season speaks to the ways in which television culture struggles to envision alternatives to the patriarchal present.
7 Banet-Weiser, *Empowered*, 32.
8 Banet-Weiser, *Empowered*, 2.
9 Banet-Weiser, *Empowered*, 33.
10 Banet-Weiser, *Empowered*, 33.
11 Bradley Jones, "An Examination of the 2016 Electorate, Based on Validated Voters," *Pew Research Center*, August 9, 2018, https://www.pewresearch.org/politics/2018/08/09/an-examination-of-the-2016-electorate-based-on-validated-voters/.
12 Michelle Goldberg, "The Future Isn't Female Anymore," *New York Times*, June 17, 2022, sec. Opinion, https://www.nytimes.com/2022/06/17/opinion/roe-dobbs-abortion-feminism.html.
13 Kaamil Ahmed, "Nine Out of 10 People Are Biased Against Women, Says 'Alarming' UN Report," *Guardian*, June 12, 2023, sec. Global Development, https://www.theguardian.com/global-development/2023/jun/12/nine-out-of-10-people-are-biased-against-women-says-alarming-un-report.

14 Anna North, "You've Heard That Women Make 80 Cents to Men's Dollar. It's Much Worse Than That," *Vox*, November 28, 2018, https://www.vox.com/policy-and-politics/2018/11/28/18116388/equal-pay-day-2019-gender-gap-equity; Jeanne Sahadi, "The US Gender Pay Gap: Why It Hasn't Narrowed Much in 20 Years | CNN Business," *CNN*, March 1, 2023, https://www.cnn.com/2023/03/01/success/gender-pay-gap-pew/index.html.

15 Nancy Fraser, *Fortunes of Feminism: From State-Managed Capitalism to Neoliberal Crisis*, 1st ed. (Brooklyn, N.Y.: Verso, 2013), 239.

16 Banet-Weiser, *Empowered*, 10, 25.

17 Rosalind Gill, "The Affective, Cultural and Psychic Life of Postfeminism: A Postfeminist Sensibility 10 Years On," *European Journal of Cultural Studies* 20, no. 6 (2017): 619.

18 Banet-Weiser, *Empowered*, 23.

19 Banet-Weiser, *Empowered*; Gill, "Affective, Cultural and Psychic Life," 606–626; Angela McRobbie, "Notes on the Perfect: Competitive Femininity in Neoliberal Times," *Australian Feminist Studies* 30, no. 83 (January 2, 2015): 3–20; Catherine A. Rottenberg, *The Rise of Neoliberal Feminism* (New York: Oxford University Press, 2018).

20 Wendy Brown, *Undoing the Demos: Neoliberalism's Stealth Revolution*, reprint ed. (New York: Zone, 2017), 106.

21 Rottenberg, *Rise of Neoliberal Feminism*, 14.

22 McRobbie, "Notes on the Perfect," 12.

23 Sarah Banet-Weiser and Laura Portwood-Stacer, "The Traffic in Feminism: An Introduction to the Commentary and Criticism on Popular Feminism," *Feminist Media Studies* 17, no. 5 (2017): 886.

24 Robin James, *Resilience & Melancholy: Pop Music, Feminism, Neoliberalism* (Winchester, U.K.: Zero, 2015), 86–87.

25 James, *Resilience & Melancholy*, 7.

26 James, *Resilience & Melancholy*, 11–12.

27 James, *Resilience & Melancholy*, 84–85. Emphasis in original.

28 Recent critiques of white feminism's contributions to white supremacy and anti-trans politics includes Ruby Hamad, *White Tears / Brown Scars: How White Feminism Betrays Women of Color* (New York: Catapult, 2020); Alison Phipps, *Me, Not You: The Trouble with Mainstream Feminism*, 1st ed. (Manchester: Manchester University Press, 2020); and Rafia Zakaria, *Against White Feminism: Notes on Disruption* (New York: W. W. Norton, 2021).

29 Eleanor Goldberg, "'Feminist' T-Shirt Backed by Women's Group Made in Sweatshop," *Huffington Post*, November 3, 2014, https://www.huffpost.com/entry/feminist-t-shirt-sweatshop_n_6094722.

30 Michael T. Heaney, "Is the Women's March Focused on White Women—or Does It Promote Intersectional Activism?," *Washington Post*, July 8, 2019, https://www.washingtonpost.com/politics/2019/07/08/is-womens-march-focused-white-women-or-does-it-promote-intersectional-activism/.

31 Tarana Burke, "#MeToo Was Started for Black and Brown Women and Girls. They're Still Being Ignored," *Washington Post*, November 9, 2017, https://www.washingtonpost.com/news/post-nation/wp/2017/11/09/the-waitress-who-works-in-the-diner-needs-to-know-that-the-issue-of-sexual-harassment-is-about-her-too/.

32 Kimberlé Crenshaw is credited for coining the term "intersectionality" in "Demarginalizing the Intersection of Race and Sex: A Black Feminist Critique of Antidiscrimination Doctrine, Feminist Theory, and Politics," *University of Chicago Legal*

Forum (1989): 139–167. See also Patricia Hill Collins and Sirma Bilge, *Intersectionality* (Cambridge, U.K.: Polity, 2016).

33 Leah Asmelash, "What Intersectionality Actually Means and Why It Matters," *CNN*, April 19, 2023, https://www.cnn.com/2023/04/19/us/intersectionality-feminism-explainer-cec/index.html; Jane Coaston, "The Intersectionality Wars," *Vox*, May 20, 2019, https://www.vox.com/the-highlight/2019/5/20/18542843/intersectionality-conservatism-law-race-gender-discrimination.

34 Bonnie J. Dow, *Prime-Time Feminism: Television, Media Culture, and the Women's Movement Since 1970* (Philadelphia: University of Pennsylvania Press, 1996), 8.

35 Jane Shattuc, "Netflix, Inc. and Online Television," in *A Companion to Television*, 2nd ed., ed. Janet Wasko and Eileen R. Meehan (New York: Wiley and Sons, 2020), 145–164; Kasey Moore, "Netflix Secret Codes 2024: Every Movie & Series Category on Netflix," *What's on Netflix*, January 5, 2024, https://www.whats-on-netflix.com/news/the-netflix-id-bible-every-category-on-netflix/.

36 "Resonate State of Streaming Report Shows That OTT Has Achieved 82% Consumer Saturation, with Cable TV Falling to 55%," *Financial Services Monitor Worldwide*, October 15, 2021, LexisNexis.

37 Shattuc, "Netflix, Inc.," 156.

38 Julia Havas and Tanya Horeck, "Netflix Feminism: Binge-Watching Rape Culture in *Unbreakable Kimmy Schmidt* and *Unbelievable*," in *Binge-Watching and Contemporary Television Studies*, ed. Marieke Jenner (Edinburgh: Edinburgh University Press, 2021), 251.

39 Havas and Horeck, "Netflix Feminism," 267.

40 "Strong Female Leads," panel discussion, February 8, 2017, by Netflix, YouTube, https://www.youtube.com/watch?v=nDmqTY67Q-Q.

41 Malina Saval, "Women Rule Drama Series Emmy Race," *Variety*, August 20, 2015, https://variety.com/2015/tv/spotlight/drama-series-emmy-race-women-strong-female-characters-1201572968/.

42 Rachel Handler, "The Best of Netflix's 'Featuring a Strong Female Lead' Categories," Vulture, October 6, 2015, https://www.vulture.com/2015/10/best-of-netflixs-strong-female-leads-categories.html.

43 "Featuring a Strong Female Lead," *The Break with Michelle Wolf*, May 24, 2018, by Netflix, YouTube, https://www.youtube.com/watch?v=8uArRFr7_YY.

44 Brit Marling, "I Don't Want to Be the Strong Female Lead," *New York Times*, February 7, 2020, sec. Opinion, https://www.nytimes.com/2020/02/07/opinion/sunday/brit-marling-women-movies.html; Zack Sharf, "Emily Blunt Rails Against 'Strong Female Lead' Label: 'It's the Worst Thing Ever' and 'I'm Bored' of It," *Variety*, November 14, 2022, https://variety.com/2022/tv/news/emily-blunt-rails-slams-strong-female-lead-label-worst-thing-ever-1235432354/; Fiona Sturges, "Tatiana Maslany: 'Strong Female Lead? It's a Box No One Fits In,'" *Guardian*, August 13, 2022, sec. Television and Radio, https://www.theguardian.com/tv-and-radio/2022/aug/13/tatiana-maslany-she-hulk-marvel-mark-ruffalo-orphan-black.

45 Marling, "I Don't Want."

46 Mary Eleanor Triece, *Protest and Popular Culture: Women in the American Labor Movement* (New York: Routledge, 2001).

47 Dow, *Prime-Time Feminism*.

48 Aviva Dove-Viebahn, *There She Goes Again: Gender, Power, and Knowledge in Contemporary Film and Television Franchises* (New Brunswick, N.J.: Rutgers University

Press, 2024); Sumiko Higashi, "Hold It! Women in Television's Adventure Series," *Journal of Popular Film and Television* 8, no. 3 (1980): 28.

49 Quoted in Julie D'Acci, *Defining Women: Television and the Case of Cagney and Lacey* (Chapel Hill: University of North Carolina Press, 1994), 69.

50 Anita Harris identifies the "can-do girl" as an "ideal late modern subject" perceived as "the most confident, resilient, and empowered of all the demographic groups affected by risk." Images of young women who are independent, successful, and ambitious provide models of ideal femininity that also function as lucrative markets for advertisers. While only a small number of girls can achieve the consumer lifestyles presented by advertisers' projections of "can-do girls," the image was a "powerful ideal" in the new millennium that restricted ideas about "what it means to be successful" in terms of personal achievement independent of family, government, or relationships influence. Anita Harris, *Future Girl: Young Women in the Twenty-First Century* (New York: Routledge, 2004), 8, 16–25.

51 Angela McRobbie, *The Aftermath of Feminism: Gender, Culture and Social Change* (London: Sage, 2009), 12.

52 Dow, *Prime-Time Feminism*, 98.

53 Elspeth Probyn, "New Traditionalism and Post-Feminism: TV Does the Home," *Screen* 31, no. 2 (1990): 147–159.

54 Dow, *Prime-Time Feminism*.

55 Sarah Kornfield, "Fixating on the Stasis of Fact: Debating 'Having It All' in U.S. Media," *Rhetoric and Public Affairs* 20, no. 2 (Summer 2017): 272.

56 Dow, *Prime-Time Feminism*, 92.

57 Laurie Ouellette, "Victims No More: Postfeminism, Television, and Ally McBeal," *Communication Review* 5, no. 4 (October 1, 2002): 332–333.

58 Mary Douglas Vavrus, "Putting Ally on Trial: Contesting Postfeminism in Popular Culture," *Women's Studies in Communication* 23, no. 3 (September 1, 2000): 413–428.

59 Allison M. Prasch, "The Two Madam Secretaries: Elizabeth McCord, Hillary Rodham Clinton, and Mimetic Representations of Twenty-First Century Feminism," in *Women, Feminism, and Pop Politics: From "Bitch" to "Badass" and Beyond*, ed. Karrin Vasby Anderson (New York: Peter Lang, 2018), 223–242.

60 Isabel Pinedo, *Difficult Women on Television Drama: The Gender Politics of Complex Women in Serial Narratives* (New York: Routledge, 2021).

61 Julia Havas, *Woman Up: Invoking Feminism in Quality Television* (Detroit, Mich.: Wayne State University Press, 2022).

62 Havas, *Woman Up*, 228.

63 Michaela D. E. Meyer, "The Good Wife's Fatalistic Feminism: Televised Feminist Failures in Work/Life Balance, Romance, and Feminist Alliances," in *Women, Feminism, and Pop Politics*, 205–222.

64 Moore, "Netflix's Secret Codes."

65 Michaela D. E. Meyer and Rachel Alicia Griffin, eds., "Introduction: Riding Shondaland's Rollercoaster: Critical Cultural Television Studies in the 21st Century," in *Adventures in Shondaland: Identity Politics and the Power of Representation* (New Brunswick, N.J.: Rutgers University Press, 2018), 1–19.

66 Meyer and Griffin, "Introduction," 8.

67 Meyer and Griffin, "Introduction," 10–11; Kristen Warner, *The Cultural Politics of Colorblind TV Casting* (New York: Routledge, 2015).

68 Milly Buonanno, ed., *Television Antiheroines: Women Behaving Badly in Crime and Prison Drama* (Bristol, U.K.: Intellect, 2017); Havas, *Woman Up*; Yael Levy, *Chick TV: Antiheroines and Time Unbound* (Syracuse, N.Y.: Syracuse University Press, 2022); Pinedo, *Difficult Women*; Meg Tully, "Watching a Trainwreck Feminism," *Women's Studies in Communication* 43, no. 4 (2020): 341.

69 Sarah Hagelin and Gillian Silverman, *The New Female Antihero: The Disruptive Women of Twenty-First-Century US Television* (Chicago: University of Chicago Press, 2022), 204.

70 Hagelin and Silverman, *New Female Antihero*, 22.

71 Anita Harris and Amy Shields Dobson, "Theorizing Agency in Post-Girlpower Times," *Continuum* 29, no. 2 (2015): 153.

72 Dow, *Prime-Time Feminism*, xv.

73 Lynn Spigel and Denise Mann, eds., *Private Screenings: Television and the Female Consumer* (Minneapolis: University of Minnesota Press, 1992), xiii.

74 Kenneth Burke, *The Philosophy of Literary Form*, 3rd ed. (Berkeley: University of California Press, 1974), 293–304.

75 Barry Brummett, "Burke's Representative Anecdote as a Method in Media Criticism," *Critical Studies in Mass Communication* 1, no. 2 (June 1984): 164.

76 Brummett, "Burke's Representative Anecdote," 165.

77 Karrin Vasby Anderson, "Introduction: Hillary Clinton from 'Bitch' to 'Badass,'" in *Women, Feminism, and Pop Politics*, 2–3.

78 Kristina Horn Sheeler and Karrin Vasby Anderson, *Woman President: Confronting Postfeminist Political Culture* (College Station: Texas A&M University Press, 2013).

79 Douglas Kellner, *Media Culture: Cultural Studies, Identity and Politics Between the Modern and the Postmodern* (New York: Routledge, 1995), 2.

80 Michael Ryan and Douglas Kellner, *Camera Politica: The Politics and Ideology of Contemporary Film* (Bloomington: Indiana University Press, 1988), 12.

81 Ryan and Kellner, *Camera Politica*, 12.

82 Amanda D. Lotz, "Unpopularity and Cultural Power in the Age of Netflix: New Questions for Cultural Studies' Approaches to Television Texts," *European Journal of Cultural Studies* 24, no. 4 (2021): 897.

83 Celeste Michelle Condit, "The Rhetorical Limits of Polysemy," *Critical Studies in Mass Communication* 6, no. 2 (1989): 103–122.

84 Kenneth Burke, *A Rhetoric of Motives* (Berkeley: University of California Press, 1969), 25–26.

85 Amanda D. Lotz, "*House*: Narrative Complexity," in *How to Watch Television*, 1st ed., ed. Ethan Thompson and Jason Mittell (New York: New York University Press, 2013), 22–29.

86 Banet-Weiser, *Empowered*, 27.

87 Sarah Kornfield, "Televisual Pregnancy Beauty," *Feminist Media Studies* 19, no. 2 (2019): 163–178.

88 Pinedo, *Difficult Women*.

89 Sayak Valencia, *Gore Capitalism* (South Pasadena, Calif.: Semiotext(e), 2018).

Chapter 1 Impossibly Resilient

1 Erika Engstrom, "'Knope We Can!' Primetime Feminist Strategies in NBC's *Parks and Recreation*," *Media Report to Women* 41, no. 4 (2013): 11.

2 Kelsey Wallace, "A Big Feminist Yep to Leslie Knope," *Bitch Media*, October 5, 2009, https://www.bitchmedia.org/post/a-big-feminist-yep-to-leslie-knope.
3 *Parks and Recreation*, season 1, episode 1, "Pilot," written by Greg Daniels and Michael Schur, original airdate April 9, 2009, NBC.
4 *Parks and Recreation*, season 3, episode 3, "Time Capsule," written by Michael Schur, original airdate February 3, 2011, NBC.
5 *Parks and Recreation*, season 3, episode 2, "Flu Season," written by Norm Hiscock, original airdate January 27, 2011, NBC.
6 *Parks and Recreation*, season 1, episode 4, "Boy's Club," written by Alan Yang, original airdate April 20, 2009, NBC.
7 Michelle Rodino-Colocino, "The Great He-Cession: Why Feminists Should Rally for the End of White Supremacist Capitalist Patriarchy," *Feminist Media Studies* 14, no. 2 (2014): 343–347.
8 Rodino-Colocino, "Great He-Cession," 344.
9 Kathleen Kuehn and Thomas F. Corrigan, "Hope Labor: The Role of Employment Prospects in Online Social Production," *Political Economy of Communication* 1, no. 1 (2013): 21.
10 Brooke Erin Duffy, *(Not) Getting Paid to Do What You Love: Gender, Social Media, and Aspirational Work* (New Haven, Conn.: Yale University Press, 2017), 4. Emphasis in original.
11 *Parks and Recreation*, "Time Capsule."
12 *Parks and Recreation*, season 5, episode 19, "Article Two," written by Matt Murray, original airdate April 18, 2013, NBC.
13 *Parks and Recreation*, "Boy's Club."
14 *Parks and Recreation*, season 1, episode 2, "Canvassing," written by Rachel Axler, original airdate April 16, 2009, NBC.
15 Lauren Berlant, *Cruel Optimism* (Durham, N.C.: Duke University Press, 2011), 176–177.
16 Berlant, *Cruel Optimism*, 6.
17 Berlant, *Cruel Optimism*, 176–177.
18 Berlant, *Cruel Optimism*, 1.
19 Berlant, *Cruel Optimism*, 2.
20 Berlant, *Cruel Optimism*, 2.
21 *Parks and Recreation*, season 4, episode 22, "Win, Lose, or Draw," written by Michael Schur, original airdate May 10, 2012, NBC.
22 *Parks and Recreation*, season 5, episode 18, "Animal Control," written by Megan Amram, original airdate April 11, 2013, NBC.
23 *Parks and Recreation*, "Animal Control."
24 Karrin Vasby Anderson, "'Rhymes with Rich': 'Bitch' as a Tool of Containment in Contemporary American Politics," *Rhetoric and Public Affairs* 2, no. 4 (1999): 599–623; Karrin Vasby Anderson, "'Rhymes with Rich' Redux: The 'Bitch' Metaphor and Campaign 2020," *Spectra*, August 4, 2020, https://www.natcom.org/communication-currents/rhymes-rich-redux-bitch-metaphor-and-campaign-2020.
25 *Parks and Recreation*, season 6, episode 10, "Second Chunce," written by Amy Poehler and Michael Schur, original airdate January 9, 2014, NBC.
26 Ijeoma Oluo, *Mediocre: The Dangerous Legacy of White Male America* (New York: Seal Press, 2020), 4.
27 *Parks and Recreation*, season 6, episode 15, "The Wall," written by Jen Statsky, original airdate March 6, 2014, NBC.

28 Mark Neocleous, "Resisting Resilience," *Radical Philosophy* 178 (2013): 4, https://www.radicalphilosophy.com/commentary/resisting-resilience.

29 Silvia Federici, *Caliban and the Witch: Women, the Body and Primitive Accumulation* (New York: Autonomedia, 2004).

30 *Parks and Recreation*, season 2, episode 15, "Sweetums," written by Alan Yang, original airdate February 4, 2010, NBC.

31 Denise Martin, "Making Bureaucracy Work," *Los Angeles Times*, November 19, 2009, https://www.latimes.com/et-parks09-story.html.

32 Wendy Brown, *Undoing the Demos: Neoliberalism's Stealth Revolution* (New York: Zone, 2015), 39.

33 Robert Asen, "Neoliberalism, the Public Sphere, and a Public Good," *Quarterly Journal of Speech* 103, no. 4 (2017): 332. Emphasis in original.

34 Asen, "Neoliberalism," 334.

35 *Parks and Recreation*, season 5, episode 22, "Are You Better Off?," original airdate May 2, 2013, NBC.

36 Kate Manne, *Down Girl: The Logic of Misogyny* (New York: Oxford University Press, 2019).

37 *Parks and Recreation*, season 5, episode 12, "Ann's Decision," written by Michael Schur, original airdate February 7, 2013, NBC.

38 Henry A. Giroux, "Beyond the Biopolitics of Disposability: Rethinking Neoliberalism in the New Gilded Age," *Social Identities* 14, no. 5 (2008): 593–594.

39 Sarah Kornfield, "Fixating on the Stasis of Fact: Debating 'Having It All' in U.S. Media," *Rhetoric and Public Affairs* 20, no. 2 (Summer 2017): 272.

40 Michelle Colpean and Meg Tully, "Not Just a Joke: Tina Fey, Amy Schumer, and the Weak Reflexivity of White Feminist Comedy," *Women's Studies in Communication* 42, no. 2 (2019): 162.

41 See the chapters by Valerie Renegar, Lacy Lowrey, and Kirsti Cole, Mary Douglas Vavrus, Tasha N. Dubriwny, and Alyssa Samek in Karrin Vasby Anderson, *Women, Feminism, and Pop Politics: From "Bitch" to "Badass" and Beyond* (New York: Peter Lang, 2018).

42 John Fiske, *Television Culture*, 2nd ed. (New York: Routledge, 2010); Lisa Glebatis-Perks, "Polysemic Scaffolding: Explicating Discursive Clashes in *Chappelle's Show*," *Communication, Culture and Critique* 3, no. 2 (2010): 270–289; Lisa Gring-Pemble and Martha Solomon Watson, "The Rhetorical Limits of Satire: An Analysis of James Finn Garner's *Politically Correct Bedtime Stories*," *Quarterly Journal of Speech* 89, no. 2 (2003): 132–153.

43 Perks, "Polysemic Scaffolding," 271.

44 *Parks and Recreation*, season 2, episode 16, "Galentine's Day," written by Michael Schur, original airdate February 11, 2010, NBC.

45 *Parks and Recreation*, season 2, episode 22, "Telethon," written by Amy Poehler, original airdate May 6, 2010, NBC.

46 *Parks and Recreation*, season 3, episode 4, "Ron and Tammy Part 2," written by Emily Kapnek, original airdate February 10, 2011, NBC.

47 Karrin Vasby Anderson, "'Yes We Can't Not. Knope.': *Parks and Recreation* and the Promise of Comic Feminist Parody," in *Women, Feminism, and Pop Politics*, 297.

48 *Parks and Recreation*, season 4, episode 8, "Smallest Park," written by Chelsea Peretti, original airdate November 17, 2011, NBC.

49 *Parks and Recreation*, season 3, episode 1, "Go Big or Go Home," written by Alan Yang, original airdate January 20, 2011, NBC.

50 *Parks and Recreation*, season 4, episode 10, "Citizen Knope," written by Dave King, original airdate December 8, 2011, NBC.

51 Robyn Stacia Swink, "Lemony Liz and Likable Leslie: Audience Understandings of Feminism, Comedy, and Gender in Women-Led Television Comedies," *Feminist Media Studies* 17, no. 1 (2017): 22–24.

52 Swink, "Lemony Liz," 24.

53 *Parks and Recreation*, season 5, episode 14, "Leslie and Ben," written by Michael Schur and Alan Yang, original airdate February 21, 2013, NBC.

54 *Parks and Recreation*, season 5, episode 10, "Two Parties," written by Dave King, original airdate January 17, 2013, NBC.

55 Trevor Parry-Giles and Shawn Parry-Giles, "The West Wing's Prime-Time Presidentiality: Mimesis and Catharsis in a Postmodern Romance," *Quarterly Journal of Speech* 88, no. 2 (May 2002): 211.

56 Amy B. Wang, "'Nevertheless, She Persisted' Becomes New Battle Cry After McConnell Silences Elizabeth Warren," *Washington Post*, February 8, 2017, https://www.washingtonpost.com/news/the-fix/wp/2017/02/08/nevertheless-she-persisted-becomes-new-battle-cry-after-mcconnell-silences-elizabeth-warren/.

57 Shane Goldmacher and Astead W. Herndon, "Elizabeth Warren, Once a Front-Runner, Drops Out of Presidential Race," *New York Times*, March 5, 2020, sec. U.S., https://www.nytimes.com/2020/03/05/us/politics/elizabeth-warren-drops-out.html.

58 Danielle Tcholakian, "Democrats Say They'll Support a Woman for President. Here's How We Know They're Lying," *Daily Beast*, June 17, 2019, sec. Politics, https://www.thedailybeast.com/democrats-say-theyll-support-a-woman-for-president-heres-how-we-know-theyre-lying.

59 Karrin Vasby Anderson, "Every Woman Is the Wrong Woman: The Female Presidentiality Paradox," *Women's Studies in Communication* 40, no. 2 (2017): 133.

60 Lisa Lerer and Susan Chira, "'There's a Real Tension.' Democrats Puzzle over Whether a Woman Will Beat Trump," *New York Times*, January 5, 2019, https://www.nytimes.com/2019/01/05/us/politics/women-candidates-president-2020.html.

61 Asen, "Neoliberalism," 340.

62 Colpean and Tully, "Not Just a Joke," 162.

63 Emily St. James, "The Democrats' Not-So-Secret Closing Argument: Hillary Clinton Is Leslie Knope," *Vox*, July 28, 2016, https://www.vox.com/2016/7/28/12306978/hillary-clinton-leslie-knope-dnc.

64 Dow, *Prime-Time Feminism*, 161. Emphasis in original.

Chapter 2 Improbably Cheerful

1 Emily Nussbaum, "Candy Girl," *New Yorker*, March 23, 2015, https://www.newyorker.com/magazine/2015/03/30/candy-girl.

2 Alice Bolin, *Dead Girls: Essays on Surviving an American Obsession* (New York: William Morrow, 2018).

3 Other scholars attending to the promotional materials surrounding the series interpret the title as a form of wordplay to highlight how women are, in fact, breakable. See Julia Havas and Tanya Horeck, "Netflix Feminism: Binge-Watching Rape Culture in *Unbreakable Kimmy Schmidt* and *Unbelievable*," in *Binge-Watching and Contemporary Television Studies*, ed. Marieke Jenner (Edinburgh: Edinburgh University Press, 2021): 251–273.

4 Shani Orgad, "The Survivor in Contemporary Culture and Public Discourse: A Genealogy," *Communication Review* 12, no. 2 (2009): 150.

5 Paul Gallagher, "Antoine Dodson: From Local News Item to Internet Sensation," *Guardian*, August 14, 2010, sec. U.S. News, https://www.theguardian.com/world/2010/aug/15/antoine-dodson-internet-sensation.

6 *Unbreakable Kimmy Schmidt*, season 1, episode 1, "Kimmy Goes Outside!," written by Tina Fey and Robert Carlock, released March 6, 2015, Netflix Original.

7 *Unbreakable Kimmy Schmidt*, season 1, episode 2, "Kimmy Gets a Job!," written by Sam Means, released March 6, 2015, Netflix Original.

8 *Unbreakable Kimmy Schmidt*, season 3, episode 4, "Kimmy Goes to College!," written by Dan Rubin, released May 19, 2017, Netflix Original.

9 *Unbreakable Kimmy Schmidt*, season 2, episode 4, "Kimmy Kidnaps Gretchen!," written by Allison Silverman, released April 15, 2016, Netflix Original.

10 Rosalind Gill and Shani Orgad, "The Amazing Bounce-Backable Woman: Resilience and the Psychological Turn in Neoliberalism," *Sociological Research Online* 23, no. 2 (2018): 477–495.

11 Responsibilization refers to the neoliberal frameworks and discourses running across legal, political, economic, and criminal justice institutions that hold individuals solely responsible for their health and safety. It tasks the individual with "discerning and undertaking the correct strategies of self-investment and entrepreneurship for thriving and surviving." See Brown, *Undoing the Demos*, 132–133. Mallory Mallock notes that responsibilization is inextricably linked to notions of risk and blame because people subjected to violence and disease must demonstrate moral competence to be treated as worthy victims deserving of public sympathy and state provision. See Mallory Mallock, "Not 'Fragrant' at All: Criminal Justice Responses to 'Risky' Women," *Critical Social Policy* 24, no. 3 (2004): 291–427.

12 *Unbreakable Kimmy Schmidt*, "Kimmy Gets a Job!"

13 *Unbreakable Kimmy Schmidt*, season 1, episode 8, "Kimmy Is Bad at Math!," written by Meredith Scardino, released March 6, 2015, Netflix Original.

14 Tanya Horeck, "Streaming Sexual Violence: Binge-Watching Netflix's *13 Reasons Why*," *Participations: Journal of Audience and Reception Studies* 16, no. 2 (2019): 143–166. For a deeper discussion of continuum thinking, see Karen Boyle, "What's in a Name? Theorizing the Inter-Relationships of Gender and Violence," *Feminist Theory* 20, no. 1 (2018): 19–36.

15 Julia Havas and Tanya Horeck argue that casting Jon Hamm in this role aids the series' efforts to spotlight the systemic nature of toxic masculinity because his star persona was defined by his previous role as Don Draper in AMC's *Mad Men*. See Havas and Horeck, "Netflix Feminism," 255. I am less convinced that Hamm's casting advances feminist critique, in part because his role as Draper also catapulted his persona as an alluring lothario, and his subsequent acting roles, including guest hosting *Saturday Night Live*, have constructed Hamm's celebrity persona as charming and likable. In *UKS*, he is more buffoonish than he is repulsive, and the contrast between his attractive physique and his character's psychopathology is likely more intended to draw laughs than advance feminist politics.

16 Natalia Vedric and Janine Little, "True Victims: Men's Privilege, Class, and Violence Against Women in *Making a Murderer* and *The Jinx*," *Feminist Media Studies* 23, no. 3 (2022): 4.

17 *Unbreakable Kimmy Schmidt*, season 4, episode 3, "Party Monster: Scratching the Surface," written by Meredith Scardino, released May 30, 2018, Netflix Original.
18 *Unbreakable Kimmy Schmidt*, season 2, episode 3, "Kimmy Goes to a Play!," written by Sam Means, released April 15, 2016, Netflix Original.
19 *Unbreakable Kimmy Schmidt*, season 3, episode 13, "Kimmy Bites an Onion!," written by Meredith Scardino and Allison Silverman, released May 19, 2017, Netflix Original.
20 *Unbreakable Kimmy Schmidt*, season 4, episode 1, "Kimmy Is . . . Little Girl, Big City!," written by Sam Means, released May 30, 2018, Netflix Original.
21 *Unbreakable Kimmy Schmidt*, season 4, episode 4, "Kimmy Disrupts the Paradigm," written by Leila Strachan, released May 30, 2018, Netflix Original.
22 *Unbreakable Kimmy Schmidt*, season 4, episode 12, "Kimmy Says Bye!," written by Robert Carlock and Tina Fey, released January 25, 2019, Netflix Original.
23 Wendy Brown, *In the Ruins of Neoliberalism: The Rise of Antidemocratic Politics in the West* (New York: Columbia University Press, 2019), 44.
24 *Unbreakable Kimmy Schmidt*, season 1, episode 6, "Kimmy Goes to School!," written by Dan Rubin and Lon Zimmet, released March 6, 2015, Netflix Original.
25 *Unbreakable Kimmy Schmidt*, season 3, episode 2, "Kimmy's Roommate Lemonades!," written by Tina Fey and Sam Means, released May 19, 2017, Netflix Original.
26 *Unbreakable Kimmy Schmidt*, "Kimmy's Roommate Lemonades!"
27 Cáit Neylon, "Irrational Exuberance: Cuteness as Affective Bubble in *Crazy Ex-Girlfriend* and *Unbreakable Kimmy Schmidt*," *Feminist Media Studies* 23, no. 5 (2022): 2.
28 *Unbreakable Kimmy Schmidt*, "Kimmy's Roommate Lemonades!"
29 Lauren Berlant, *Cruel Optimism* (Durham, N.C.: Duke University Press, 2011), 167.
30 *Unbreakable Kimmy Schmidt*, season 2, episode 7, "Kimmy Walks into a Bar!," written by Leila Strachan, released April 15, 2016, Netflix Original.
31 *Unbreakable Kimmy Schmidt*, season 3, episode 10, "Kimmy Pulls Off a Heist!," written by Nick Bernardone and Bridger Winegar, released May 19, 2017, Netflix Original.
32 Rahul Rao, "Neoliberal Antiracism and the British University," *Radical Philosophy* 208 (2020): 49.
33 *Unbreakable Kimmy Schmidt*, season 3, episode 12, "Kimmy and the Trolley Problem!," written by Sam Means, released May 19, 2017, Netflix Original.
34 *Unbreakable Kimmy Schmidt*, "Kimmy and the Trolley Problem!"
35 Orgad, "Survivor," 150.
36 Orgad, "Survivor," 150.
37 Orgad, "Survivor," 152.
38 *Unbreakable Kimmy Schmidt*, season 2, episode 11, "Kimmy Meets a Celebrity!," written by Josh Siegal and Dylan Morgan, released April 15, 2016, Netflix Original.
39 *Unbreakable Kimmy Schmidt*, "Kimmy Meets a Celebrity!"
40 *Unbreakable Kimmy Schmidt*, "Kimmy and the Trolley Problem!"
41 *Unbreakable Kimmy Schmidt*, season 2, episode 10, "Kimmy Goes to Her Happy Place!," written by Emily Altman and Robert Carlock, released April 15, 2016, Netflix Original.
42 Rosalind Gill, "The Affective, Cultural and Psychic Life of Postfeminism: A Postfeminist Sensibility 10 Years On," *European Journal of Cultural Studies* 20, no. 6 (2017): 607.

43 Akane Kanai, "On Not Taking the Self Seriously: Resilience, Relatability and Humour in Young Women's Tumblr Blogs," *European Journal of Cultural Studies* 22, no. 1 (2019): 60–77.
44 Rosalind Gill, "Post-Postfeminism? New Feminist Visibilities in Postfeminist Times," *Feminist Media Studies* 16, no. 4 (2016): 618. Emphasis in original.
45 Kanai, "Not Taking," 67.
46 Rebecca Traister, *Good and Mad: The Revolutionary Power of Women's Anger* (New York: Simon and Schuster, 2018), 209.
47 Traister, *Good and Mad.*
48 Brittney Cooper, *Eloquent Rage: A Black Feminist Discovers Her Superpower* (New York: St. Martin's, 2018), 204.
49 Kanai, "Not Taking"; Gill, "Post-Postfeminism?," 610–630.
50 Alex Abad-Santos and Caroline Framke, "Why Does Kimmy Schmidt Keep Choosing Race as a Hill to Die On?," *Vox*, April 19, 2016, https://www.vox.com/2016/4/19/11441502/unbreakable-kimmy-schmidt-race-season-2.
51 *Unbreakable Kimmy Schmidt*, "Kimmy Goes to a Play!"
52 David Chison Oh, "'Opting Out of That': White Feminism's Policing and Disavowal of Anti-Racist Critique in *The Unbreakable Kimmy Schmidt*," *Critical Studies in Media Communication* 37, no. 1 (2020): 59.
53 Christopher Medjesky, "How Can Rape Be Funny: Comic Persona, Irony, and the Limits of Rape Jokes," in *Standing Up, Speaking Out: Stand-Up Comedy and the Rhetoric of Social Change*, ed. Matthew R. Meier and Casey R. Schmitt (New York: Routledge, 2017), 208.
54 Oh, "Opting Out," 62.
55 Oh, "Opting Out," 65.
56 *Unbreakable Kimmy Schmidt*, season 2, episode 8, "Kimmy Goes to a Hotel!," written by Tina Fey and Sam Means, released April 15, 2016, Netflix Original.
57 *Unbreakable Kimmy Schmidt*, season 3, episode 5, "Kimmy Steps on a Crack!," written by Leila Strachan, released May 19, 2017, Netflix Original.
58 *Unbreakable Kimmy Schmidt*, "Kimmy Is . . . Little Girl."
59 Sarah Kornfield and Hannah Jones, "#MeToo on TV: Popular Feminism and Episodic Sexual Violence," *Feminist Media Studies* 22, no. 7 (2022): 1657–1672.
60 Hilary Lewis, "Inside 'Kimmy Schmidt's' Sexual Harassment Storyline," *Hollywood Reporter*, June 1, 2018, https://www.hollywoodreporter.com/tv/tv-news/kimmy-schmidt-sexual-harassment-storyline-explained-1116416/.
61 Lewis, "Inside 'Kimmy.'"
62 *Unbreakable Kimmy Schmidt: Kimmy vs. the Reverend*, screenplay by Robert Carlock, Tina Fey, Meredith Scardino, and Sam Means, released May 12, 2020, Netflix Original.
63 *Unbreakable Kimmy Schmidt*, season 3, episode 8, "Kimmy Does a Puzzle!," written by Tina Fey, released March 19, 2017, Netflix Original.
64 Dana Cloud, "The Irony Bribe and Reality Television: Investment and Detachment in *The Bachelor*," *Critical Studies in Media Communication* 27, no. 5 (2010): 413–437.
65 Cloud, "Irony Bribe," 431.
66 *Unbreakable Kimmy Schmidt*, "Kimmy Says Bye!"
67 Havas and Horeck, "Netflix Feminism."

Chapter 3 Exquisitely Lonely

1 Malina Saval, "Women Rule Drama Series Emmy Race," *Variety*, August 20, 2015, https://variety.com/2015/tv/spotlight/drama-series-emmy-race-women-strong-female-characters-1201572968/.

2 Saval, "Women Rule."

3 Willa Paskin, "Nothing like a Jew Eating a Pickle and You Put Some Christmas Carols Over It," Vulture, November 27, 2017, https://www.vulture.com/2017/11/amy-sherman-palladino-the-marvelous-mrs-maisel.html.

4 Alexis Soloski, "Did You Hear the One About the Housewife Who Walks into a Comedy Club?," *New York Times*, November 21, 2017, https://www.nytimes.com/2017/11/21/arts/television/marvelous-mrs-maisel-amazon-amy-sherman-palladino.html.

5 Jeremy Shere, host, *Adventures in Jewish Studies: The Association for Jewish Studies Podcast*, episode 7, "The Marvelous Mrs. Carroll," December 16, 2019, https://www.associationforjewishstudies.org/podcasts/the-marvelous-mrs-carroll-episode-transcript.

6 "The Marvelous Mrs. Maisel: Awards," IMDb, accessed April 28, 2025, https://www.imdb.com/title/tt5788792/awards/?ref_=tt_awd.

7 Emily Farra, "Power Dressing *The Marvelous Mrs. Maisel* Way," *Vogue*, January 9, 2019, https://www.vogue.com/article/marvelous-mrs-maisel-fashion-best-outfits-golden-globes.

8 Faith Karimi, "'The Queen's Gambit' Is Sparking a Surge of Interest in Chess," *CNN*, December 6, 2020, https://www.cnn.com/2020/12/06/us/queens-gambit-chess-popularity-trnd/index.html.

9 Peter White, "'The Queen's Gambit' Becomes Netflix's Biggest Scripted Limited Series with 62M Checking Chess Drama," *Deadline*, November 23, 2020, https://deadline.com/2020/11/queens-gambit-62m-viewers-netflix-1234620378/.

10 Karimi, "Queen's Gambit."

11 Dylan Loeb McClain, "How 'The Queen's Gambit' Is Inspiring Women to Take Up Chess," *New York Times*, December 10, 2020, https://www.nytimes.com/2020/12/10/arts/television/queens-gambit-netflix-chess.html.

12 Bonnie J. Dow, "Femininity and Feminism in *Murphy Brown*," *Southern Communication Journal* 57, no. 2 (1992): 144.

13 Betty Friedan, *The Feminine Mystique*, reissue ed. (New York: Dell/Laurel, 1984), 15.

14 *The Queen's Gambit*, episode 4, "Middle Game," written by Scott Frank, released October 23, 2020, Netflix Original.

15 *The Marvelous Mrs. Maisel*, season 2, episode 9, "Vote for Kennedy, Vote for Kennedy," written by Daniel Palladino, released December 5, 2018, Amazon Prime Video Original.

16 *The Queen's Gambit*, episode 1, "Openings," written by Scott Frank, released October 23, 2020, Netflix Original.

17 *Queen's Gambit*, "Openings."

18 Rachel Syme, "'The Queen's Gambit' Is the Most Satisfying Show on Television," *New Yorker*, November 13, 2020, https://www.newyorker.com/culture/on-television/the-queens-gambit-is-the-most-satisfying-show-on-television.

19 James Poniewozik, "Review: In 'The Marvelous Mrs. Maisel,' a Comic Asks, Take My Strife, Please," *New York Times*, November 28, 2017, https://www.nytimes.com/2017/11/28/arts/television/marvelous-mrs-maisel-tv-review.html.

20 *The Marvelous Mrs. Maisel*, season 3, episode 8, "A Jewish Girl Walks into the Apollo . . . ," written by Amy Sherman-Palladino, released December 6, 2019, Amazon Prime Video Original.
21 *The Marvelous Mrs. Maisel*, season 3, episode 5, "It's Comedy or Cabbage," written by Amy Sherman-Palladino, released December 6, 2019, Amazon Prime Video Original.
22 *The Marvelous Mrs. Maisel*, season 4, episode 8, "How Do You Get to Carnegie Hall," written by Amy Sherman-Palladino, released April 14, 2023, Amazon Prime Video Original.
23 *The Queen's Gambit*, episode 5, "Fork," written by Scott Frank, released October 23, 2020, Netflix Original.
24 *The Queen's Gambit*, episode 2, "Exchanges," written by Scott Frank, released October 23, 2020, Netflix Original.
25 *The Queen's Gambit*, episode 7, "End Game," written by Scott Frank, released October 23, 2020, Netflix Original.
26 Aja Romano, "What We Still Haven't Learned from Gamergate," *Vox*, January 7, 2021, https://www.vox.com/culture/2020/1/20/20808875/gamergate-lessons-cultural-impact-changes-harassment-laws.
27 Sarah Banet-Weiser, *Empowered: Popular Feminism and Popular Misogyny* (Durham, N.C.: Duke University Press, 2018), 154.
28 *The Marvelous Mrs. Maisel*, season 5, episode 8, "The Princess and the Plea," written by Daniel Palladino, released May 19, 2023, Amazon Prime Video Original.
29 John Stuart Mill, *The Subjection of Women*, 2nd ed. (London: Longmans, Green, Reader, and Dyer, 1869), 32–34.
30 Mill, *Subjection of Women*, 48–49.
31 Kristen Hoerl, *The Bad Sixties: Hollywood Memories of the Counterculture, Antiwar, and Black Power Movements* (Jackson: University Press of Mississippi, 2018), 15.
32 Kristen Hoerl, "Selective Amnesia and Racial Transcendence in News Coverage of President Obama's Inauguration," *Quarterly Journal of Speech* 98, no. 2 (2012): 180.
33 Lynn Spigel, "Postfeminist Nostalgia for a Prefeminist Future," *Screen* 54, no. 2 (2013): 271.
34 Spigel, "Postfeminist Nostalgia," 275.
35 Willa Paskin, "Amy Sherman-Palladino Is About to Debut Her Most Ambitious Show Yet," Vulture, November 28, 2017, https://www.vulture.com/2017/11/amy-sherman-palladino-the-marvelous-mrs-maisel.html.
36 Sarah Ahmed, *The Promise of Happiness* (Durham, N.C.: Duke University Press, 2010), 65.
37 Banet-Weiser, *Empowered*, 15; Rosalind Gill and Akane Kanai, "Mediating Neoliberal Capitalism: Affect, Subjectivity and Inequality," *Journal of Communication* 68, no. 2 (2018): 322.
38 Alexis Soloski, "'The Marvelous Mrs. Maisel' Takes Its Final Curtsy," *New York Times*, April 11, 2023, https://www.nytimes.com/2023/04/11/arts/television/the-marvelous-mrs-maisel-final-season.html.
39 Rhonda Garelick, "The Sorcerer of Costumes," *New York Times*, August 1, 2023, https://www.nytimes.com/2023/08/01/style/maisel-costume-designer.html.
40 Garelick, "Sorcerer of Costumes."
41 Jessica Radloff, "The Marvelous Mrs. Maisel Finale: We Bet You Didn't Catch These Hidden Details," *Glamour*, May 26, 2023, https://www.glamour.com/story/the-marvelous-mrs-maisel-series-finale-recap-details.

42 Soloski, "Marvelous Mrs. Maisel."

43 Julia Hobbs, "'The Queen's Gambit' Costume Designer Reveals the Hidden Meanings Behind Anya Taylor-Joy's Winning On-Screen Style," *Vogue*, November 8, 2020, https://vogue.sg/the-queens-gambit-costume-designer-reveals-the-hidden-meanings-behind-anya-taylor-joys-winning-on-screen-style/#:~:text=We%20wanted%20to%20create%20a,her%20mother%20is%20with%20her.

44 Rachael Burrow Rummel, "We Can't Stop Thinking About 'The Queen's Gambit' Midcentury Maximalism," *Veranda*, February 28, 2021, https://www.veranda.com/home-decorators/g34752693/queens-gambit-set-design/; Sidra Khokhar, "An Architectural Review of *The Queen's Gambit*," *Rethinking the Future* (blog), accessed April 28, 2025, https://www.re-thinkingthefuture.com/rtf-architectural-reviews/a6251-an-architectural-review-of-the-queens-gambit/; Julie Vadnal, "*The Queen's Gambit* Set Designer Tells Us How to Get That '60s Look at Home," *Domino*, October 12, 2018, https://www.domino.com/content/queens-gambit-set-design/.

45 Julia Felsenthal, "You're Going to Want to Watch 'The Marvelous Mrs. Maisel,'" *Vogue*, November 29, 2017, https://www.vogue.com/article/marvelous-mrs-maisel-amazon-review.

46 Dominic Patten, "Netflix Hit with $5M Suit over 'Sexism' of 'Queen's Gambit' Line About Soviet Chess Legend," *Deadline*, September 16, 2021, https://deadline.com/2021/09/queens-gambit-lawsuit-netflix-nona-gaprindashvili-1234838186/.

47 Syme, "Queen's Gambit."

48 Danielle Braff, "'Queen's Gambit' Costumes Make Us Want to Toss Our Leggings," *New York Times*, November 10, 2020, https://www.nytimes.com/2020/11/10/style/queens-gambit-clothes.html.

49 Andrea Wurzburger, "Ranking Anya Taylor-Joy's Winning Outfits in 'The Queen's Gambit,'" *People*, November 14, 2022, https://people.com/style/queens-gambit-costumes-ranked/.

50 Cristina Corvino, "Take a Walk Down 'Maisel' Memory Lane with Midge's Best Looks," *Town and Country*, April 21, 2023, https://www.townandcountrymag.com/leisure/arts-and-culture/g43555281/best-marvelous-mrs-maisel-outfits/; Jake Dee, "Netflix's *The Queen's Gambit*: Beth's 10 Best Outfits, Ranked," *ScreenRant*, November 17, 2020, https://screenrant.com/netflix-the-queens-gambit-beth-best-outfits-ranked/; Sophie Leen, "15 Best Fashion Moments from *The Queen's Gambit*," *Cosmopolitan*, November 20, 2020, https://www.cosmopolitan.com/uk/fashion/style/g34687342/the-queens-gambit-fashion/; Hannah Malach, "The Best Looks from Season Five of 'The Marvelous Mrs. Maisel' So Far," *Women's Wear Daily*, April 30, 2023, https://wwd.com/pop-culture/culture-news/marvelous-mrs-maisel-season-five-best-looks-1235632588/.

51 Lara Walsh, "10 of Midge's Best Outfits in 'The Marvelous Mrs. Maisel,'" *Insider*, October 22, 2018, https://www.insider.com/the-marvelous-mrs-maisel-best-outfits-2018-10; Wurzburger, "Ranking Anya Taylor-Joy's Winning Outfits"; National Women's History Museum. "History of Paper Dolls and Popular Culture," November 20, 2016, https://www.womenshistory.org/articles/history-paper-dolls-and-popular-culture.

52 Nicola Dall'Asen, "*The Marvelous Mrs. Maisel* Is Back for Season 3, and We Have All the Details on Midge's Beauty Look," *Allure*, December 5, 2019, https://www.allure.com/story/marvelous-mrs-maisel-hair-makeup-products; Farra, "Power Dressing"; Kia D. Goosby, "How to Recreate 7 'Queen's Gambit' Outfits," *Vanity Fair*, March 24, 2021, https://www.vanityfair.com/style/2021/03/how-to-recreate

-7-queens-gambit-outfits; Christie Griffin, "'Marvelous Mrs. Maisel' Lipstick: A Clean Beauty Fave," *CNN*, January 2, 2020, https://www.cnn.com/2020/01/02/cnn-underscored/marvelous-mrs-maisel-lipstick; Kara Kia, "The Queen's Gambit: How to Dress Like Grandmaster and '60s Babe Beth Harmon," *PopSugar*, November 10, 2020, https://www.popsugar.com/fashion/beth-harmons-style-in-the-queens-gambit-47957461; Bee Shapiro, "What the Marvelous Mrs. Maisel Wears Offscreen," *New York Times*, November 27, 2019, https://www.nytimes.com/2019/11/27/style/skin-care-beauty-what-the-marvelous-mrs-maisel-wears-offscreen.html; Phebe Wahl, "Anya Taylor-Joy Is a Master of Her Craft," *Gotham*, November 16, 2022, http://gothammag.com/anya-taylor-joy-cover-story-interview.

53 Cal McNeil, "Bid Now! Marvelous Mrs. Maisel Coat Benefits Fashion Manufacturing Initiative," CDFA, October 24, 2019, https://cfda.com/news/bid-now-marvelous-mrs-maisel-coat-benefits-fashion-manufacturing-initiative.

54 Garelick, "Sorcerer of Costumes."

55 *The Marvelous Mrs. Maisel*, season 1, episode 2, "Ya Shivu v Bolshom Dome Na Kholme," written by Amy Sherman-Palladino, released November 29, 2017, Amazon Prime Video Original.

56 Robert Goldman, Deborah Heath, and Sharon Smith, "Commodity Feminism," *Critical Studies in Mass Communication* 8, no. 3 (1991): 338.

57 Goldman et al., "Commodity Feminism," 336.

58 Joe Tompkins, "The Makings of a Contradictory Franchise: Revolutionary Melodrama and Cynicism in *The Hunger Games*," *JCMS: Journal of Cinema and Media Studies* 58, no. 1 (2018): 70–90.

59 *Marvelous Mrs. Maisel*, "It's Comedy or Cabbage."

60 *The Queen's Gambit*, episode 6, "Adjournment," written by Scott Frank, released October 23, 2020, Netflix Original.

61 Sarah Miller, "The Fatal Flaw of 'The Queen's Gambit,'" *New Yorker*, December 1, 2020, https://www.newyorker.com/culture/culture-desk/the-fatal-flaw-of-the-queens-gambit.

62 Goldman et al., "Commodity Feminism," 338.

63 Lindsay Geller, "Why the Color Pink in 'Marvelous Mrs. Maisel' Is So Important, According to Amy Sherman-Palladino," *Women's Health*, December 6, 2019, https://www.womenshealthmag.com/life/a30125402/marvelous-mrs-maisel-pink-hidden-meaning/.

64 Radloff, "Marvelous Mrs. Maisel Finale."

65 Hobbs, "Queen's Gambit."

66 Alex Bevan, *The Aesthetics of Nostalgia TV* (New York: Bloomsbury, 2019), 135.

67 Bevan, *Aesthetics*, 135.

68 Bevan, *Aesthetics*, 16, 139.

69 *Creating the Queen's Gambit*, directed by Scott Frank, released January 10, 2021, Netflix Original.

70 Goldman et al., "Commodity Feminism," 338.

71 Susan Douglas, *Enlightened Sexism: The Seductive Message That Feminism's Work Is Done* (New York: Henry Holt, 2010), 10.

72 Douglas, *Enlightened Sexism*, 9.

73 Douglas, *Enlightened Sexism*, 16–17.

74 *The Marvelous Mrs. Maisel*, season 2, episode 7, "Look, She Made a Hat," written by Amy Sherman-Palladino, released December 5, 2018, Amazon Prime Video Original.

75 Catherine A. Rottenberg, *The Rise of Neoliberal Feminism* (New York: Oxford University Press, 2018).
76 Angela McRobbie, "Notes on the Perfect: Competitive Femininity in Neoliberal Times," *Australian Feminist Studies* 30, no. 83 (January 2, 2015): 4.
77 Angela McRobbie, *Feminism and the Politics of Resilience: Essays on Gender, Media and the End of Welfare* (Medford, Mass.: Polity, 2020), 43.
78 McRobbie, *Feminism*, 43.
79 McRobbie, *Feminism*, 44.
80 McRobbie, *Feminism*, 49, 66–69.
81 Robin James, *Resilience & Melancholy: Pop Music, Feminism, Neoliberalism* (Winchester, U.K.: Zero, 2015), 85.
82 James, *Resilience & Melancholy*, 84. Emphasis in original.
83 James, *Resilience & Melancholy*, 80.
84 Elspeth Probyn, "New Traditionalism and Post-Feminism: TV Does the Home," *Screen* 31, no. 2 (1990): 147–159.
85 Michaela D. E. Meyer, "The Good Wife's Fatalistic Feminism: Televised Feminist Failures in Work/Life Balance, Romance, and Feminist Alliances," in *Women, Feminism, and Pop Politics: From "Bitch" to "Badass" and Beyond*, ed. Karrin Vasby Anderson (New York: Peter Lang, 2018), 213.
86 Soloski, "Marvelous Mrs. Maisel."
87 Paskin, "Nothing like a Jew."
88 *Creating the Queen's Gambit*.
89 *Queen's Gambit*, "Middle Game."
90 *Creating the Queen's Gambit*.
91 Rottenberg, *Rise of Neoliberal Feminism*.
92 *Queen's Gambit*, "End Game."
93 Casey Ryan Kelly, "Donald J. Trump and the Rhetoric of White Ambivalence," *Rhetoric and Public Affairs* 23, no. 2 (2020): 195–224.
94 Kelly, "Donald J. Trump," 197.
95 Kelly, "Donald J. Trump," 197.
96 *Marvelous Mrs. Maisel*, "Jewish Girl Walks."
97 *The Marvelous Mrs. Maisel*, season 4, episode 1, "Rumble on the Wonder Wheel," written by Amy Sherman-Palladino, released February 17, 2022, Amazon Prime Video Original.
98 *The Marvelous Mrs. Maisel*, season 4, episode 2, "Billy Jones and the Orgy Lamps," written by Amy Sherman-Palladino, released February 17, 2022, Amazon Prime Video Original.
99 See Ruby Hamad, *White Tears / Brown Scars: How White Feminism Betrays Women of Color* (New York: Catapult, 2020); Dreama G. Moon and Michelle A. Holling, "'White Supremacy in Heels': (White) Feminism, White Supremacy, and Discursive Violence," *Communication and Critical/Cultural Studies* 17, no. 2 (2020): 253–260; Rafia Zakaria, *Against White Feminism: Notes on Disruption* (New York: W. W. Norton, 2021).
100 Meredith Neville-Shepard, "'Better Never Means Better for Everyone': White Feminist Necropolitics and Hulu's *The Handmaid's Tale*," *Quarterly Journal of Speech* 109, no. 1 (2023): 5.
101 *The Marvelous Mrs. Maisel*, season 4, episode 5, "How to Chew Quietly and Influence People," written by Kate Fodor, released March 4, 2022, Amazon Prime Video Original.

102 Neville-Shepard, "Better Never Means Better," 6.

103 Hamad, *White Tears*, 108–109. Emphasis in original.

104 Gillian Bennett, "*Marvelous Mrs. Maisel* Season 5, Midge, and Amy Sherman-Palladino's Bad, Funny Ladies," *Paste*, May 12, 2023, https://www.pastemagazine.com/tv/amazon-prime-video/marvelous-mrs-maisel-season-5-episode-6-midge-antihero; Arielle Bernstein, "Midge Goes Straight Up Antihero in a Rollercoaster of a Season Finale on *The Marvelous Mrs. Maisel*," *AV Club*, December 8, 2019, https://www.avclub.com/midge-goes-straight-up-antihero-in-a-rollercoaster-of-a-1840303055.

105 For a discussion of responsibilization in neoliberal feminist discourse, see McRobbie, *Feminism*, 47.

106 Aviva Dove-Viebahn, *There She Goes Again: Gender, Power, and Knowledge in Contemporary Film and Television Franchises* (New Brunswick, N.J.: Rutgers University Press, 2024), 4. Emphasis in original.

Chapter 4 Insanely Gifted

1 Andrew Romano, "Why *Game of Thrones* Is the Best Fantasy Show Ever and You'll Love Season 4," *Daily Beast*, July 12, 2017, https://www.thedailybeast.com/why-game-of-thrones-is-the-best-fantasy-show-ever-and-youll-love-season-4; Tim Goodman, "*Game of Thrones* Season 2: Tim Goodman, 'Game of Thrones' Season 2: TV Review," *Hollywood Reporter*, March 27, 2012, https://web.archive.org/web/20170125162126/http://edit.hollywoodreporter.com/review/game-of-thrones-hbo-peter-dinklage-george-martin-304869.

2 James Hibberd, "*Game of Thrones* Makes Emmy History: Most Awards Ever," *Entertainment Weekly*, September 18, 2016, https://ew.com/article/2016/09/18/game-thrones-emmys-2/.

3 Gaby Del Valle, "'Khaleesi' Became Shorthand for a Strong Empowered Woman," *Vox*, April 26, 2019, https://www.vox.com/the-goods/2019/4/26/18516599/daenerys-targaryen-feminism-merch-game-of-thrones.

4 Tanya Ghahremani, "Daenerys Targaryen Is a Feminist," *Bustle*, November 7, 2013, https://www.bustle.com/articles/8327-game-of-thrones-daenerys-targaryen-is-a-feminist-first-mother-of-dragons-second.

5 Del Valle, "'Khaleesi' Became Shorthand."

6 Del Valle, "'Khaleesi' Became Shorthand."

7 Laura Bogart, "The Rise of the Political She-ro," *Week*, July 17, 2017, https://web.archive.org/web/20200121212727/https://theweek.com/articles/709496/rise-political-shero.

8 Concepción Cascajosa Virino and Vicente Rodriquez Ortega, "Daenerys Targaryen Will Save Spain: *Game of Thrones*, Politics, and the Public Sphere," *Television and New Media* 20, no. 5 (2019): 423–442.

9 Elizabeth Warren, "The World Needs Fewer Cersei Lannisters," *Cut*, April 21, 2019, https://www.thecut.com/2019/04/elizabeth-warren-review-game-of-thrones-season-8.html.

10 Parker Richards, "How *Game of Thrones* Lost Its Way as a Political Drama," *Atlantic*, May 24, 2019, https://web.archive.org/web/20190607115317/https://www.theatlantic.com/entertainment/archive/2019/05/game-thrones-lost-its-way-political-drama/590260/.

11 Emily St. James, "Why Everybody's So Mad About Daenerys Targaryen," *Vox*, May 17, 2019, https://www.vox.com/culture/2019/5/17/18624767/game-of-thrones-series-finale-season-8-episode-5-the-bells-daenerys-dany-kings-landing-targaryen.

12 Keshav Kant, "Daenerys Stormborn: Annoying White Saviour of House Targaryen," *Off Colour*, August 25, 2017, https://offcolour.org/2017/08/25/daenerys-stormborn-annoying-white-saviour-of-house-targaryen/.

13 Helen Young, "*Game of Thrones*' Racism Problem," *Public Medievalist*, July 21, 2017, https://publicmedievalist.com/game-thrones-racism-problem.

14 Raka Shome, *Diana and Beyond: White Femininity, National Identity, and Contemporary Media Culture* (Urbana: University of Illinois Press, 2014), 2.

15 *Game of Thrones*, season 1, episode 1, "Winter Is Coming," written by David Benioff and D. B. Weiss, original airdate April 17, 2011, HBO Original.

16 For a discussion of racist tropes used in Hollywood portrayals of Arabs, see Jack Shaheen, *Reel Bad Arabs: How Hollywood Vilifies a People* (Ithaca, N.Y.: Olive Branch, 2012).

17 Sarah Hagelin and Gillian Silverman, *The New Female Antihero: The Disruptive Women of Twenty-First-Century US Television* (Chicago: University of Chicago Press, 2022), 28–29.

18 Jill Gutowitz, "I'm Tired of Male Screenwriters Using Rape as a Convenient Backstory for Women," *Glamour*, January 18, 2018, https://www.glamour.com/story/keira-knightley-on-rape-backstory-in-movies-tv-shows; Ellen Vanstone, "How Has Rape Become Such a Common Trope of Television Drama," *Globe and Mail*, September 16, 2016, https://www.theglobeandmail.com/arts/television/how-has-rape-become-such-a-common-trope-of-television-drama/article31931181.

19 Sarah Projansky, *Watching Rape: Film and Television in Postfeminist Culture* (New York: New York University Press, 2001), 97.

20 Tanya Horeck, *Public Rape: Representing Violation in Fiction and Film* (New York: Routledge, 2003), 17.

21 Sarah Hagelin, *Reel Vulnerability: Power, Pain, and Gender in Contemporary American Film and Television* (New Brunswick, N.J.: Rutgers University Press, 2013).

22 Hagelin, *Reel Vulnerability*, 15.

23 Helen Young, *Race and Popular Fantasy Literature: Habits of Whiteness* (New York: Routledge, 2016).

24 Jenny Sharpe, *Allegories of Empire: The Figure of Woman in the Colonial Text* (Minneapolis: University of Minnesota Press, 1993).

25 *Game of Thrones*, season 1, episode 6, "A Golden Crown," written by David Benioff, D. B. Weiss, and Jane Espenson, original airdate May 22, 2011, HBO Original.

26 Alison Phipps cites Achille Mbembe to discuss the female characters on *Game of Thrones* as illustrations of white feminism's imbrications with necropolitics. Alison Phipps, *#MeToo Not You: The Trouble with Mainstream Feminism* (Manchester: Manchester University Press, 2020), 120–123; Achille Mbembe, "Necropolitics (Translated by Libby Meintjes)," *Public Culture* 15, no. 1 (2003): 11–40.

27 Gayatri Chakravorty Spivak, "Can the Subaltern Speak," in *Marxism and the Interpretation of Culture*, ed. Cary Nelson and Lawrence Grossberg (Urbana: University of Illinois Press, 1988), 297.

28 María Menéndez Menéndez and Marta Fernández Morales, "Every Flight Begins with a Fall: Approaching Sexual Violence in Game of Thrones," *Cuadernos* 47 (2019): 224.

29 Menéndez and Morales, "Every Flight," 223.

30 Kathleen Murphey, "The Phoenix Moment as Another Vehicle for Normalizing Rape Culture," *Pennsylvania Literary Journal* 11, no. 2 (2019): 190.
31 *Game of Thrones*, season 3, episode 4, "And Now His Watch Has Ended," written by David Benioff and D. B. Weiss, original airdate April 21, 2013, HBO Original.
32 Hagelin and Silverman, *New Female Antihero*, 34.
33 Hagelin and Silverman, *New Female Antihero*, 38–39.
34 Hagelin and Silverman, *New Female Antihero*, 38.
35 Rikke Schubart, "Woman with Dragons: Daenerys, Pride, and Postfeminist Possibilities," in *Women of Ice and Fire: Gender,* Game of Thrones, *and Multiple Media Engagements*, ed. Anne Gjelsvik and Rikke Schubart (New York: Bloomsbury Academic), 106.
36 See Hagelin and Silverman, *New Female Antihero*, 31–33.
37 Shome, *Diana and Beyond*, 5.
38 Shome, *Diana and Beyond*, 113.
39 Shome, *Diana and Beyond*, 113.
40 *Game of Thrones*, season 1, episode 8, "The Pointy End," written by Geroge R. R. Martin, original airdate June 5, 2011, HBO Original.
41 Sharpe, *Allegories of Empire*, 11.
42 *Game of Thrones*, "Pointy End."
43 Young, *Race and Popular Fantasy Literature*, 68.
44 Sharpe, *Allegories of Empire*, 4.
45 Raka Shome, "Transnational Feminism and Communication Studies," *Communication Review* 9, no. 4 (2006): 261.
46 Sharpe, *Allegories of Empire*, 10.
47 Sharpe, *Allegories of Empire*, 10.
48 *Game of Thrones*, season 3, episode 10, "Mhysa," written by David Benioff and D. B. Weiss, original airdate June 9, 2013, HBO Original.
49 Shome, *Diana and Beyond*, 121.
50 Shome, *Diana and Beyond*, 121. See also Richard Dyer, *White* (New York: Routledge, 1997).
51 *Game of Thrones*, "Mhysa."
52 *Game of Thrones*, season 1, episode 10, "Fire and Blood," written by David Benioff and D. B. Weiss, original airdate June 19, 2011, HBO Original.
53 Lila Abu-Lughod, *Do Muslim Women Need Saving?* (Cambridge, Mass.: Harvard University Press, 2013).
54 See Chandra Talpade Mohanty, *Feminism Without Borders: Decolonizing Theory, Practicing Solidarity* (Durham, N.C.: Duke University Press, 2003).
55 Jenna N. Hanchey, *The Center Cannot Hold: Decolonial Possibility in the Collapse of a Tanzanian NGO* (Durham, N.C.: Duke University Press, 2023), 62.
56 Dakota J. Sandras and Kristen Hoerl, "The Next [White] Thing: Neocolonial White Feminism in Disney's *Frozen II*," *Critical Studies in Media Communication* 41, no. 2 (2024): 105–120.
57 *Game of Thrones*, season 4, episode 3, "Breaker of Chains," written by David Benioff and D. B. Weiss, original airdate April 20, 2014, HBO Original.
58 *Game of Thrones*, season 4, episode 10, "The Children," written by David Benioff and D. B. Weiss, original airdate June 15, 2014, HBO Original.
59 Saidiya Hartman, *Scenes of Subjection: Terror, Slavery, and Self-Making in Nineteenth-Century America* (Oxford: Oxford University Press, 1997), 116.
60 Hartman, *Scenes of Subjection*, 6.

61 Hartman, *Scenes of Subjection*, 117.
62 *Game of Thrones*, season 6, episode 3, "Oathbreaker," written by David Benioff and D. B. Weiss, original airdate May 8, 2016, HBO Original.
63 *Game of Thrones*, season 5, episode 2, "The House of Black and White," written by David Benioff and D. B. Weiss, original airdate April 19, 2015, HBO Original.
64 *Game of Thrones*, season 5, episode 1, "The Wars to Come," written by David Benioff and D. B. Weiss, original airdate April 12, 2015, HBO Original.
65 *Game of Thrones*, season 5, episode 8, "Hardhome," written by David Benioff and D. B. Weiss, original airdate May 31, 2015, HBO Original.
66 *Game of Thrones*, "Hardhome."
67 *Game of Thrones*, season 8, episode 5, "The Bells," written by David Benioff and D. B. Weiss, original airdate May 12, 2019, HBO Original.
68 *Game of Thrones*, season 7, episode 7, "The Spoils of War," written by David Benioff and D. B. Weiss, original airdate August 6, 2017, HBO Original.
69 *Game of Thrones*, season 7, episode 2, "Stormborn," written by Bryan Cogman, original airdate July 23, 2017, HBO Original.
70 *Game of Thrones*, season 7, episode 5, "Eastwatch," written by Dave Hill, original airdate August 27, 2017, HBO Original.
71 *Game of Thrones*, season 8, episode 4, "The Last of the Starks," written by David Benioff and D. B. Weiss, original airdate May 5, 2019, HBO Original.
72 *Game of Thrones*, "Last of the Starks."
73 *Game of Thrones*, "Bells."
74 Karrin Vasby Anderson, "Every Woman Is the Wrong Woman: The Female Presidentiality Paradox," *Women's Studies in Communication* 40, no. 2 (2017): 132–135.
75 *Game of Thrones*, "Bells."
76 *Game of Thrones*, season 8, episode 6, "The Iron Throne," written by David Benioff and D. B. Weiss, original airdate May 19, 2019, HBO Original.
77 Mikkel Bolt Rasmussen, *Late Capitalist Fascism* (Medford, Mass.: Polity, 2022), 5.
78 *Game of Thrones*, "Iron Throne."
79 Mel Robbins, "Hillary Clinton and the Clueless Hormone Argument," *CNN*, April 21, 2015, https://www.cnn.com/2015/04/20/opinions/robbins-hillary-clinton.
80 Hagelin and Silverman, *New Female Antihero*, 204.
81 Abigail Kahler, "Mother of Dragons: White Feminist Imperialism in HBO's Game of Thrones" (master's thesis, College of William and Mary, 2020), 30.

Chapter 5 Gangster Girlboss

1 *Queen of the South*, season 3, episode 12, "Justicia," written by Dailyn Rodriguez and Ryan O'Nan, original airdate September 6, 2018, USA Network.
2 Catherine A. Rottenberg, *The Rise of Neoliberal Feminism* (New York: Oxford University Press, 2018), 148.
3 Javier Ramirez, "Prestige Adaptation by Design: The Commercial Appeal of Latinx Tropes in *Queen of the South*," in *Prestige Television: Cultural and Artistic Value in Twenty-First-Century America*, ed. Seth Friedman and Amanda Keeler (New Brunswick, N.J.: Rutgers University Press, 2023), 95–112.
4 Ramirez, "Prestige Adaptation," 97.
5 Ramirez, "Prestige Adaptation," 102–103.

6 Ramirez, "Prestige Adaptation," 99.
7 Ramirez, "Prestige Adaptation," 99.
8 Sayak Valencia, *Gore Capitalism* (South Pasadena, Calif.: Semiotext(e), 2018), 58–142.
9 Valencia, *Gore Capitalism*, 143. See also Misha Glenny, *McMafia: A Journey Through the Global Criminal Underworld* (New York: Random House, 2008), xv–xvi.
10 Valencia, *Gore Capitalism*, 28.
11 *Queen of the South*, season 3, episode 2, "El Colgado," written by Benjamin Daniel Lobato, original airdate June 28, 2018, USA Network.
12 Valencia, *Gore Capitalism*, 20–21.
13 *Queen of the South*, "Justicia."
14 *Queen of the South*, season 1, episode 1, "Piloto," written by M. A. Fortin and Joshua John Miller, original airdate June 23, 2016, USA Network.
15 *Queen of the South*, "Piloto."
16 *Queen of the South*, "Piloto."
17 *Queen of the South*, "Piloto."
18 *Queen of the South*, season 1, episode 4, "Lirio de los Valles," written by Scott Rosenbaum, original airdate July 14, 2016, USA Network.
19 Valencia, *Gore Capitalism*, 65.
20 *Queen of the South*, season 1, episode 6, "El Engaño Como la Regla," written by Scott Rosenbaum, original airdate July 28, 2016, USA Network.
21 Valencia, *Gore Capitalism*, 143.
22 Valencia, *Gore Capitalism*, 126.
23 *Queen of the South*, "Piloto."
24 *Queen of the South*, season 3, episode 9, "El Diablo," written by Dailyn Rodriquez and Mark Valadez, original airdate August 16, 2018, USA Network.
25 Valencia, *Gore Capitalism*, 55.
26 *Queen of the South*, season 1, episode 9, "Coge Todo lo Que Puede Llevar," written by Benjamin Daniel Lobato and David Ehrman, original airdate August 18, 2016, USA Network.
27 Aviva Dove-Viebahn, *There She Goes Again: Gender, Power, and Knowledge in Contemporary Film and Television Franchises* (New Brunswick, N.J.: Rutgers University Press, 2024), 32.
28 Dove-Viebahn, *There She Goes Again*, 28, 32.
29 *Queen of the South*, season 2, episode 12, "Todas las Horas Hieren," written by Ryan O'Nan, original airdate August 24, 2017, USA Network.
30 Ana Peluffo, "Necrofeminism and Networks of Indignatión in Gertrudis Gómez de Avellaneda and Emilia Pardo Bazán," *Revista Hispánica Moderna* 73, no. 1 (2020): 61–75.
31 Valencia, *Gore Capitalism*, 219.
32 *Queen of the South*, season 2, episode 7, "El Precio de la Fe," written by Jorge A. Reyes, original airdate July 20, 2017, USA Network.
33 *Queen of the South*, "Justicia."
34 Jen Silverman, "Art Isn't Supposed to Make You Comfortable," *New York Times*, April 28, 2024, https://www.nytimes.com/2024/04/28/opinion/art-morality-discomfort.html.
35 *Queen of the South*, season 2, episode 1, "El Cuerpo de Cristo," written by Natalie Chaidez, original airdate June 8, 2017, USA Network.
36 Catherine Rottenberg, "The Rise of Neoliberal Feminism," *Cultural Studies* 28, no. 3 (2014): 422.

37 *Queen of the South*, season 4, episode 5, "Noche de las Chicas," written by Tom Garrigus and Davia Carter, original airdate July 4, 2019, USA Network.
38 Katie Mettler, "Hillary Clinton Just Said It, but 'The Future Is Female' Began as a 1970s Lesbian Separatist Slogan," *Washington Post*, February 8, 2017, https://www.washingtonpost.com/news/morning-mix/wp/2017/02/08/hillary-clinton-just-said-it-but-the-future-is-female-began-as-a-1970s-lesbian-separatist-slogan/.
39 Rottenberg, *Rise of Neoliberal Feminism*, 145.
40 *Queen of the South*, season 5, episode 2, "Me Llevo Manhattan," written by Tom Garrigus, original airdate April 14, 2021, USA Network.
41 Jodi Melamed, *Represent and Destroy: Rationalizing Violence in the New Racial Capitalism* (Minneapolis: University of Minnesota Press, 2011).
42 Alyssa Hardy, "Alexandria Ocasio-Cortez Wore Suffragette White to Be Sworn into Congress," *Teen Vogue*, January 3, 2019, https://www.teenvogue.com/story/alexandria-ocasio-cortez-wore-suffragette-white-sworn-into-congress.
43 *Queen of the South*, season 2, episode 6, "El Camino de la Muerte," written by Ryan O'Nan, original airdate July 13, 2017, USA Network.
44 Valencia, *Gore Capitalism*, 26. Emphasis in original.
45 Valencia, *Gore Capitalism*, 26, 74.
46 Valencia, *Gore Capitalism*, 115–116.
47 Valencia, *Gore Capitalism*, 118.
48 *Queen of the South*, "Cuerpo de Cristo."
49 *Queen of the South*, season 2, episode 9, "Sólo el Amor de una Madre," written by Tina Mabry and Dailyn Rodriguez, original airdate August 3, 2017, USA Network.
50 *Queen of the South*, season 3, episode 7, "Reina de Espadas," written by Tony Puryear, original airdate August 2, 2018, USA Network.
51 *Queen of the South*, season 4, episode 11, "Mientras Dormías," written by Fernanda Coppel, original airdate August 15, 2019, USA Network.
52 Melamed, *Represent and Destroy*, 42.
53 Héctor Parra García, "Escape Routes to *Capitalismo Gore*," *Social Text Online*, November 8, 2019, https://socialtextjournal.org/periscope_article/escape-routes-to-capitalismo-gore/.
54 Valencia, *Gore Capitalism*, 55.
55 Valencia, *Gore Capitalism*, 55.
56 James W. Messerschmidt, "Donald Trump, Dominating Masculine Necropolitics, and COVID-19," *Men and Masculinities* 24, no. 1 (2021): 190.
57 Valencia, *Gore Capitalism*, 134.
58 *Queen of the South*, season 3, episode 3, "Reina de Oros," written by Ryan O'Nan, original airdate July 5, 2018, USA Network.
59 *Queen of the South*, "Reina de Oros."
60 In his explanation of racial realism, Derrick Bell explains that the formal achievements of the civil rights era of the Black Freedom Struggle did not put an end to racially motivated exclusions and affronts because subsequent decades demonstrated powerful whites' "willingness . . . to subvert (black) rights in furtherance of political or economic ends." Derrick A. Bell, "Racial Realism," in *Critical Race Theory: The Key Writings That Formed the Movement*, ed Kimberlé Crenshaw, Neil Gotanda, Gary Peller, and Kendall Thomas (New York: New Press, 1995), 306.
61 See Cristina Beltrán, *Cruelty as Citizenship: How Migrant Suffering Sustains White Democracy* (Minneapolis: University of Minnesota Press, 2020).

62 Beltrán, *Cruelty as Citizenship*, 17.

63 Beltrán, *Cruelty as Citizenship*, 14–19. Beltrán credits Pierre L. van den Berge, *Race and Racism: A Comparative Perspective* (New York: John Wiley, 1967) with the term "Herrenvolk democracy," noting that the concept is rooted in Nazi ideology but applies to other political regimes organized around democratic processes for a privileged race and the tyrannical rule of subordinated groups.

64 *Queen of the South*, season 3, episode 5, "El Juicio," written by Jorge A. Reyes, original airdate July 19, 2018, USA Network.

65 Beltrán, *Cruelty as Citizenship*, 18.

66 Lisa A. Flores, *Deportable and Disposable: Public Rhetoric and the Making of the "Illegal" Immigrant* (University Park, Penn.: Penn State University Press, 2020).

67 *Queen of the South*, season 4, episode 1, "Bienvenidos a Nueva Orleans," written by Dailyn Rodriguez, original airdate June 6, 2019, USA Network.

68 *Queen of the South*, season 4, episode 13, "Vienen Por Ti," written by Dailyn Rodriguez and Tom Garrigus, original airdate August 29, 2019, USA Network.

69 J. David Cisneros, "Contaminated Communities: The Metaphor of 'Immigrant as Pollutant' in Media Representations of Immigration," *Rhetoric and Public Affairs* 11, no. 4 (2008): 593. See also Otto Santa Ana, *Brown Tide Rising: Metaphors of Latinos in Contemporary Public Discourse* (Austin: University of Texas Press, 2002).

70 Casey Ryan Kelly, *Caught on Tape: White Masculinity and Obscene Enjoyment* (New York: Oxford University Press, 2023), 58.

71 Kelly, *Caught on Tape*, 58.

72 *Queen of the South*, "Mientras Dormías."

73 William Robinson, "The Next Economic Crisis: Digital Capitalism and Global Police State," *Race and Class* 60, no. 1 (2018): 4.

74 Robinson, "Next Economic Crisis," 9.

75 *Queen of the South*, "Me Llevo Manhattan."

76 *Queen of the South*, season 4, episode 12, "Diosa de la Guerra," written by Benjamin Daniel Lobato and Matthew J. Lieberman, original airdate August 22, 2019, USA Network.

77 *Queen of the South*, "Diosa de la Guerra."

78 Gargi Bhattacharyya, *The Futures of Racial Capitalism* (Cambridge, U.K.: Polity, 2024).

79 Michael C. Dawson, "Hidden in Plain Sight: A Note on Legitimation Crises and the Racial Order," *Critical Historical Studies* 3, no. 1 (2016): 147; Nancy Fraser, "Expropriation and Exploitation in Racialized Capitalism: A Reply to Michael Dawson," *Critical Historical Studies* 3, no. 1 (2016): 166.

80 Dawson, "Hidden in Plain Sight," 148.

81 Alexander Cockburn and Jeffrey St. Clair, *Whiteout: The CIA, Drugs, and the Press* (New York: Verso, 1999).

82 Valencia, *Gore Capitalism*, 244.

83 Melamed, *Represent and Destroy*, 42.

84 García, "Escape Routes," para. 9.

Epilogue

1 Javier Ramirez, "Prestige Adaptation by Design: The Commercial Appeal of Latinx Tropes in *Queen of the South*," in *Prestige Television: Cultural and Artistic Value in Twenty-First-Century America*, ed. Seth Friedman and Amanda Keeler (New Brunswick, N.J.: Rutgers University Press, 2023), 103.
2 bell hooks, *Feminist Theory: From Margin to Center* (Boston, Mass.: South End, 1984), 24.
3 Amy Shields Dobson and Akane Kanai, "From 'Can-Do' Girls to Insecure and Angry: Affective Dissonances in Young Women's Post-Recessional Media," *Feminist Media Studies* 19, no. 6 (2019): 777.
4 Dobson and Kanai, "From 'Can-Do' Girls," 778.
5 Diane Negra and Yvonne Tasker, "Introduction: Gender and Recessionary Culture," in *Gendering the Recession: Media and Culture in an Age of Austerity*, ed. Diane Negra and Yvonne Tasker (Durham, N.C.: Duke University Press, 2014), 3. See also William Joseph Sipe, "The New American Dream: Neoliberal Transformation as Character Development in *Schitt's Creek*," *International Journal of Communication* 17 (2022): 388–404.
6 Sarah Hagelin and Gillian Silverman, *The New Female Antihero: The Disruptive Women of Twenty-First-Century US Television* (Chicago: University of Chicago Press, 2022), 23.
7 Meg Tully, "Watching a Trainwreck Feminism," *Women's Studies in Communication* 43, no. 4 (2020): 341.
8 Hagelin and Silverman, *New Female Antihero*, 23, 205.
9 My reference to new traditionalism draws from Elspeth Probyn's work on eighties-era television programs that portrayed the home as the site of ultimate fulfillment for women. See Elspeth Probyn, "New Traditionalism and Post-Feminism: TV Does the Home," *Screen* 31, no. 2 (1990): 147–159. As part of its plan for Trump's anticipated second term in office, the conservative Project 2025's "Family Agenda" aims to promote a "biblically based" definition of marriage. See Melissa Quinn, "What Is Project 25? What to Know About the Conservative Blueprint for a Second Administration," *CBS News*, July 11, 2024, https://www.cbsnews.com/news/what-is-project-2025-trump-conservative-blueprint-heritage-foundation/. Harrison Butker's 2024 commencement speech at Benedictine College is a dark illustration of Christian nationalism's investment in the "remasculinization of men." See the full text at the *National Catholic Register*, May 16, 2024, https://www.ncregister.com/news/harrison-butker-speech-at-benedictine.
10 Hanna Lustig, "Misogyny Is the Biggest—and Most Unflattering—Trend of 2023," *Glamour*, March 16, 2023, https://www.glamour.com/story/misogyny-the-biggest-and-most-unflattering-trend-of-2023.
11 Jilly Boyce Kay, "The Reactionary Turn in Popular Feminism," *Feminist Media Studies*, August 2024, 1–18, https://www.tandfonline.com/doi/full/10.1080/14680777.2024.2393187.
12 Jeff Stein, "Kamala Harris Vows to Revive Biden's Defeated 'Care Economy' Plans," *Washington Post*, July 24, 2024, https://www.washingtonpost.com/business/2024/07/24/kamala-harris-care-economy-biden/.
13 Jeet Heer, "No, Kamala Harris Staffers Did Not Run a 'Flawless' Campaign," *Nation*, December 10, 2024, https://www.thenation.com/article/politics/harris-democratic-staff-defeat-responsibility/.

14 *Someday You'll Die*, written by Nikki Glaser, original airdate May 11, 2024, HBO Original.

15 Ebony Elizabeth Thomas, *The Dark Fantasies: Race and the Imagination from Harry Potter to the Hunger Games* (New York: New York University Press, 2019).

16 Jenna N. Hanchey, *The Center Cannot Hold: Decolonial Possibility in the Collapse of a Tanzanian NGO* (Durham, N.C.: Duke University Press, 2023), 189.

Index

Abu-Lughod, Lila, 107
abuse, gendered forms of, 60–61
abuse, sexual: on *Queen of the South*, 133; of Daenerys Targaryen, 96, 99–100; Donald Trump's conviction for, 144; on *Unbreakable Kimmy Schmidt*, 46, 47, 48, 51, 53, 56–57. *See also* rape; rape culture; violence
Access Hollywood, 3
aesthetics, 50, 75, 77–79, 81–82, 105, 111, 121, 140–141
Against Our Will, 99–100
Ally McBeal, 17, 142
Amazon Prime, 72
ambition TV, 18
Americans, The, 18
Anderson, Karrin Vasby, 20, 39, 43
Andromedon, Titus (*Unbreakable Kimmy Schmidt*), 48, 50, 53–54, 59
anger, 53, 57, 75, 141
Arpaio, Joe, 134
Asen, Robert, 35, 44
aspirationalism, 18, 28, 40, 86
aspirational labor, 29
Atlantic, The, 97
Avengers: Endgame, 96

Bachelor, The, 61
Baldwin, Shy (*The Marvelous Mrs. Maisel*), 90, 141
Banet-Weiser, Sarah, 4, 5, 8, 9, 72
beauty: trailblazer, 24, 64, 66, 74–84, 93–94, 126; and whiteness, 77, 81, 100, 103, 141; of women characters, 35, 140; of women comedians, 65
Bell, Derrick, 170n60
Beltik, Harry (*The Queen's Gambit*), 83–84
Beltrán, Cristina, 133–134
Berlant, Lauren, 29–30, 54
Berry, Amanda, 48
Bevan, Alex, 82
Beyoncé, 9
Binder, Gabriele, 76, 81, 82
Bionic Woman, The, 15
Bitch, 25
Blunt, Emily, 14
Borgov, Vasily (*The Queen's Gambit*), 89
Boyle, Karen, 157n14
Breaking Bad, 118
Broad City, 142
Brosnahan, Rachel, 65, 77, 87–88. *See also* Maisel, Midge
Brown, Wendy, 10, 35, 157n11
Brownmiller, Susan, 99–100
Bruce, Lenny (comedian), 70
Bruce, Lenny (*The Marvelous Mrs. Maisel*), 70, 83, 87
Brummett, Barry, 20
Burke, Kenneth, 20, 22
Burke, Tarana, 11–12
Bustle, 97
Butker, Harrison, 172n9

"can-do" girls, 16, 152n50
capitalism, 9, 34, 54, 86, 119–120, 135, 139. *See also* gore capitalism; neoliberalism; racial capitalism
capitalist realism, 5, 36–37
care labor, 9, 143
Carlock, Robert, 60
Carroll, Jean, 65
Castro, Ariel, 46, 48
Charlie's Angels, 15, 124
cheerfulness, 23, 26, 40, 47, 49, 53, 64, 141. *See also* positivity
Chilling Adventures of Sabrina, 2, 4, 95–96
CIA (Central Intelligence Agency), 137
Cisneros, J. David, 135
Clinton, Hillary, 7, 8, 25, 26, 43, 97, 115, 127, 128
Cloud, Dana, 61
colonialism, 55, 101, 104, 133
color-blind television, 18
Colpean, Michelle, 38
competitive individualism: alignment with necropolitics, 125, 130; fruitlessness of, 142; of Beth Harmon, 68, 85–86, 88, 89; of Leslie Knope, 39; of Midge Maisel, 70, 85–86, 89; of Teresa Mendoza, 117, 118, 127; and neoliberalism, 35, 44, 85–86, 93, 127; as rationale for liberal feminism, 73
Cooper, Brittney, 57
costuming, 64, 76, 81–83, 105, 121
Crazy Ex-Girlfriend, 142
Crenshaw, Kimberlé, 150n32
Cut, The, 97
cynicism, 7, 53, 58–61, 79, 88

Daily Mail, 11
Dávila, Guero (*Queen of the South*), 119, 122, 130
Dawson, Michael, 136
decolonial feminism, 6, 62, 116
DeJesus, Gina, 48
Del Valle, Gaby, 97
DeSantis, Ron, 12
Diana, Princess of Wales, 104, 105
Dobson, Amy Shields, 142
Dodd, Fran, 50, 51, 60
Dodson, Antoine, 49
Douche, The (*Parks and Recreation*), 36
Douglas, Susan, 83
Dove-Viebahn, Aviva, 93, 124
Dow, Bonnie, 17, 19, 45
Downton Abbey, 14, 63
Draper, Don (*Mad Men*), 92, 157n15
Drogo, Khal (*Game of Thrones*), 96, 104, 106
Dr. Phil, 56
Duffy, Brooke Erin, 29
Dumas, Marcel (*Queen of the South*), 127, 136
Durst, Robert, 59
Durst, Robert (*Unbreakable Kimmy Schmidt*), 59–60

Eleven (*Stranger Things*), 2
Elle, 11
endriago subject, 129–130, 131, 132, 137
Engstrom, Erika, 25
Equalizer, The, 2
Equal Rights Amendment, 66
Ettenberg, Benjamin (*The Marvelous Mrs. Maisel*), 83, 87

Faludi, Susan, 12
fascism, 113
Fashion Designers of America, Council of, 78
Federici, Silvia, 34
Felsenthal, Julia, 77
Feminine Mystique, The, 66
feminism: backlash against, 7, 17, 18; coalitional, 144–145; as a commodity, 79, 82, 84; and consumerism, 14; decolonial feminism, 99, 109; intersectional, 12, 18, 62, 150n32; postfeminism, 6, 17, 53, 64, 82, 87, 142; reactionary, 143; second-wave, 9, 15–16, 56, 64, 78; socialist, 9; on television, 2–3, 13, 21, 23, 37, 140, 145. *See also* liberal feminism; neoliberal feminism; popular feminism; white feminism
Fey, Tina, 50, 58
Fisher, Mark, 5
Fleabag, 142
Flores, Lisa, 134
Frank, Scott, 88
Fraser, Nancy, 9, 136
Friedan, Betty, 66, 67

Galvez, Pote (*Queen of the South*), 120, 126, 136, 137
Game of Thrones, 4, 18, 95–116. *See also* Targaryen, Daenerys

Gamergate, 72
García, Héctor Parra, 139
Garelick, Rhonda, 75
Gato (*Queen of the South*), 122–123
Get Christie Love, 18
Ghahremani, Tanya, 97
gifted woman (myth), 72–73, 93
Gill, Rosalind, 9, 57
Gilmore Girls, 65
Girls, 142
Giroux, Henry, 36
Glamour, 143
Glaser, Nikki, 144
Glebatis-Perks, Lisa, 38–39
Glenny, Misha, 119
global mother figure, 103–104, 116
go-getter, 6, 16
Goldberg, Michelle, 8, 12
Goldman, Robert, 79, 81
Goldman, Ronald, 50
Good Girls Revolt, 64
Good Wife, The, 17, 18, 87
gore capitalism, 24, 120, 122–123, 126, 128–132, 133, 137, 138–139
Grand Theft Auto, 137
Great Recession, 28, 142
Griselda, 118

Hagelin, Sarah, 18, 99, 100, 102, 103, 115–116, 142
Hamad, Ruby, 92
Hamm, Jon, 50, 157n15
Hanchey, Jenna, 107, 145
Handmaid's Tale, The, 14
Hanisch, Uli, 76
Harmon, Beth, 24, 65–66, 68–69; addiction of, 88; attractiveness of, 81; costuming of, 77–78, 81–82; loneliness of, 89; male admirers, 71–72, 82–83; as a neoliberal subject, 85, 89; sexuality of, 83–84; traumatic losses of, 88; whiteness of, 89–90, 141. See also *Queen's Gambit, The*; Taylor-Joy, Anya
Harris, Anita, 19, 152n50
Harris, Kamala, 8, 97, 143–144
Hartman, Saidiya, 108
Havas, Julia, 13, 17, 156n3, 157n15
Haverford, Tom (*Parks and Recreation*), 44
having-it-all debate, 16, 37, 125, 130
HBO (television network), 96
HeForShe Alliance, 7
Herrenvolk democracy, 134, 171n63
Homeland, 14, 18
homo oeconomicus, 35, 126
homophobia, 66, 89, 90
hooks, bell, 142, 145
Horeck, Tanya, 13, 62, 99, 156n3, 157n15

immigration (U.S.), 131, 133–136
imperialism (Western), 100, 107, 116, 142
impossible woman figure, 2–6; cultural ambivalence regarding, 37, 40, 61; emergence of, 25; historical conditions, 7–13; ideological status of, 142; and lack of feminist imagination, 62, 144; and limits of neoliberal feminism, 37, 141–142; in relation to ambition TV, 18–19; satiric portrayals of, 27, 61; as a television product, 14, 16–17, 21; tensions facing, 40–45, 87, 96, 98, 119, 125
Insecure, 142
irony, 61

James, Robin, 10, 86
Jamm, Jeremy (*Parks and Recreation*), 31, 35
Jinx, The, 59
Jolene (*The Queen's Gambit*), 89–90
Jones, Hannah, 60

Kahler, Abigail, 116
Kanai, Akane, 57, 142
Kaushtupper, Lillian (*Unbreakable Kimmy Schmidt*), 51, 52, 53, 55, 56, 59, 60
Kay, Jilly Boyce, 143
Kellner, Douglas, 20
Kelly, Casey Ryan, 90, 92, 135
Killing, The, 17
Killing Eve, 2, 118, 122, 141
killjoy, feminist, 75
Kimmy vs. the Reverend, 61
Knight, Michelle, 46, 48
Knope, Leslie (*Parks and Recreation*), 2, 3, 23, 25–44, 47, 58, 131, 141, 142
Kornfield, Sarah, 16, 60

Lafayette, Cecil (*Queen of the South*), 134–135, 136
Lannister, Cersei (*Game of Thrones*), 111, 113

Lannister, Tyrion (*Game of Thrones*), 108, 110, 111, 112–113, 114
La Reina del Sur, 2
Lean In, 10, 28, 84, 142
Levy, Erin, 63
liberal feminism, 6–7, 9–10, 11–12, 21, 25, 29, 67, 79, 128
likeability, 18, 19; of Leslie Knope, 40; of Teresa Mendoza, 126, 138; of Kimmy Schmidt, 61; of Daenerys Targaryen, 112, 115
Little, Janine, 50
Lotz, Amanda, 21
Ludgate, April (*Parks and Recreation*), 31
Lustig, Hanna, 143

MacGyver (*MacGyver*), 120, 132
Madam Secretary, 17
Mad Max: Fury Road, 145
Mad Men, 14, 63, 64, 82, 93, 157n15
Maisel, Joel (*The Marvelous Mrs. Maisel*), 66–67, 68, 79, 86–87
Maisel, Midge (*The Marvelous Mrs. Maisel*), 24, 65, 66–68, 69; and beauty, 79–80; costuming of, 75–79, 81–82; male admirers of, 70, 82–83; as a neoliberal subject, 85, 89; personal relationships of, 83, 86–87; as a white feminist, 90–92, 141. See also Brosnahan, Rachel; *Marvelous Mrs. Maisel, The*
Making a Murderer, 50
Mallock, Mallory, 157n11
Malwae-Tweep, Shauna (*Parks and Recreation*), 32–33, 42
Mann, Denise, 20
Manne, Kate, 36
Marling, Brit, 14
Martin, George R. R., 96, 97
Marvelous Mrs. Maisel, The, 2, 14, 24, 63, 64–65, 72, 75–76, 126. *See also* Maisel, Midge
Mary Tyler Moore Show, The, 15
Maslany, Tatiana, 14
Mayo, Jed (*Queen of the South*), 133–134
Mbembe, Achille, 166n26
McRobbie, Angela, 10, 16, 85, 86
Meagle, Donna (*Parks and Recreation*), 44
Medjesky, Christopher, 59
Melamed, Jodi, 139, 143
Mendoza, Teresa (*Queen of the South*), 24, 117–139, 141
Menéndez, María Menéndez, 101
Messerschmidt, James, 132
Me Too, 7, 11–12, 60, 63, 123
Meyer, Michaela, 18, 87
Milano, Alyssa, 11
Mill, John Stuart, 73, 93
Miller, George, 145
Miller, Sarah, 81
Minor, Jerry, 50
misogyny: causes of, 26; cultural, 2, 52, 61, 144; and feminist agency, 103, 124; and feminist television, 12, 18, 100, 140–141, 144; in *Game of Thrones*, 96, 102; in gaming, 72; and global capitalism, 120; and gore capitalism, 123–124, 132; growth of, 143; and neoliberal feminism, 73, 126, 129; in *Parks and Recreation*, 26, 31, 36–37; and the period trailblazer TV trope, 72, 73, 74; and sexist realism, 6, 11; in *Unbreakable Kimmy Schmidt*, 46–52, 58, 60–62. *See also* popular misogyny
Morales, Marta Fernández, 101
Mormont, Jorah (*Game of Thrones*), 104, 106
MTV Video Music Awards, 9
multicultural neoliberalism, 133, 135, 139, 143
Murphey, Kathleen, 101
Murphy Brown, 16, 45
Myerson, Susie (*The Marvelous Mrs. Maisel*), 67, 87

Naharis, Daario (*Game of Thrones*), 108, 110
narcofeminism, 125, 127, 130
Narcos, 118
necrofeminism, 125, 128, 130
necropolitics, 100, 125, 166n26
Neocleous, Mark, 33
neocolonial dreamwork, 145
neoliberal feminism, 10, 11, 28, 89, 116; and competitive individualism, 85; differences from other feminisms, 109; dominance on television, 21; and gendered hierarchies, 139; of Leslie Knope, 28–29, 42; in literature, 142; on *The Marvelous Mrs. Maisel*, 88; of Teresa Mendoza, 126–128; mockery of, 53–54, 115, 127; and neoliberal antiracism, 55; and perfectionism, 85; and racial capitalism, 138–139; and recessionary

politics, 28; in relation to misogyny, 126; and trailblazer beauty, 84–85; and white supremacy, 120. *See also* neoliberalism
neoliberalism: and care labor, 10, 39; challenges to, 143; as a cultural logic, 27; as economic system, 9, 42, 135, 136; as an embodied subjectivity, 54, 56, 85; and incompatibility with feminism, 132, 141; and narcotics trafficking, 119, 125, 126; and necropolitics, 125; and popular feminism, 23; and private prison contracts, 136; and publics, 35, 39, 52, 55; and responsibilization, 49, 56, 93, 117, 157n11, 165n105; and sexism, 34–38, 44, 52, 58; and sexual violence, 58; television's disinvestment from, 142; values of, 139. *See also* multicultural neoliberalism; neoliberal feminism
Netflix, 13–14, 62, 65, 82, 145
Neville-Shepard, Meredith, 91, 92
Newport, Bobby (*Parks and Recreation*), 31
new traditionalism, 16, 143, 172n9
New Yorker, 46, 70, 81
New York Times, 8, 12, 44, 66, 70, 75, 77, 88
Neylon, Cáit, 53
Nussbaum, Emily, 46

objectification, women's, 64, 66, 75, 77, 79, 82
Ocasio-Cortez, Alexandria, 128
Oh, David, 59
Oluo, Ijeoma, 33
optimism, 53; cruel, 29–30, 43–44
Orange Is the New Black, 17
Orgad, Shani, 56
Ouelette, Laurie, 17
Outlander, 17

Pan Am, 64
Paper Girls, 149n6
Parks and Recreation, 2, 3, 23, 25–45, 116, 131, 136
Paskin, Willa, 75
patriarchy: facing impossible women characters, 27, 34, 47, 69, 72, 91, 103, 113; and geek masculinity, 72; as global phenomenon, 115; intersectionality's challenge to, 62; investments in, 72; and neoliberal feminism, 28; periodization of, 63, 74; and popular feminism, 5, 10; and resilience, 11; retrenchment of, 143; and sexist realism, 19, 144; as subject of *Parks and Recreation*, 30, 33; and viewing pleasure, 75, 79; and white feminism, 92, 115; and white supremacy, 47, 94, 113, 115
Pecas (*Queen of the South*), 124, 134
Peluffo, Ana, 125
People (magazine), 77
Pérez-Reverte, Arturo, 118
perfection: and emotional regulation, 57; and imperfect women on tv, 142; of Leslie Knope, 26–27, 38; as neoliberal feminist demand, 10, 45, 64, 93; women's physical appearance, 78, 85. *See also* resilience
Perkins, Ann (*Parks and Recreation*), 36, 39, 40
Phipps, Alison, 166n26
phoenix moment, 101, 122
Playboy Club, The, 64
Podemos (Spanish political party), 97
Poehler, Amy, 25, 26. *See also* Knope, Leslie
popular feminism, 4–5; and economies of visibility, 9; and emotional regulation, 57; and sexist realism, 11, 115; and the strong female lead, 14; and television narrative, 22–23, 64
popular misogyny, 4–5, 7–8, 140
positivity, 10, 26, 38, 40, 47, 49, 57–58, 103, 141, 142
postfeminist nostalgia, 74
postracialism, 18
Prasch, Allison, 17
prestige television, 118, 122
Prime-Time Feminism, 19–20
prison-industrial complex, 135–136
Probyn, Elsbeth, 87, 172n9
Projansky, Sarah, 99
Project 2025, 172n9
public good, 26, 35, 52, 54, 131

Queen of the South, 2, 24, 99, 117–139. *See also* Mendoza, Teresa
Queen's Gambit, The (miniseries), 24, 64, 65, 93. *See also* Harmon, Beth
Queen's Gambit, The (novel), 65, 89

racial capitalism, 24, 136–137
racial realism, 116, 133, 170n60

racism, 18, 58–59, 66, 89, 111, 128, 132–136. *See also* white supremacy
Ramirez, Javier, 118
Ramsey, Charles, 48
Rao, Rahul, 55
rape, 96, 99–100; as backstory, 99, 101; in feminist literature, 99–100; television depictions of, 104–122. *See also* violence: sexual
rape culture, 7, 145; television commentary about, 47, 49, 50
reflexivity (as critical practice), 38
Reina del Sur, La, 118
representative anecdote, 20
Reprisal, 149n6
resilience, 10, 23, 86; of Beth Harmon, 86; of Leslie Knope, 29–34, 38, 39–40; of Midge Maisel, 86, 88; of Teresa Mendoza, 117, 120–122, 129; perfect-imperfect, 85–86; in relation to violence, 122; of Kimmy Schmidt, 46, 47, 49, 53, 55–56, 57, 61; and upbeat feminism, 57
rhetorical criticism, 19–22
Rhimes, Shonda, 18
Richards, Parker, 97
Richard Wayne Gary Wayne (*Unbreakable Kimmy Schmidt*), 50, 60
Rivers, Joan, 65
Robinson, William, 135–136
Rodino-Colocino, Michelle, 28
Roe v. Wade, 8
Rottenberg, Catherine, 10, 55
Ryan, Michael, 20

Sandberg, Sheryl, 10, 28, 84, 142
satire, 30, 38–40, 58–62
Saturday Night Live, 26, 157n15
Saval, Malina, 63, 74
Scandal, 17, 18
Schmidt, Kimmy (*Unbreakable Kimmy Schmidt*), 23, 46–62
Schubart, Rikke, 103
selective amnesia, 74
Selmy, Ser Barristan (*Game of Thrones*), 108
Sex and the City, 17, 142
Sex Education, 145
sexism, 72, 74, 114; and the beauty industry, 79; as a commodity, 79, 141; enlightened, 83; and machismo, 132. *See also* misogyny
sexist realism, 5, 7, 19, 37, 62, 124; and economic conditions, 131; and electoral politics, 43, 113, 115, 144; and retrenchment of patriarchy, 143; violence against women, 122; and women's suffering, 62, 89
sex trafficking, 132–133
sexual harassment, 32, 42, 60–61, 72, 124
Shaibel, William (*The Queen's Gambit*), 69, 88
Shapiro, Ben, 12
Sharma, Sarah, 6
Sharpe, Jenny, 104–105
Shattuc, Jane, 13
Shere, Jeremy, 65
Sherman-Palladino, Amy, 65, 75, 76, 87, 88
Shome, Raka, 98, 104
Silverman, Gillian, 18, 99, 102, 103, 115–116, 142
Simpson, Nicole Brown, 50
Snow, Jon (*Game of Thrones*), 97, 111, 112, 113, 114
Soloski, Alexis, 75
Songify the News, 48–49
Song of Ice and Fire, A, 96
Sopranos, The, 137
Southern Poverty Law Center, 8
Spellman, Sabrina (*Chilling Adventures of Sabrina*), 2
Spigel, Lynn, 20, 74
Spivak, Gayatri, 101
Staircase, The, 50
St. James, Emily, 97–98
Stranger Things, 2
strong female lead, 13–15, 21, 138, 140
Subjection of Women, The, 73
suffering actors, girls as, 19
survivor: as a cultural formation, 58; discourse about, 11–12, 47, 56–57; Teresa Mendoza as a, 120; Kimmy Schmidt as a, 46–47, 49; sexual assault, 11, 23; Daenerys Targaryen as a, 99–100
Swanson, Ron (*Parks and Recreation*), 28, 33, 34, 39, 40–44
Swink, Robin Stacia, 40
Syme, Rachel, 70, 77

Targaryen, Daenerys (*Game of Thrones*), 2, 24, 95–116, 141
Tate, Andrew, 143

Taylor-Joy, Anya, 77, 89. *See also* Harmon, Beth
Taza (*Queen of the South*), 127, 134
Telemundo, 139
temporality, 6
Tevis, Walter, 65, 81
thirtysomething, 16
Thomas, Ebony Elizabeth, 145
Tompkins, Joe, 79
trainwreck feminism, 142, 143
Traister, Rebecca, 57
transphobia, 143
trauma, 48, 53, 56, 86, 88, 130
Trump, Donald, 2, 8, 12, 32, 43, 50, 66, 135, 143–144, 172n9
Trump, Ivanka, 117
Tully, Meg, 38, 142

Unbreakable Kimmy Schmidt, 2, 23, 46–62, 99, 136, 141
United Nations, 7, 8
USA (television network), 118, 139

Valdez, James (*Queen of the South*), 117, 119–120, 123, 124, 125, 131, 137
Valencia, Sayak, 24, 119, 125, 129–130, 132, 137
Van den Berge, Pierre L., 171n63
Vargas, Camila (*Queen of the South*), 118, 119, 122, 123–124, 125, 126, 128, 130
Vargas, Epifanio (*Queen of the South*), 119, 123–124
Variety, 14
Varys (*Game of Thrones*), 110, 112–113
Vedric, Natalia, 50
Veep, 17
Villanelle (*Killing Eve*), 141
violence: on *Game of Thrones*, 111, 115, 128; gendered, 56, 104, 132; of narcotics trafficking, 128, 132; on *Queen of the South*, 130–131, 138; sexual, 50–53, 58, 61, 90, 96, 99, 103, 122, 124. *See also* abuse, sexual; gore capitalism; rape; rape culture
Vogue, 77
Voorhees, Jacqueline (*Unbreakable Kimmy Schmidt*), 48, 53–55, 141
Voorhees, Zan (*Unbreakable Kimmy Schmidt*), 49, 57
Vox, 97
Vulture, 14, 75

wage gap, 8
Wallace, Kelsey, 25
Warren, Elizabeth, 43, 97
Watson, Emma, 7, 11
Watts, Benny (*The Queen's Gambit*), 83–84
Weeds, 118
Weissman, Abe (*The Marvelous Mrs. Maisel*), 72
Wheatley, Allston (*The Queen's Gambit*), 68–69
Wheatley, Alma (*The Queen's Gambit*), 68–69
white ambivalence, 90
white feminism, 44, 59, 62, 90–92, 98, 99, 103, 104, 107, 109, 115
whiteness, 11–12, 13, 33, 54–55, 62, 90, 111, 133, 141; in fantasy fiction, 100, 112, 115–116, 145
white pantsuit, 14, 121, 128
white savior, 98, 106–107, 109
white supremacy, 11, 24, 62, 107, 133, 134, 135, 136, 143; as social structure, 90, 92
Wolf, Michelle, 14
Women's Health, 81
Women's March in Washington, D.C., 11
Women Who Work, 117
Wonder Woman, 15
Wyatt, Ben (*Parks and Recreation*), 37

Young, Helen, 98

Zakowska, Donna, 75, 77–78, 81

About the Author

KRISTEN HOERL is associate professor of rhetoric and public culture at the University of Nebraska–Lincoln and author of *The Bad Sixties: Hollywood Memories of the Counterculture, Antiwar, and Black Power Movements* with the University Press of Mississippi. She is a past editor of *Women's Studies in Communication*.